If you're serious about exam success, it's time to *Concentrate!*

Each guide in the **Concentrate** series shows you what to expect in your law exam, what examiners are looking for, and how to achieve extra marks.

* Written by experts
* Developed with students
* Designed for success

For a full list of titles available and forthcoming please visit the website

If you're struggling with your course or worried about exams, don't panic, just

concentrate!

Buy yours from your campus book online from O

www.oxfordtextbooks.co.uk/law/rev

Visit **www.oxfordtextbooks.co.uk/orc/concentrate/** for a wealth of online resources including a podcast of exam and revision guidance, diagnostic tests, understanding your marks, interactive flashcard questions

Acknowledgements

For my father

I would like to thank Professor Luke Clements for providing an invaluable source of knowledge for this book and Dr Melanie Smith and my colleagues at Cardiff Law School for all their help and encouragement during the writing process. I would also like to acknowledge the invaluable support I continually receive from my mother, family, and friends.

QR Code images are used throughout this book. QR Code is a registered trademark of DENSO WAVE INCORPORATED. You can scan the code with your mobile device to launch the relevant webpage from the Online Resource Centre. If your mobile device does not have a QR Code reader try this website for advice: www.mobile-barcodes.com/qr-code-software.

Human Rights Law
Concentrate

Bernadette Rainey

Lecturer in Law, Cardiff University

OXFORD
UNIVERSITY PRESS

OXFORD
UNIVERSITY PRESS

Great Clarendon Street, Oxford OX2 6DP

Oxford University Press is a department of the University of Oxford.
It furthers the University's objective of excellence in research, scholarship,
and education by publishing worldwide in

Oxford New York

Auckland Cape Town Dar es Salaam Hong Kong Karachi
Kuala Lumpur Madrid Melbourne Mexico City Nairobi
New Delhi Shanghai Taipei Toronto

With offices in

Argentina Austria Brazil Chile Czech Republic France Greece
Guatemala Hungary Italy Japan Poland Portugal Singapore
South Korea Switzerland Thailand Turkey Ukraine Vietnam

Oxford is a registered trade mark of Oxford University Press
in the UK and in certain other countries

Published in the United States
by Oxford University Press Inc., New York

British Library Cataloguing in Publication Data
Data available

Library of Congress Cataloging in Publication Data
Data available

Typeset by Newgen Imaging Systems (P) Ltd, Chennai, India
Printed in Great Britain
on acid-free paper by
Ashford Colour Press Ltd, Gosport, Hampshire

ISBN 978-0-19-969594-2

10 9 8 7 6 5 4 3 2 1

Contents

Table of cases   vi
Table of legislation   xii

1 Introduction   1

2 European Convention on Human Rights   20

3 The Human Rights Act 1998 (HRA)   38

4 Right to life and freedom from ill treatment   56

5 Right to liberty and right to fair trial   76

6 Right to family and private life   98

7 Freedom of religion and expression   116

8 Freedom of assembly and association   137

9 Freedom from discrimination   153

10 Terrorism   172

Exam essentials   A1
Outline answers   A5
Glossary   A10
Index   A12

Table of cases

97 Members of the Gldani Congregation of Jehovah's Witnesses v Georgia (2007) (Application No 71156/01) . . . 119

A, B, and C v Ireland (2010) (Application No 25579/05) . . . 61

A and others v Secretary of State for the Home Department (No 2) [2005] UKHL 71; [2006] 1 All ER 575 . . . 72, 187

A and others v UK (2009) (Application No 3455/05) . . . 178, 179, 186

A and others v Secretary of State for the Home Department [2005] 2 All ER 169; [2005] 2 WLR 87 . . . 47, 51, 53, 169, 183, 184, 187, 189

A v UK (1998) 27 EHRR 611 . . . 64, 71

A v UK (2009) 49 EHRR 29 . . . 33, 90, 94, A9

Abdulaziz, Cabales and Balkandali v UK (1985) 7 EHRR 471 . . . 159, 160

Age Concern England (Case 388/07) (2009) . . . 167

Ahmet Arslan and Others v Turkey (2010) (Application No 41135/98) . . . 123, A7

Airey v Ireland (1979) 2 EHRR 305 . . . 31

Aksoy v Turkey (1996) 23 EHRR 533 . . . 179

Al Rawi and others (Respondents) v The Security Service and others (Appellants) [2011] UKSC 34 . . . 187

Al Saadoon and Mufdhi v UK (2010) (Application No 61498/08) . . . 63, 64, A5

Al-Skeini v UK (2011) (Application No 55721/07) . . . 67

Alinak v Turkey (2005) (Application No 40287/98) . . . 129

Angelini v Sweden (1986) 51 DR 41 . . . 119

Anguelova v Bulgaria (2004) 38 EHRR 659 . . . 162

Anufrijeva and others v Southwark LBC and others [2004] 1 All ER 833 . . . 48

Appleby v UK (2003) 37 EHRR 38 . . . 140

Arrowsmith v UK (1978) 18 DR 5 . . . 118, 120

Assenov v Bulgaria (1998) 28 EHRR 652 . . . 72

Associated Society of Locomotive Engineers & Firemen (ASLEF) v the UK (2007) 45 EHRR 793 . . . 142, 146, 150

Austin v Commissioner of Police of the Metropolis [2009] UKHL 5 . . . 86, 95, 96, 147, A6

Ayadin v Turkey (1997) 25 EHRR 251 . . . 70

B and P v UK (2002) 34 EHRR 529 . . . 90

Baczkowski v Poland (2009) 48 EHRR 475 . . . 140, A7

Baranowski v Poland (2000) (Application No 28358/95) . . . 80

Barfuss v Czech Republic (2000) 34 EHRR 948 . . . 83

Belfast City Council v Miss behaving Ltd (Northern Ireland) [2008] HRLR 11 . . . 51

Belgian Linguistics Case (1968) (1979–80) 1 EHRR 241 . . . 159, 163, A8

Bellinger v Bellinger [2003] 2 AC 467 . . . 46, 169

Beoku-Betts (FC) v Secretary of State for the Home Department [2008] UKHL 39 . . . 112

Berrehab v Netherlands (1989) 11 EHRR 332 . . . 101

Botta v Italy (1998) 26 EHRR 241 . . . 101

Boultif v Switerland (2001) 33 EHRR 1179 . . . 106

Brand v Netherlands (2004) 17 BHRC 398 . . . 80

Brannigan and McBride v UK (1993) 17 EHRR 539 . . . 179, 180

Brogan v UK (1988) 11 EHRR 117 . . . 83, 179

Brown v Board of Education (1954) US Supreme Court . . . 156, 163

Brown v Stott [2001] 2 WLR 817 . . . 92, 95

Brumarescu v Romania (1999) 33 EHRR 862 . . . 91

Bryan v UK (1995) 21 EHRR 342 . . . 89

Buckley v UK (1996) 23 EHRR 101 . . . 35, 104

Burden v UK (2008) 47 EHRR 857 . . . 160

Cadder v HM Advocate (2010) UKSC 43 . . . 93, A6

Campbell v Mirror Group Newspapers [2004] 2 All ER 192 . . . 44, 112, 113, 114, 132, A6

Campbell and Cosens v UK (1982) 4 EHRR 293 . . . 119

Campbell and Fell v UK (1984) 4 EHRR 165 . . . 89, A6

Castells v Spain (1992) 14 EHRR 445 . . . 129

Chahal v UK (1996) 23 EHRR 413 . . . 71, 176, 182, 188, A9

Christians against Racism and Fascism v UK (1980) (Application No 8440/78) . . . 144

Church of Scientology Moscow v Russia (2007) 46 EHRR 304 . . . 118

Cisse v France (2002) (Application No 51346/99) . . . 139, 140, A7

Clark v Novacold Ltd [1999] EWCA Civ 1091 . . . 169

Coleman v Attridge Law [2008] ECR I-5603 . . . 166

Connors v UK (2004) 40 EHRR 9 . . . 102

Copland v UK (2007) 45 EHRR 37 . . . 102, A6

Cossey v UK (1991) (Application No 10843/84) . . . 29

Council of Civil Service Unions v UK (1987) (Application No 11603/85) . . . 146

Cyprus v Turkey (2001) 35 EHRR 371 . . . 101

D v UK (1997) 24 EHRR 423 . . . 72

Darby v Sweden (1990) 13 EHRR 774 . . . 119, 161

De Freitas v Permanent Secretary of Ministry of Agriculture, Fisheries, Land and Housing [1999] 1 AC 69 . . . 50

Demir and Baykara v Turkey (2009) 48 EHRR 1272 . . . 141

D.H. and Others v Czech Republic (2008) 47 EHRR 59 . . . 164, 165, 170, 171, A8

Dickson v UK (2007) 46 EHRR 927 . . . 109

Dobson v Thames Water Utilities Ltd [2009] EWCA Civ 28 . . . 48

Donoghue v Poplar Housing & Regeneration Community Association & Sec State DETR [2001] 4 All ER 604 . . . 42

Douglas v Hello! Ltd (No 6) [2005] EWCA Civ 595 . . . 44, 53, 113, 132, A6

Dudgeon v UK (1981) 4 EHRR 149 . . . 35, 104, 109, 162

East African Asians case (Patel v UK) (1993) 3 EHRR 76 . . . 70

E.B. v France (2008) ECHR 74 . . . 161, A8

Edwards v UK (1992) 15 EHRR 417 . . . 90

Edwards v UK (2002) 35 EHRR 13 . . . 64, A5

Engel v Netherlands (1976) 1 EHRR 647 . . . 30, 79, 81, 88

Evans v UK (2006) 43 EHRR 43 . . . 61

Evans v UK (2007) 46 EHRR 728 . . . 109

Eweida v British Airways (2009) IRLR 78 . . . 126, 169

Ezelin v France (1991) 14 EHRR 362 . . . 145

Fedeyeva v Russia (2005) 49 EHRR 295 . . . 110

Fox, Campbell and Hartley v UK (1990) 13 EHRR 157 . . . 81, 82

Frette v France (2004) 38 EHRR 438 . . . 161, A8

Gafgen v Germany (2010) (Application No 22978/05) . . . 68, 74, 91

Galstyan v Armenia (2007) (Application No 26986/03) . . . 142

Garaudy v France (2003) (Application No 65831/01) . . . 130, A7

Gaygusuz v Austria (1997) 23 EHRR 364 . . . 160

Ghaidan v Mendoza [2004] 3 All ER 411 . . . 45, 53, 169

Gillan and Quinton v UK (2010) (Application No 4158/05) . . . 102, 107, 114, 177, 182, 188

Gillow v UK (1986) 11 EHRR 335 . . . 102

Golder v UK (1978) 1 EHHR 524 . . . 30, 90, 95, A6

Goodwin v UK (1996) 22 EHRR 123 . . . 129

Goodwin v UK (2002) 35 EHRR 447 . . . 29, 35, 46, 104, 109

Gorzelik v Poland (2004) 40 EHRR 76 . . . 141

Government of South Africa v Grootboom, Constitutional Court of South Africa, Case CCT 11/00 October 2000 . . . 13, 17

Table of cases

✳✳✳✳✳✳✳✳✳✳

Greek Case (1969) 12 YB 1 . . . 69, 70, 179

Guerra v Italy (1998) 26 EHRR 357 . . . 110, 127

Gulec v Turkey (1998) 28 EHRR 121 . . . 60

Guzzardi v Italy (1980) 3 EHRR 333 . . . 79, 84, 95, 186, A5, A9

H v Norway (1992) 73 DR 155 . . . 61

H v UK (1993) 16 EHRR 44 . . . 118

Haas v Switzerland (2011) (Application No 31322/07) . . . 62

Halford v UK (1997) 24 EHRR 523 . . . 107, A6

Handyside v UK (1976) 1 EHRR 737 . . . 34, 36, 103, 117, 127, 128, A7

Hasan and Chaush v Bulgaria (2000) 34 EHRR 1339 . . . 119, 121

Hatton v UK (2003) 37 EHRR 611 . . . 35, 104, 110, 111, 114

Heather v Leonard Cheshire Foundation [2002] EWCA Civ 366 . . . 42

Hirst v UK (2005) 42 EHRR 849 . . . 35

H.L. v UK (2004) 40 EHRR 761 . . . 79, 80

H.M. v Switzerland (2004) 38 EHRR 314 . . . 79

Hoffman v Austria (1994) 17 EHRR 293 . . . 160

Hood v UK (1999) 26 EHRR 365 . . . 83

Hornsby v Greece (1997) 24 EHRR 250 . . . 88

Huang v Secretary of State for the Home Department [2007] 2 AC 167 . . . 50, 112

Ireland v UK (1978) 2 EHRR 25 . . . 69, 70, 71, 73, 181, A5

Islington LBC v Ladele (2009) IRLR 154 . . . 126

Johansen v Norway (1996) 23 EHRR 33 . . . 105

Johnston v Chief Constable of the Royal Ulster Constabulary (Case 222/84) (1986) . . . 167

Jordan v UK (2001) 37 EHRR 52 . . . 65

Kalac v Turkey (1997) 27 EHRR 552 . . . 120, A7

Kamal v United Kingdom DR 20/168 . . . 101

Karaduman v Turkey (1993) 74 DR 93 . . . 120

Kay v Commissioner of Police of Metropolis [2008] UKHL 69 . . . 148

Kay v Lambeth LBC [2006] UKHL 10 . . . 44

Kaya v Germany (2007) (Application No 31753/02) . . . 106

Kaya v Turkey (1998) 28 EHRR 1 . . . 65

Keenan v UK (2001) 33 EHRR 39 . . . 71, A5

Khamila Isayeva v Russia (2007) (Application No 6846/02) . . . 64

Kingsley v UK (2002) 35 EHRR 177 . . . 89

Klass v Germany (1978) 2 EHRR 214 . . . 35, 177

Koch v Germany (2011) (Application No 497/09) . . . 62

Kokkinakis v Greece (1993) 17 EHRR 397 . . . 118, 120

Koniarska v UK (2000) (Application No 33670/96) . . . 81

Konig v FRG (1978) 2 EHRR 170 . . . 89

Konttinen v Finland (1996) (Application No 24949/94) . . . 120

Kurt v Turkey (1998) 27 EHRR 373 . . . 78

Kutzner v Germany (2002) 35 EHRR 653 . . . 105

Kyrtatos v Greece (2003) 40 EHRR 390 . . . 110

Labita v Italy (2000) 46 EHRR 1228 . . . 83

Laskey, Jaggard and Brown v UK (1997) (Application No 21627/93) . . . 35, 104, 109

Lautsi v Italy (2011) (Application No 30814/06) . . . 122

Lawless v Ireland (1961) 1 EHRR 15 . . . 179

Le Compte, Van Leuven and De Meyere v Belgium (1981) 4 EHRR 1 . . . 89, 141, A6

Leander v Sweden (1987) 9 EHRR 433 . . . 108

Lebbink v Netherlands (2004) (Application No 45582/99) . . . 101

Lewisham LBC v Malcolm [2008] UKHL 45 . . . 169

Leyla Sahin v Turkey (2005) 44 EHRR 99 . . . 120, 123, 124, 125, 134, 135, A7

Lingens v Austria (1981) 8 EHRR 407 . . . 128

Lithgow v UK (1986) 8 EHRR 329 . . . 159–60

Lopez Ostra v Spain (1994) 20 EHRR 227 . . . 110

McCann, Farrell & Savage v UK (1995) 31 EHRR 97 . . . 59, 60, 73

McCaughey's Application for Judicial Review, Re [2011] UKSC 20 . . . 66

McFeeley v UK (1980) 3 EHRR 161 . . . 141

McKay v UK (2006) 44 EHRR 827 . . . 83

McKennit v Ash [2007] EWCA Civ 1714 . . . 112, A6

McVeigh, O'Neill and Evans v UK (1981) 5 EHRR 71 . . . 81

Makaratzis v Greece (2004) 41 EHRR 1092 . . . 58

Marckx v Belgium (1979) 2 EHRR 330 . . . 101, 160, 162

Marshall v Southampton and South West Hampshire Area Health Authority (Teaching) (Case 152/84) [1986] 2 All ER 584 . . . 167

Marzari v Italy (1999) 28 EHRR 175 . . . 101

Matznetter v Austria (1969) 1 EHRR 198 . . . 83, A6

Minelli v Switzerland (1983) 5 EHRR 554 . . . 91

Mitchell v Glasgow City Council [2009] UKHL 11 . . . 66

Moldovan v Romania (2005) 44 EHRR 302 . . . 70

Mosley v News Group Newspapers Ltd [2008] EWHC 2341 (QB) . . . 113, 132, 134

Munim Abdul and Others Appellants v Director of Public Prosecutions [2011] EWHC 247 (Admin) . . . 133, 148

Murray v Big Pictures [2008] EWCA Civ 446 . . . 113

Murray v UK (1994) 19 EHRR 193 . . . 81

Murray v UK (1996) 22 EHRR 29 . . . 91

N v UK (2008) (Application No 26565/05) . . . 72

Nachova v Bulgaria (2005) 42 EHRR 933 . . . 59, 62, 65, 160, 162, 163, 164, 170

Napier v Scottish Minister [2002] UKHRR 308 . . . 44

Nasri v France (1996) 21 EHRR 458 . . . 106

National Union of Belgian Police v Belgium (1975) 1 EHRR 578 . . . 141

Niemietz v Germany (1993) 16 EHRR 97 . . . 102, 107, A6

Novoseletskiy v Ukraine (2005) (Application No 47148/99) . . . 101

Ocalan v Turkey (2005) 41 EHRR 985 . . . 63, A5

Olga Tellis v Bombay Municipal Corporation, Supreme Court of India AIR 1986 Supreme Court 18 . . . 14, 17

Ollinger v Austria (2006) 46 EHRR 849 . . . 140, 151, A8

Olsson v Sweden (1992) 17 EHRR 134 . . . 89

Öneryildiz v Turkey (2004) 41 EHRR 20 . . . 10, 64, 71

Opuz v Turkey (2009) (Application No 33401/02) . . . 64

Orsus v Croatia (2010) (Application No 15766/03) . . . 165, A8

Osman v UK (1998) 29 EHRR 245 . . . 31, 32, 36, 64, 66, 71, 73, A5

Osmani v FYRM (2001) (Application No 50841/99) . . . 145

Otto-Preminger-Institut v Austria (1994) 19 EHRR 34 . . . 130

Oyal v Turkey (2010) (Application No 4864/05) . . . 65

Parish of Aston Cantlow v Wallbank [2003] 3 All ER 1213 . . . 42, 43

Paton v UK (1979) 19 DR 244 . . . 61

Peck v UK (2003) 36 EHRR 719 . . . 101, 107

Peers v Greece (2001) 33 EHRR 51 . . . 71

Phillips v UK (2001) (Application No 41087/98); (2001) *The Times*, 13 August . . . 91

Piersack v Belgium (1982) 5 EHRR 169 . . . 89, A6

Pini and others v Romania (2005) 40 EHRR 412 . . . 101

Plattform 'Ärzte für das Leben' v Austria (1988) 13 EHRR 204 . . . 139, 140, 150, A8

Playfoot v Millais School Governing Body [2007] EWHC 1698 (Admin) . . . 125

Pretty v UK (2002) 35 EHRR 1 . . . 61, 73, 101, 119

Price v UK (2001) 34 EHRR 1285 . . . 71

Purdy v DPP (2009) UKHL 45 . . . 62, 74

R (Animal Defenders International) v Secretary of State for Culture, Media and Sport [2008] 2 WLR 781 . . . 49

Table of cases

✳✳✳✳✳✳✳✳✳✳

R (Bernard) v London Borough of Enfield [2002] EWHC 2282 (Admin) . . . 48

R (Brooke and another) v Parole Board and another [2008] EWCA Civ 29 . . . 85

R (Daly) v Secretary of State for the Home Department [2001] 2 All ER 43 . . . 50

R (F) v Secretary of State Home Dept [2010] UKSC 17 . . . 47

R (Ghai) v Newcastle City Council and others [2010] EWCA Civ 59 . . . 126

R (Greenfield) v Secretary of State for the Home Department [2005] UKHL 14 . . . 48, 53

R (Mohammed) v Chief Constable of West Midlands [2010] EWHC 1228 (Admin) . . . 48

R (Suryananda) v Welsh Ministers [2007] EWCA Civ 893 . . . 125

R (Weaver) v London & Quadrant Housing Trust [2009] EWCA Civ 587 . . . 43

R (on the application of Amin (Imtiaz)) v Secretary of State for the Home Department [2003] UKHL 51 . . . 67

R (on the application of Anderson) v Secretary of State for the Home Department [2002] UKHL 46 . . . 45, 46

R (on the application of Begum) v Denbigh High School [2006] UKHL 15 . . . 125, 134, 135, A7

R (on the application of Brehony) v Chief Constable of Greater Manchester [2005] EWHC 640 (Admin) . . . 148

R (on the application of E) v Governing Body of JFS [2009] UKSC 15 . . . 168, 170

R (on the application of Gillan and another) v Police Commissioner of the Metropolis [2006] UKHL 12 . . . 182

R (on the application of Laporte) v Chief Constable of Gloucestershire Constabulary [2006] UKHL 55 . . . 147, 149, 150, A7

R (on the application of Moos) v Commissioner of Police of the Metropolis [2011] EWHC 957 (Admin) . . . 86, 147–8, A6

R (on the application of Mousa) v Secretary of State for Defence [2010] EWHC 3304 (Admin) . . . 72

R (on the application of Pro Life Alliance) v BBC [2003] 2 All ER 977 . . . 51, 133, 134, A7

R (on the application of Smith) v Oxfordshire Assistant Deputy Coroner [2010] UKSC 29 . . . 67

R v A (No 2) [2001] 3 All ER 1 . . . 45

R v Horncastle [2009] UKSC 14 . . . 44

R v Howell (1981) 3 WLR 501 . . . 147

R v Lord Chancellor, ex p Witham [1997] 2 All ER 779 . . . 15, 18

R v MHRT & Secretary of State for Health, ex p KB [2003] 2 All ER 209 . . . 48

R v MHRT, North & East London Region & the Secretary of State for Health, ex p H [2001] EWCA Civ 415 . . . 49, 86

R v Secretary of State DETR, ex p Alconbury Developments Ltd et al [2001] 2 WLR 1389 . . . 94, A6

R v Secretary of State for the Home Department, ex p Adam and Limbuela [2005] UKHL 66 . . . 72, 74

R v Secretary of State for the Home Department, ex p Simms [1999] 3 All ER 400 . . . 16, 18

R v Special Adjudicator, ex p Ullah [2004] UKHL 26 . . . 44

Rasmussen v Denmark (1985) 7 EHRR 372 . . . A8

Rees v UK (1981) (Application No 9532/81) . . . 29

Refah Partisi v Turkey (2001) 37 EHRR 1 . . . 145–6

Rekvenyi v Hungary (2000) 30 EHRR 519 . . . 146

Re S (children: case plan) [2002] 2 All ER 192 . . . 45

S and Marper v UK (2009) 48 EHRR 1169 . . . 101, 108, 111, 114

Saadi v Italy (2008) 49 EHRR 730 . . . 71, 177, A9

Saadi v UK (2008) 44 EHRR 1005 . . . 82

Sadik v Greece (1996) . . . 129

Salabiaku v France (1988) 13 EHRR 379 . . . 91

Salduz v Turkey (2009) 49 EHRR 19; (2008) 26 BHRC 223, ECtHR (GC) . . . 93

Salgueiro da Silva Mouta v Portugal (2001) 31 EHRR 1055 . . . 160

Savage v South Essex Partnership NHS Foundation Trust [2008] UKHL 74 . . . 66

Schalk and another v Austria (2010) (Application No 30141/04) . . . 101, 109

Schiesser v Switzerland (1979) 2 EHRR 417 . . . 83

Schmidt and Dahlström v Sweden (1976) 1 EHRR 632 . . . 142

Schuler-Zgraggen v Switzerland (1993) 16 EHRR 405 . . . 89

Secretary of State for the Home Department v AF (No 3) [2009] UKHL 28 . . . 94, 95, 186, 188, A9

Secretary of State for the Home Department v E [2007] All ER (D) 27 . . . 84, 85, 185, 186, A9

Secretary of State for the Home Department v JJ and Others [2007] All ER (D) 489 . . . 84, 85, 95, 185, 186, A9

Secretary of State for the Home Department v MB, AF [2007] UKHL 46 . . . 186

Sejdic v Bosnia and Herzegovina (2011) 28 BHRC 201 . . . 165

Selmouni v France (1999) 29 EHRR 403 . . . 70

Sen and Cinar v Turkey (2006) 46 EHRR 374 . . . 146

Shtukaturov v Russia (2008) (Application No 44009/05) . . . 83

Soering v UK (1989) 11 EHRR 439 . . . 62, 63, 71, A5

Somerset v Steuart (1772) 98 ER 499 . . . 15

Sommerfield v Germany (2004) 36 EHRR 565 . . . 106

Sorenson and Rasmussen v Denmark (2008) 46 EHRR 572 . . . 141

Stafford v UK (2002) 35 EHRR 1121 . . . 80, 81, 83

Stankov and United Macedonian Organisation Ilinden v Bulgaria (2001) (Application No 29221/95) . . . 144

Stedman v United Kingdom (1997) (Application No 29107/95) . . . 120

Steel and Morris v UK (2005) 41 EHRR 403 . . . 90, 129, 134

Stewart v UK (1984) (Application No 10044/82) . . . 60

Storck v Germany (2005) 43 EHRR 96 . . . 81

Sunday Times v UK (1979) 2 EHRR 245 . . . 129, 135, A7

Surek and Ozdemir v Turkey (2002) ECHR 606 . . . 131, A7

Surek v Turkey (No 1) (1999) (Application No 26682/95) . . . 131, A7

Swedish Engine Driver's Union v Sweden (1976) 1 EHRR 617 . . . 141

Tabernacle v Secretary of State for Defence [2009] EWCA Civ 23 . . . 149, 150

Thlimmenos v Greece (2001) 31 EHRR 411 . . . 59, 163, A8

Timurtas v Turkey (2000) 33 EHRR 121 . . . 59

TSE v News Group Newspapers Ltd [2011] EWHC 1308 (QB) . . . 113, 132

Tyrer v UK (1978) 2 EHRR 1 . . . 28

United Communist Party of Turkey and others v Turkey (1998) 26 EHRR 121 . . . 141, 145, 151

V and T v UK (1999) 30 EHRR 121 . . . 90, A6

Van Colle v Chief Constable of Hertfordshire [2008] UKHL 50 . . . 65, 74

Vereinigung Bildender Kunstler v Austria (2008) 47 EHRR 189 . . . 130

Vo v France (2004) 40 EHRR 12 . . . 61

Von Hannover v Germany (2004) 43 EHRR 2 . . . 111, 113, 131, A6

Wainwright v Home Office [2003] UKHL 53 . . . 111

Wainwright v UK (2006) 44 ECHR 809 . . . 111

Watkins-Singh v Aberdare Girls' High School Governors [2008] EWHC 1865 (Admin) . . . 125, A7

Weber v Switzerland (1990) 12 EHRR 508 . . . 88

Wells v Secretary of State for Justice (Parole Board Intervening) [2009] UKHL 22 . . . 85

Wemhoff v FRG (1968) 1 EHRR 91 . . . 83

Wilson v UK (2002) 35 EHRR 523 . . . 141, 142

Table of legislation

✳✳✳✳✳✳✳✳✳✳

Wingrove v UK (1996) 24 EHRR 1 . . . 130

Winterwerp v Netherlands (1979) 2 EHRR 387 . . . 80, 82, 86

Wood v Commissioner of Police of the Metropolis [2009] EWCA Civ 414 . . . 111

X (Ahmad) v United Kingdom (1981) 22 DR 27 . . . 120, A7

X v FRG (1975) DR 3/92 . . . 81

X v Switzerland DR 13/248 . . . 101

X and Y v Netherlands (1985) 8 EHRR 235 . . . 108

Yasa v Turkey (1998) 28 EHRR 408 . . . 58

YL v Birmingham City Council and others [2007] UKHL 27 . . . 42, 43, 54

Young, James and Webster v UK (1981) 4 EHRR 38 . . . 141

Z v Finland (1997) 25 EHRR 371 . . . 108

Z & others v UK (2002) 34 EHRR 97 . . . 71

Zana v Turkey (1997) 27 EHRR 667 . . . 131

Table of legislation

UK Statutes

Anti-Social Behaviour Act 2003
s.30 . . . 149
Anti-terrorism, Crime and Security Act 2001 . . . 181, 188
Pt.4 . . . 181, 182
s.22 . . . 182, 183
s.23 . . . 47, 183, 184

Bill of Rights 1689 . . . 15, 17

Children Act 1989 . . . 45
Civil Emergencies Act 2004 . . . 181
Communications Act 2003 . . . 49
Contempt of Court Act 1981 . . . 132
Counter-Terrorism Act 2008 . . . 181
Crime (Sentences) Act 1997 . . . 46
Criminal Justice Act 2003 . . . 46, 181
Criminal Justice and Public Order Act 1984
s.68 . . . 148

Disability Discrimination Act 1995 . . . 167

Emergency Provisions Act (NI) 1973–1998 . . . 180
Equal Pay Act 1970 . . . 167
Equality Act 2006 . . . 167
s.21 . . . 168
s.30 . . . 168

Equality Act 2010 . . . 125, 153, 157, 161, 167
s.1 . . . 167
s.13 . . . 166
s.15 . . . 169

Freedom of Information Act 2000 . . . 131–2

Gender Recognition Act 2004 . . . 47

Health and Social Care Act 2008
s.145 . . . 43
Highways Act 1980
s.137 . . . 148
Human Rights Act 1998 . . . 1, 15, 16, 17, 32, 34, 38–55, 66, 76, 83, 92, 98, 99, 111, 112, 113, 125, 132, 147, 148, 169, A6
s.2 . . . 39, 44, A8
s.3 . . . 39, 44–6, 47, 51, 52, 55, 94, 126, 186, 188
s.4 . . . 39, 45, 46, 47, 51, 52, 53, 55, 184, 188
s.4(3) . . . 46
s.4(6) . . . 46
s.6 . . . 39, 41, 43, 54, A5, A6, A7, A8
s.6(1) . . . 41
s.6(3) . . . 41
s.6(5) . . . 41
s.7 . . . 39, 41, A5
s.8 . . . 39, 47–9
s.8(3)–(4) . . . 48
s.10 . . . 39, 49

s.12 . . . 41, 53, 113, 132, A6, A7
s.12(3) . . . 113
s.13 . . . 41, 125
s.14 . . . 39, 50, 183
s.15 . . . 39, 50
s.19 . . . 39, 49
Sch.1 *see* European Convention on Human
 Rights

Magna Carta 1215 . . . 3, 11, 15, 17, 76, 77, 83, 92
Matrimonial Causes Act 1973 . . . 46
Mental Health Act 1983 . . . 49

National Assistance Act 1948
 s.21 . . . 43
Northern Ireland Act 1998
 s.75 . . . 157

Official Secrets Act 1989 . . . 132

Police and Criminal Evidence Act 1984 . . . 77,
 92
Prevention of Terrorism Acts 1974–1999 . . .
 180
Prevention of Terrorism Act 2005 . . . 47, 181,
 184, 185
 ss.2–4 . . . 185
Public Order Act 1986
 ss.1–4 . . . 148
 s.4A . . . 148
 s.5 . . . 133, 148
 ss.11–14 . . . 148
 ss.14A–14C . . . 148

Race Relations Act 1976 . . . 167, 168, 170
Racial and Religious Hatred Act 2006 . . . 125
Rent Act 1977 . . . 45

Serious Organised Crime and Police Act 2005
 Pt.4 . . . 148, 181
Sex Discrimination Act 1975 . . . 167

Terrorism Act 2000 . . . 107, 148, 177, 181
 s.1 . . . 172
 s.44 . . . 181, 182, 188
 s.45 . . . 181, 182
Terrorism Act 2006 . . . 181

Youth Justice and Criminal Evidence Act
 1999 . . . 45

UK Secondary legislation

Employment Equality (Age) Regulations
 2006 . . . 167
Employment Equality (Religion or Belief)
 Regulations 2003 . . . 167
Employment Equality (Sexual Orientation)
 Regulations 2003 . . . 167
Equality Act (Sexual Orientation) Regulations
 2007 . . . 167

Human Rights Act 1998 (Designated
 Derogation) Order 2001 . . . 183, 184

Bills before Parliament

Protection of Freedoms Bill 2011 . . . 182

European Union legislation

Charter of Fundamental Rights . . . 10
 Art.21 . . . 166

Lisbon Treaty 2009 . . . 10

Treaty on the Functioning of the European Union
 Art.13 . . . 166
 Art.157 (ex 119 EC Treaty) . . . 166

France legislation

Declaration of the Rights of Man and Citizen
 1789 . . . 4

International legislation

African Charter of Human Rights and Peoples'
 Rights 1981 (AU) . . . 10, 110
American Convention of Human Rights 1969
 (OAS) . . . 10
American Convention on Human Rights in the
 Area of Economic, Social and Cultural Rights
 Protocol of San Salvador 1999 . . . 14
Arab Charter on Human Rights 1994
 (LAS) . . . 10

Commonwealth of Independent States Treaty
 on Human Rights . . . 10
Convention against Torture and Other Cruel,
 Inhuman or Degrading Treatment or
 Punishment 1984 . . . 7, 68–9
 Art.1 . . . 68
 Art.16 . . . 68–9

Table of legislation

****

Convention on the Elimination of All Forms of Discrimination Against Women 1979 . . . 7, 157

Convention on Preventing and Combating Violence against Women and Domestic Violence 2011 . . . 23

Convention for the Protection of All Persons from Enforced Disappearance 2006 . . . 7

Convention on the Rights of the Child 1989 . . . 7, 157

Convention on Rights of Migrant Workers and Their Families 1990 . . . 7, 157

Convention on the Rights of Persons with Disabilities 2008 . . . 7, 157

Council of Europe Charter for Regional or Minority Languages 1992 . . . 22

Council of Europe Convention on Action against Trafficking in Human Beings 2005 . . . 23

Council of Europe Convention on the Exercise of Children's Rights 1996 . . . 23

Council of Europe Convention for the Prevention of Torture 1961 . . . 22

Council of Europe Framework Convention for the Protection of National Minorities 1995 . . . 23

European Convention on Human Rights 1950 . . . 1, 10, 16, 20, 61, 157, 169
Art.1 . . . 31, 34, 100
Art.2 . . . 23, 31, 32, 33, 36, 40, 56, 57, 58–67, 72, 73, 100, 110, 119, 122, 144, 162, 163, 164, 170, 176, 178, A1, A5
Art.2(1) . . . 58, 60–3, 62, 63, A5
Art.2(2) . . . 58, 59, 62, A1
Art.3 . . . 23, 31, 32, 33, 40, 44, 56, 57, 62, 63, 64, 67–73, 74, 100, 106, 110, 119, 159, 162, 172, 176, 177, 178, 183, 187, A5, A8
Art.4 . . . 23, 32, 33, 40, 122, 178
Art.4(1) . . . 33, 40
Art.5 . . . 30, 32, 33, 40, 47, 51, 53, 76, 77, 78–87, 137, 142, 147, 176, 178, 179, 183, 184, 188, A1, A5, A6, A9
Art.5(1) . . . 32, 78, 80, 83, 85
Art.5(1)(a)–(b) . . . 78, 81, 84
Art.5(1)(c) . . . 78, 81, 82, 84, A5
Art.5(1)(d) . . . 78, 81, 84
Art.5(1)(e) . . . 78, 80, 82, 84
Art.5(1)(f) . . . 78, 82, 84
Art.5(2) . . . 78, 82

Art.5(3) . . . 78, 82, A6
Art.5(4) . . . 79, 83, 85, 178
Art.5(5) . . . 79, 83
Art.6 . . . 23, 30, 32, 33, 40, 45, 46, 63, 76, 77, 87–92, 93, 94, 110, 122, 129, 176, 178, 186, A1, A5, A6, A9
Art.6(1) . . . 32, 87, 88, 92, 93, A6
Art.6(2) . . . 87, 88, 91, 93
Art.6(3) . . . 87, 88, 91, 92, 93
Art.6(3)(a)–(b) . . . 87, 92
Art.6(3)(c) . . . 87, 92, 93, A6
Art.6(3)(d) . . . 87, 92
Art.6(3)(e) . . . 88, 92
Art.7 . . . 23, 32, 33, 40
Art.8 . . . 23, 29, 30, 32, 33, 40, 42, 44, 45, 47, 61, 62, 73, 98–111, 112, 113, 114, 119, 121, 122, 127, 159, 176, 177, 182, A1, A6, A7, A8
Art.8(1) . . . 100, 101–2, 105
Art.8(2) . . . 100, 102, 105, 177
Art.9 . . . 23, 32, 33, 40, 116, 117, 119–24, 125, 126, 128, 142, 147, 163, A1, A7
Art.9(1) . . . 119, 120, 121, 124, 127, 128, A7
Art.9(2) . . . 119, 120, 121–2, 125, 127, A7
Art.10 . . . 23, 32, 33, 34, 36, 40, 44, 111, 112, 113, 114, 116, 117, 121, 126–32, 133, 137, 140, 142, 144, 146, 147, 148, 149, 151, 176, A1, A7
Art.10(1) . . . 126, 127, 128, 130, 131
Art.10(2) . . . 127, 128, 130, 131, 146, A7
Art.11 . . . 23, 32, 33, 40, 86, 87, 112, 137, 138–50, 151, A1, A7
Art.11(1) . . . 137, 139, 140, 141, 142, 143
Art.11(2) . . . 139, 142, 143, 146, A7
Art.12 . . . 23, 29, 30, 40
Art.13 . . . 23, 40
Art.14 . . . 23, 45, 47, 119, 153, 154, 158–64, 165, 166, 170, 183, 184, A1, A8
Art.15 . . . 33, 178, 183, 184, A1
Art.15(1) . . . 178
Art.15(2) . . . 176, 178
Art.15(3) . . . 178
Art.16 . . . 40
Art.17 . . . 130, 131
Art.18 . . . 40
Art.27 . . . 26
Art.28 . . . 26
Art.30 . . . 26
Art.33 . . . 24
Art.34 . . . 24, 27, 41, A5, A8
Art.35 . . . 26, 27, 28, A5, A8

Art.43 . . . 26
Art.45 . . . 26
Protocol 1 . . . 23
  Art.1 . . . 23, 40, 140
  Art.2 . . . 23, 40, 122, 164, 166, A8
  Art.3 . . . 23, 40, 165, 166
Protocol 2 . . . 23
Protocol 4 . . . 40
  Arts.1–3 . . . 23
  Art.4 . . . 24
Protocol 6 . . . 24, 62, 63
Protocol 7 . . . 40
  Arts.1–5 . . . 24
Protocol 11 . . . 24, 25
Protocol 12 . . . 24, 40, 153, 154, 159, 165–6
  Art.1 . . . 165, 166
  Art.1(1)–(2) . . . 165
Protocol 13 . . . 24, 40, 62, 63
Protocol 14 . . . 24, 25, 26, 27, 36
Protocol 14bis . . . 26
European Social Charter 1996 . . . 10, 22

Inter-American Convention on Human Rights 1969
  Art.4 . . . 61
International Convention on the Elimination of All Forms of Racial Discrimination 1966 . . . 7, 157
International Covenant on Civil and Political Rights 1966 . . . 6, 7, 12, 21, 58, 68, 99, 137, 138, 139, 180
  Art.2(1) . . . 6
  Art.4 . . . 180
  Art.21 . . . 138, 157
  Art.22 . . . 138
  Optional Protocol . . . 7
International Covenant on Economic, Social and Cultural Rights 1966 . . . 6, 12, 13
  Art.2(1) . . . 6
  Art.2(2) . . . 157

Izmir Declaration on the Future of the European Court of Human Rights, April 2011 . . . 26

Nuremberg Statute
  Art.6 . . . 5
  Art.7 . . . 5

Vienna Declaration 1993 . . . 12

Indian legislation
Constitution
  Art.21 . . . 14, 17
  Art.39 . . . 14, 17

South African legislation
Constitution
  s.26 . . . 13, 17

United Nations
Charter . . . 6

Declaration on the Elimination of All Forms of Intolerance and of Discrimination Based on Religion or Belief (General Assembly Resolution 36/55) . . . 118, 157
Declaration on the Rights of Persons Belonging to National or Ethnic, Religious and Linguistic Minorities 1992 . . . 157

Universal Declaration of Human Rights (UDHR) 1948 . . . 6, 58, 68, 99, 157
  see also **International legislation** for Treaties and Conventions

United States legislation
Constitution 1789 . . . 4
  First Amendment . . . 127
  Fourteenth Amendment . . . 155

Declaration of Independence 1776 . . . 4

#1

Introduction

- The meaning and content of human rights is debated and challenged.

- The development of human rights protection has been influenced by natural rights theory and challenged by other philosophies such as utilitarianism.

- The period after the Second World War witnessed a growth in international protection for individual rights and enforcement mechanisms.

- There are debates over different types of rights such as civil/political and social/economic rights. Should they be treated differently or are they indivisible?

- Human rights in the UK have developed in a common law system with no codified constitution or Bill of Rights. The **Human Rights Act 1998** enabled the **European Convention of Human Rights** to become directly enforceable in UK courts.

Chapter overview

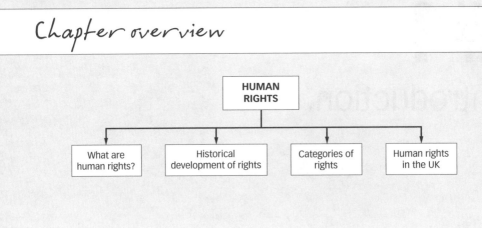

What are human rights?

Many people take for granted that there is human rights protection within society. But human rights are still contested and our ideas about rights have changed over time. The American revolutionaries in the eighteenth century declared that all 'men are born equal' in an era when slavery was acceptable. Ideas of equality have changed and transformed the protection given to sexual rights, ethnic minorities, women, children, the disabled, etc.

Natural rights and dignity

The modern conception of human rights has its roots in the intellectual enlightenment of the eighteenth century. The idea of 'self-evident' rights espoused by the US Declaration of Independence comes from the idea of **natural rights**. Philosophers like St Thomas Aquinas argued that man is made in God's image and certain inalienable rights flow from this. The Enlightenment thinkers such as John Locke began to move away from God as the giver of rights to arguing that reason means that man has intrinsic 'goods'. Locke argued that the state could only rule with the consent of its people and that the people had certain rights that the state had a duty to refrain from abusing. Other philosophers such as Kant argued that the human ability to reason meant that as humans we have a moral imperative known as the 'categorical imperative'. This means that humans have an inherent dignity that cannot be violated. It commands that we never treat another human being as a means to an end, but should always be treated as an end in itself. For example, a human being should not be tortured to gain information because this is treating the person as an instrument; a means by which the information is gathered. This view is still very influential in rights protection. Modern philosophers such as Alan Gerwith (who argues that as rational human agents we should respect each other's rights) and John Rawls (who argues that rational human beings should act reciprocally with fairness) have also justified the protection of rights through arguments of rationality.

Challenges to human rights

As noted below, the nineteenth century witnessed the rise of consequentialist philosophers who believed in the promotion of a common good or welfare. In other words, the end goal of maximising a kind of good such as happiness or welfare may override the individual and is instrumentalist; the end may justify the means. Marx argued that the idea of individual rights was a tool of the powerful to subdue the masses. Utilitarians argued that the goal should be the maximisation of the happiness of the greatest number. Jeremy Bentham famously argued that natural rights are 'nonsense on stilts' and that if the pain of one individual was the price to pay for the maximum happiness of the greatest number, then it may be justified. Utilitarians such as J S Mill did recognise the importance of rights such as freedom of expression but noted that it could be limited if necessary to protect others from harm. More recent critiques have been made by cultural relativists who question the universality of human rights and by others such as feminists, who assert the gendered nature of individual rights classifications.

These arguments about whether rights should be absolutely protected as inherent to human dignity and what rights can be limited for the protection of the community are still contested today.

Revision tip

You may find podcasts on legal theories such as utilitarianism useful. They are free to download and can be found on Philosophy Bites http://philosophybites.com. It can be downloaded to a computer or MP3 player from the website or is available free on itunes.

Historical development of rights

Discussion about rights has been part of philosophical debate for centuries. Legal documents containing rights were not common in earlier centuries. One of the first documents to guarantee protection under the law was the **Magna Carta 1215**. However, it was not until the eighteenth century that philosophers influenced the revolutionary constitutions of the newly liberated states.

Eighteenth century: rights and revolution

The ideas of the intellectual 'Enlightenment' heavily influenced the documents that were created after two major revolutions in the western world. In France, the revolution overthrew the regime of the sovereign and replaced it with a republic. In America, the revolution against the British colonial power led to the formation of the United States of America.

French Declaration of the Rights of Man and Citizen 1789

The Declaration established a constitution based on the democratic idea of separation of powers. It defined liberty in a negative way as being able to do anything as long as it is not 'injurious to others'. The Declaration was explicitly based on the idea of natural rights which could only be limited so as to guarantee those rights to all and any limits would only be determined by law. The rights listed are what we now view as classic civil and political rights such as right to life, due process, and freedom of expression.

US Declaration of Independence and the American Constitution

The Declaration of Independence in 1776 established the United States as a democratic state based on the principle of governance by consent. Similar to France, the Declaration was based on the idea of natural rights stating that 'all men are created equal, that they are endowed by their creator with certain unalienable rights that among these are life, liberty and the pursuit of happiness'. In 1789, the US Constitution included just a few due process rights. However the first 10 amendments to the Constitution were ratified in 1791. This 'Bill of Rights' guarantees protection under the law for speech, religion, freedom from cruel and unusual punishment, fair trial protections, and the right to bear arms.

These documents transformed the idea of natural rights and democratic principles from theory into practice. Rights were enshrined in legal documents which gave the individual the protection of the law. However, although the US Declaration may have stated all men are equal, it did not refer to slaves nor did it allow women equal rights with men.

Nineteenth century challenges to natural rights

By the end of the eighteenth century, the idea of civil and political rights stemming from the natural state of man was the predominant philosophy of constitutional documents. The early nineteenth century witnessed the growth of anti-slavery movements. Freedom from slavery became recognised as an individual human right and was recognised as such at an international as well as domestic level in many states.

However, the rise of **utilitarianism** and other consequentialist movements challenged this predominance of individual rights based on natural law. Philosophers such as Bentham derided the idea of rights preceding law and Marx believed natural rights to be a tool of the powerful. The nineteenth century also witnessed the rise of social movements such as trade unions who argued for the rights of workers and the suffragettes arguing for women's rights. These movements emphasised rights beyond the negative idea of civil and political rights where the state refrains from interfering. They argued for social and economic rights where the state was under a duty to take positive steps to provide fair employment rights etc. The nineteenth century also saw the development of international humanitarian law with the founding of the Red Cross. This led to codified rules to protect victims of warfare.

Twentieth century: the development of international protection

The international protection of human rights developed in the twentieth century as a result of war and atrocity. Following the First World War, the League of Nations was formed with the primary aim of preventing war and maintaining peace. Human rights were not part of its agenda. However, it did afford group protection to minorities. The First World War led to the break-up of large empires and the creation of new nation states. The redrawing of state borders left ethnic minorities within the new states. The League of Nations negotiated treaties between states protecting minority rights.

The war crime trials: Nuremberg and Tokyo

However, the Second World War demonstrated that the group protection regime failed to protect individuals when faced with the mass discrimination and the abuse of individuals which led to atrocities and the Holocaust. The war crime trials marked an important development in international law. Traditionally, individuals were not the subjects of international law. Only states could be held responsible for the violation of international treaties etc. However, the war crime trials at Nuremberg and Tokyo changed this. For the first time individuals were held liable for international crimes against individuals.

Nuremberg principles

- Crimes against the peace, war crimes, conspiracy to wage war and a newly developed crime—crimes against humanity (**Article 6 of the Nuremberg Statute**).
- Removal of individual immunity and superior order defence—this could no longer be used for the above crimes. An individual could not avoid liability by claiming he was only following orders or that the state was responsible (**Article 7 of the Nuremberg Statute**). This has been an important principle for the protection of human rights. (The International Criminal Court has jurisdiction for bringing individuals to trial.)

✳✳✳✳✳✳✳✳✳✳

✅ *Looking for extra marks?*

It is worth reading criticisms of Nuremberg as being victors' justice and for ignoring the 'crimes' of the allies as well as being guilty of charging individuals with a crime (crime against humanity) that did not exist—it is argued this violated the principle of retrospectivity (a person cannot be charged with an offence that did not exist at the time of the alleged act).

The United Nations (UN)

The formation of the United Nations after the Second World War witnessed the return of natural rights as the dominant influence on rights protection. The emphasis was again placed on individual rights. Unlike the League of Nations, human rights were integral to the aims of the new body. The Charter which established the United Nations included express reference to the protection of rights.

UN Declaration of Human Rights (UDHR) 1948

The Declaration enunciated the rights to be protected. This was a non-binding document but it has important symbolic effect and some of it is now international customary law (binding on states due to state practice). The list of rights included civil/political and economic/social rights. It was to be the basis for a binding Convention on rights.

Treaties

However, the beginning of the Cold War between the Soviet bloc of states and the western states meant it was difficult to agree one covenant containing the rights in the UDHR. The western states championed civil and political rights whilst the Soviet bloc was only interested in social and economic rights. In response, two covenants were agreed:

International Covenant on Civil and Political Rights (ICCPR) 1966

This general universal treaty covers the classic civil and political rights and contains a non-discrimination clause. States are under a duty to 'to respect and to ensure to all individuals within its territory and subject to its jurisdiction the rights recognized in the present Covenant' (**Article 2(1)**).

International Covenant on Economic, Social and Cultural Rights (ICESCR) 1966

This general universal treaty covers economic and social rights such as housing, health, education, and culture. It also includes a non-discrimination clause. States are under a duty to 'take steps…to the maximum of its available resources, with a view of achieving progressively the full realization of the rights recognized in the present Covenant' (**Article 2(1)**).

Specific treaties

- UN International Convention on the Elimination of All Forms of Racial Discrimination, 1966
- UN Convention on the Elimination of All Forms of Discrimination Against Women, 1979
- UN Convention Against Torture, 1984
- UN Convention on the Rights of the Child, 1989
- UN Convention on Rights of Migrant Workers and Their Families, 1990
- UN Convention for the Protection of All Persons from Enforced Disappearance, 2006
- UN Convention on the Rights of Persons with Disabilities, 2008

The United Nations has also agreed declarations on human rights in education and other areas such as religion.

Enforcing the UN treaties?

This is an area in which there has been much criticism of the United Nations. International law is based on consensus and so is very different from domestic law where enforcement of the law is usually done through compulsion (eg criminal law). There are two available mechanisms within some of the treaties: quasi-judicial mechanisms where an individual can petition to get the case heard, and reporting mechanisms where states report back to the United Nations on how they are fulfilling their obligations under the convention. Each convention has a committee responsible for monitoring implementation of the obligations of states. For example, the ICCPR has the Human Rights Committee. It can deal with individual petition (under the Optional Protocol to the ICCPR) and it reviews state reports.

Human Rights Committee (ICCPR)

- Individual petition: petitions brought before the Committee are known as communications and the Committee can make its views known to states. These are not binding on states as a legal judgment.
- Reporting mechanism: Each state party sends a periodic report to the Committee on measures taken to fulfil its obligations under the treaty. The Committee can ask the state for more information and can consult other bodies within the UN and non-governmental organisations (NGOs). It also holds a session where a representative from the state answers questions from the Committee. It then issues a final report making recommendations if necessary.

Historical development of rights

✱✱✱✱✱✱✱✱✱✱

Charter-based bodies

As well as human rights protections guaranteed through binding treaties, the United Nations has established bodies under the Charter to examine human rights protection. The General Assembly is responsible for passing resolutions and for the agreement of treaties. All other bodies below report to the General Assembly. The body delegated by the Assembly to oversee human rights is the Economic and Social Council (ECOSOC). ECOSOC established the Commission on Human Rights under **Article 62** of the UN Charter. In 2006, the Commission was abolished and replaced by the Human Rights Council (General Assembly Resolution 60/251).

United Nations Human Rights Council

The Human Rights Council consists of representatives from 47 member states. Each state on the Council is elected from their different regional groupings every three years. The Council is responsible for the promotion and protection of human rights through dialogue and review. The Council undertakes a 'universal periodic review' of every state's human rights record. Each state that is a member of the Council must also be reviewed whilst serving its membership. A member state can be suspended from the Council by a two-thirds majority if gross and systemic abuse of human rights is attributed to that state. The Council also passes recommendations and reports to the General Assembly.

There are procedures in place to allow the Council to investigate state compliance with human rights protection. These procedures can be used to put political pressure on states to comply with their obligations and can lead to the 'naming and shaming' of states that systematically violate human rights.

The Complaints Procedure (ECOSOC Resolution 1503 as revised by HR Council Resolution 5/1)

The procedure examines communications from NGOs and individuals. These will be examined by the Working Group on Communications of the Advisory Committee to the Human Rights Council. If it is decided the allegations are admissible, the report will be passed to the Working Group of the Human Rights Council on Situations to see if it 'may reveal a consistent pattern of gross and reliably attested violations of human rights'. The Working Group has several options:

1. take no action;
2. keep the situation under review; or
3. pass the report to Human Rights Council. The report is confidential and the state has to consent in order to investigate.

The Human Rights Council has several options at the end of this procedure:

1. take no action;
2. refer to special procedures—the complaints procedure is confidential;

3. appoint an ad hoc conciliation committee with the consent of the state;

4. appoint an independent expert or rapporteur for the state under Special Procedures; or

5. keep the situation under review.

Special Procedures (set up under ECOSOC Resolution 1235 as revised by HR Council Resolution 5/1) (Referral from complaint procedure or initiated by states)

This procedure is not confidential as reports are made public. Under these procedures the Human Rights Council has several options when a report is referred from the complaints procedure or allegations made by states:

1. take no action;

2. provide advisory services;

3. ask for further information to consider later;

4. ask the government to respond to accusations;

5. adopt a resolution condemning the state;

6. appoint a rapporteur—country or thematic mandate; or

7. refer to the Security Council.

Rapporteurs

The rapporteurs investigate and report on state compliance with their human rights obligations. There are many rapporteurs on themes such as torture, arbitrary detention, and disappearances. They can also be appointed to investigate specific countries where the procedures have revealed systematic abuse of human rights.

Security Council

- Five permanent members with a veto, (UK, USA, France, China, Russia).
- Ten rotating members for two-year terms.
- Nine votes required for decisions taken including the votes of all five permanent members.
- Resolutions can be legally binding.

The Security Council is not directly responsible for the enforcement of human rights protection, However it has increasingly become involved in protection measures. It has recognised the link between human rights violations and threats to peace. It has the power to order sanctions against states, to deploy peacekeepers with the consent of the state, and can order the use of force. This final option is controversial and rarely used. It is difficult to get agreement in the Security Council as the five permanent members have a veto over action and political self-interest can prevent action. One example where agreement has been reached is the use of force against Gaddaffi forces in Libya (March 2011) by UN Security Council Resolution 1973 which authorises the use of force to protect civilians.

Revision tip
An exam question may ask about the enforcement of international human rights. It may focus on the effectiveness of the UN or on the comparison between judicial, quasi-judicial, and reporting mechanisms. It is worth reading H. Steiner and P. Alston, *International Human Rights in Context: Law, Politics, Morals*, 3rd edn (OUP, 2008) chs 9 and 10.

Regional agreements

There are also regional agreements that set out obligations on state parties in those regions. These articulate similar rights to the UN treaties, but may particularly address regional cultures and have enforcement mechanisms; the most developed being the European Court of Human Rights:

- **European Convention on Human Rights and Fundamental Freedoms 1950** (Council of Europe) (Court)
- **European Social Charter** (revised) (Council of Europe) (European Committee of Social Rights—reporting and collective complaints mechanism)
- **EU Charter of Fundamental Rights** (Lisbon Treaty 2009) (European Union) (Court)
- **African Charter of Human Rights and Peoples Rights 1981** (African Union) (Commission and Court)
- **American Convention of Human Rights 1969** (Organisation of American States) (Commission and Court)
- **Arab Charter on Human Rights 1994** (revised 2004) (League of Arab States) (Committee (reporting): no mechanism for individual complaint).

The Commonwealth of Independent States made up of former Soviet states has signed a treaty on human rights and the Asian states have developed a Charter on Human Rights but these are still developing. The Association of Southeast Asian Nations (ASEAN) established an Intergovernmental Commission on Human Rights in 2009.

Human rights today

Human rights are now high on the political agenda. With the end of the Cold War, human rights were integral to the establishment of the newly independent ex-Soviet states. However the terrorist attack on September 11, 2001 on the USA and other attacks have created challenges to rights protection. The 'war on terror' challenged rights such as the absolute protection from torture, the right not to be arbitrarily detained, and privacy and expression rights. Other challenges include the continuing global conflicts, governments that fail to comply with international obligations, global poverty, and the challenge of environmental degradation.

Revision tip

An exam question on the historical development of human rights may examine the change of focus from individual to group protection in the nineteenth century with the challenges to natural rights, then the reversion back to individual rights after the Second World War.

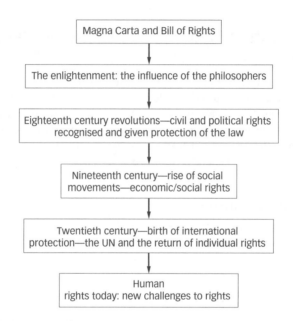

Fig 1.1 Historical development of human rights

Categories of rights

As noted above, rights have been classified historically as different types of rights.

Exam tip

An exam question may ask about the different generation of rights and arguments for and against treating the rights differently. Be aware of the arguments outlined below and reinforce with examples such as UN Committee reports, case law, and academic opinion.

First generation rights: civil and political rights

These rights include the right to life, freedom from torture and arbitrary detention, the right to privacy, and freedom of expression. These have traditionally been considered to be fundamental rights in a liberal, democratic society. These are seen as negative rights, in the sense that the state is being asked to refrain from acting in a way that would violate these rights. These were championed by western, liberal states during the Cold War. These rights have traditionally been seen as being '**justiciable**', meaning that they can be interpreted and determined by national and possibly international courts.

Second generation rights: social, economic, and cultural rights

These rights include the right to food, water, housing, education, and employment rights. These rights have been seen as positive rights as they place an obligation on the state to act in order to ensure that these rights are provided. These rights were championed by China and the Soviet states during the Cold War. They have traditionally been considered to be 'non-justiciable', meaning they are difficult to interpret by the judiciary and are issues for government policy that should not be determined by courts.

Third generation rights

This type of right covers a variety of issues, such as the right to economic development, group rights, right to peace, and also rights related to the environment. This is a developing area.

Separate or interdependent?

Although rights have traditionally been divided into generational rights, these traditional distinctions are no longer seen by all commentators as accurate. All rights are now argued to be 'indivisible, interrelated and interdependent' and were described as such by the UN Vienna Declaration in 1993. This means that these rights cannot exist in isolation from each other. What good is the right to life if people are suffering from severe malnutrition or have no health care?

The distinctions between the different generations have influenced how such rights are to be enforced through international mechanisms. It has been argued that first generation rights are legally enforceable whereas second and third generation rights are aspirational and not legally enforceable by individuals (see different wording in obligations on states under ICCPR and ICESCR).

Arguments for separation and different enforcement measures:

- Civil/political (negative) rights involve little cost to the state whereas economic/social rights require positive measures which carry an economic cost/burden.
- Civil/political rights easily justiciable—not difficult for a court to adjudicate on meaning and content of civil/political rights whereas social/economic rights are difficult to measure.
- Economic/social rights require judges to make decisions best reserved for an elected body on economic and social issues.

However, those who advocate the indivisible approach argue that all rights involve some cost to the state. For example, the right to a fair trial requires the state to put procedures etc in place. It has also been argued that economic and social rights are measurable. This can be done by examining a state's spending policy (the Economic and Social Committee of the ICESCR has done this when looking at health care in states) or looking at unemployment rates in local areas. Some states have included economic and social rights in their constitutions which have been held by the courts to be justiciable:

Government of South Africa v Grootboom, Constitutional Court of South Africa, Case CCT 11/00, October 2000

The South African Constitution gives full recognition to economic and social rights. **Section 26** states that everyone has the right to housing and the state should take reasonable measures, within its available resources, to progressively realise the right.

The respondents in the case lived in extremely poor conditions and had been on a seven-year waiting list for low cost housing. They moved on to private land in temporary shacks. They were evicted from this land, having their possessions destroyed and were left without shelter. The Constitutional Court had to interpret the obligation on the state under **s 26**.

The court held that the state had to take reasonable steps to fulfil its obligation under **s 26**.

The court examined the approach of the Economic and Social Committee of the ICESCR. It acknowledged the difficulties of determining the needs of those claiming protection of the right to housing but held that it was possible to identify the minimum core obligation under the right, which depended on various factors including poverty and availability of land etc. The court had to decide if the state had taken reasonable steps to meet the core obligation with regard to access to housing. Measures must establish a coherent programme, the content of which is left to the state to decide within its resources. However, the facts of the case demonstrate the measures taken especially for those most in need were not reasonable as they did not meet even the minimum requirements. The court held the state to account without ordering specific measures and specific spending targets. The state must take reasonable steps to provide access to housing that does not undermine the dignity of the respondents.

. . . .

Olga Tellis v Bombay Municipal Corporation, Supreme Court of India, AIR 1986 Supreme Court 18

The Indian Constitution has a list of directive principles that cover economic and social rights. These are not directly enforceable in court but the state has a duty to apply the principle in making law.

The petitioners lived on the pavements and slums in Bombay and their eviction was ordered. They argued that this would remove their livelihood which was inextricably linked to where they lived. **Article 39** of the Constitution has a directive principle on the right to a livelihood and **Article 21** guarantees the right to life.

The Supreme Court held eviction in this case would undermine the right to livelihood which would also undermine the right to life as both are inextricably linked.

The Court noted the interdependence of the right to a livelihood and the right to life. It found the right to life under **Article 21** was far-reaching and included the right to livelihood. The Court ordered that the slum dwellers should be given alternative sites to settle and should not be evicted until after the winter rains.

. . . .

✅ *Looking for extra marks?*

There has been much academic writing on this area and there is also case law from regional areas such as the Inter-American Court of Human Rights. See also Additional Protocol to the American Convention on Human Rights in the Area of Economic, Social and Cultural Rights, 'Protocol of San Salvador' 1999. See H. Steiner and P. Alston, *International Human Rights in Context: Law, Politics, Morals,* 3rd edn, (OUP, 2008) ch 4, which has useful abstracts from numerous writers and from UN reports.

Human rights in the UK

Constitutional settlement and rights

Any discussion of human rights in the UK needs to be placed in context of the constitutional position. Unlike most modern constitutions, the UK Constitution is not codified. It does not have a written Bill of Rights. Instead rights have been protected by a few written documents, by legislation made by Parliament, and by **common law**. The UK Constitution is premised on separation of powers and the rule of law.

The legislature is the primary law-making body and the doctrine of parliamentary supremacy applies. This means that Parliament can make or unmake any law whatsoever. It can repeal its own laws and can make new ones without restraint (although it has been argued that EU law has limited this supremacy). The judiciary are guardians of the rule of law. However, the courts, including the Supreme Court, have no power to overturn or declare void primary legislation made by Parliament (though they can void secondary legislation such as orders and regulations under judicial review procedures). The courts can interpret legislation but they cannot undermine the intention of Parliament.

The uncodified constitution of the UK has evolved over hundreds of years and can be found in a number of sources:

- Constitutional documents: there are several written documents which are said to be constitutional in nature. These have involved the protection of subjects from the arbitrary use of power by the Crown. **Magna Carta 1215** was an agreement between the King and his barons, which guaranteed certain protections for subjects such as **Habeas Corpus** and trial by jury. The **Bill of Rights 1689** was part of the settlement between Parliament and the Crown. The name is misleading as it is not a modern Bill of Rights but it did guarantee certain protections such as freedom of speech in Parliament and also contained a prohibition on arbitrary use of cruel and unusual punishments.

- Legislation: the legislature has also laid down important constitutional protections such as the **Human Rights Act**. These of course may be repealed as Parliament is supreme.

- Constitutional conventions: these are rules that have developed over time. Although not legally binding, they are generally followed by those in power, an example being the collective responsibility of the Cabinet of the government for decisions taken by it.

- Common law: the UK has a common law system based on **precedent**. Legal protections have been developed by the courts over time

- Royal Prerogative: The Crown is still the head of state in the UK Constitution. Much of the power of the Crown has been ceded to Parliament but any residual power that has not been legislated on remains under the Royal Prerogative, such as pardons for prisoners and declarations of war. In practice, most of these powers are carried out by the government of the Crown (the executive).

Common law and rights

As few rights protections were written down, the common law has been important for developing protections recognised by the courts. These were limited but an important historical example is the slavery case *Somerset v Steuart* **(1772) 98 ER 499**, where the court refused to allow a recaptured slave to be forcibly removed to the Americas. In more recent times (pre **Human Rights Act**) the court recognised some rights protections as constitutionally important which could only be abrogated by the express will of Parliament.

....

R v Lord Chancellor, ex p Witham [1997] 2 All ER 779

The issue was access to a court and therefore fair trial rights as the applicant could not get legal aid to pay court fees in a defamation case.

The Court of Appeal held that the common law clearly afforded special protection to a person's right of access to a court as a constitutional right. This means that the executive could not abrogate that right without express provision being enacted by Parliament.

....

Similarly, the court recognised the importance of expression in:

R v Secretary of State for the Home Department, ex p Simms [1999] 3 All ER 400

This case concerned freedom of expression. The applicant was a prisoner who wished to discuss an appeal against his conviction with a journalist but the prison imposed a blanket ban on professional interviews.

The House of Lords held, whilst recognising that the public authority could limit freedom of expression as it is not an absolute right, the expression at issue in the case was specific and valuable. The applicant wished to challenge his conviction and so freedom of expression was of great importance. Though the Prison Rules may not be inherently unlawful, the blanket ban curtailed the applicant's right to freedom of expression.

✅ Looking for extra marks?

There has also been criticism of the common law and the judiciary for failing to provide protection for some rights such as freedom of association.

Human Rights Act 1998

The UK ratified the **European Convention on Human Rights**. However the UK is a dualist system with regard to the incorporation of international law into domestic systems. In monist states, an international treaty automatically becomes part of domestic law. However in the UK, an international treaty is only binding on the UK between itself and state parties to the treaty. Parliament must enact legislation to make treaty provisions part of domestic law and so directly enforceable in a domestic court. Before 1998, a person could bring a case to the European Court of Human Rights but could not argue Convention rights directly before a UK court. The UK courts could use the Convention to help interpret ambiguous wording or clauses in legislation but could not decide a case on a Convention right alone.

The **Human Rights Act** incorporated the **European Convention on Human Rights** into UK law. Convention rights are now directly enforceable against public bodies by any person who can demonstrate that he or she is a victim under the Act. The Act maintains the constitutional position as the courts cannot overturn primary legislation but can declare (with no legal effect on the validity of the legislation) legislation incompatible with a Convention right (**s 4**). The courts have also a power of interpretation which allows them to interpret legislation so as to be compatible with Convention rights even where not ambiguous (**s 3**). There is debate as to whether the Act has given too much power to the judiciary and so undermining parliament supremacy in practice if not in theory (see Chapter 3, 'The Human Rights Act 1998', pp 44–47).

Fig 1.2 Historical development of rights protection in the UK

Revision tip

There are many articles and books written on public law and human rights in the UK. There is still an ongoing debate on the role of the judiciary and the possible need for a 'British Bill of Rights' as well as criticism of the European Court of Human Rights for interfering in domestic affairs. See Chapter 3, 'The Human Rights Act 1998', p 54.

✱ Key cases

Case	Facts	Principle
Government of South Africa v Grootboom **Constitutional Court of South Africa, Case CCT 11/00 October 2000**	The respondents were evicted and left without shelter. The Supreme Court had to interpret the obligation on the state under s 26 of Constitution: right to housing.	The Supreme Court held that there was a minimum core obligation on the state under the right to housing. The state had to take reasonable steps within its resources to meet the core obligation with regard to access to housing.
Olga Tellis v Bombay Municipal Corporation, **Supreme Court of India AIR 1986 Supreme Court 18**	The petitioners lived in slums in Bombay and their eviction was ordered. Article 39 of the Constitution is a directive principle on the right to a livelihood and Article 21 guarantees the right to life.	Eviction in this case would undermine the right to livelihood which would also undermine the right to life as both are inextricably linked.

Key debates

✱✱✱✱✱✱✱✱✱✱

Case	Facts	Principle
R v Lord Chancellor, ex p Witham [1997] 2 All ER 779	The applicant could not get legal aid to pay court fees in a defamation case (pre HRA).	The common law afforded special protection to a person's right of access to a court as a constitutional right. The executive could not abrogate that right without express provision being enacted by Parliament.
R v Secretary of State for the Home Department, ex p Simms [1999] 3 All ER 400	The applicant was a prisoner who wished to discuss an appeal against his conviction with a journalist but the prison imposed a blanket ban on interviews (pre HRA).	Though the public authority could limit freedom of expression as it is not absolute, the applicant wished to challenge his conviction and so this expression was of great importance. The blanket ban curtailed the applicant's right to freedom of expression.

(🔢) Key debates

Topic	'New horizons: incorporating socio-economic rights in a British Bill of Rights'
Author	Sandra Fredman
Viewpoint	Argues that there should be no distinct classification between rights. Primary responsibility for determining how to fulfil positive duties should be with the legislature and executive. The role of the judiciary is to enhance democratic accountability.
Source	(2010) *Public Law*, Apr, 297–320

Topic	'Reconceiving The UN Human Rights Regime: Challenges Confronting The New UN Human Rights Council'
Author	Philip Alston
Viewpoint:	Examines the challenges facing the UN Human Rights Council in addressing the criticisms of the Commission it replaced and examines further reform that may be needed.
Source	(2006) *Melbourne Journal of International Law* vol 7

(?) Exam question

Essay question

'Both freedom and bread are necessary for the all-round human being. Instead of undermining each other, they are interrelated and interdependent.'
(A Sachs, 'The Judicial Enforcement of Socio-economic Rights')

Civil/political rights and economic/social rights have been treated differently in international law despite this argument and United Nations statements to the contrary.

(a) Explain how and why, historically, rights have been treated differently.

and

(b) Evaluate the question of whether there should be a hierarchy of rights protection.

 Scan here

Scan this QR code image with your mobile device to see an outline answer to this question or log onto www.oxfordtextbooks.co.uk/orc/concentrate/

#2

European Convention on Human Rights

Key Facts

- The **European Convention on Human Rights** was developed in the aftermath of the Second World War and reflects the ideology of the Western European states; mainly consisting of civil and political rights.

- The European complaints system has been reformed several times in an attempt to deal with an increasing caseload.

- The European Court of Human Rights (ECtHR) is the most advanced international court of human rights.

- The European Court of Human Rights uses a number of interpretative principles to develop and expand protection of the ECHR.

- Rights are classified as absolute, limited, or qualified.

- When adjudicating on qualified rights the ECtHR Rights uses the doctrines of proportionality and margin of appreciation.

Chapter overview

```
                    European
                  Convention on
                  Human Rights
```

| Background and rationale | The Convention rights | The European Court of Human Rights | Interpreting the rights: principles | Nature of the rights | Proportionality and the margin of appreciation |

Background and rationale

Council of Europe

The Council of Europe was created in 1949 after the devastation of the Second World War. It was designed to prevent another European war and reflected the rationale and aims of the newly created United Nations. The emphasis was placed on the prevention of authoritarianism in Europe and to counter ideology of the Soviet states at the beginning of the Cold War. The establishing treaty underlines the importance of liberal democracy and the rule of law and 'the maintenance and further realisation of human rights and fundamental freedoms'. It should be noted that the states involved until the late 1980s were the Western European states. The Council of Europe now has 47 members. The collapse of the Soviet Union led to the growth of the Council of Europe and over 800 million people now live in the Council of Europe states.

Structure of Council of Europe

* Committee of Ministers—consists of Ministers from the member states and their permanent representatives based in Strasbourg. The Committee is responsible for policy, promulgating the treaties, and the supervision/enforcement of compliance with the decisions of the European Court of Human Rights.
* Parliamentary Assembly—the 318 members of the Parliamentary Assembly are elected from national parliaments. The Assembly can make non-binding recommendations

and resolutions, monitor member state compliance with treaties, and elects posts such as the judges to the Court, the Secretary General, and the Commissioner for Human Rights. The Legal Affairs Committee of the Assembly prepares proposals for treaties, which are then referred by the Committee of Ministers to a group of legal experts who prepare treaty texts to be approved by the Committee of Ministers.

- Secretariat—administrative arm of the Council of Europe led by the Secretary General.

- European Commissioner for Human Rights—the post was created in 2000 to promote awareness and monitor observance of member states with the obligations under the treaties dealing with human rights.

- Congress of Local and Regional Authorities—advises the Strasbourg institutions on local and regional issues.

A convention on rights

To further the aim of the protection of democracy and the rule of law encompassing rights, the Council of Europe formulated the **European Convention for the Protection of Human Rights and Fundamental Freedoms** (ECHR) in 1950 which came into force in 1953. The ECHR reflects the liberal western states that were responsible for its drafting. It includes civil and political rights and does not include a list of economic and social rights. It reflects the first generation rights in a similar way to the ICCPR (see Chapter 1, 'First generation rights: civil and political rights', p 12). This reflected the ideology of the West and acted as a counter to the Soviet states who advocated economic and social protections. The original Convention has been added to by later protocols of rights that could not be agreed upon in 1950 or became increasingly recognised in later years.

Other human rights instruments

The focus of this guide will be on the ECHR but it should be noted that other treaties also include rights protection. These include:

- **European Social Charter 1961** (revised 1996)—these instruments cover social and economic rights. (See Chapter 1, 'Second generation rights: social, economic, and cultural rights', pp 12–14 on the categories of rights and why they have been treated separately.) It has a reporting mechanism and collective complaints system but no individual petition.

- **European Convention for the Prevention of Torture 1961**—this convention created a monitoring body, the European Committee for the Prevention of Torture. The Committee has powers to investigate member states.

- **European Charter for Regional or Minority Languages 1992**—member states agreed to certain measures to protect minority languages. It has a reporting mechanism but no individual petition.

- **Framework Convention for the Protection of National Minorities 1995**—this provides protection for minorities. It has a reporting mechanism but no individual petition.
- **European Convention on the Exercise of Children's Rights 1996**—the convention includes protections similar to the UN Convention on the Rights of the Child and includes a committee to monitor state compliance. There is no individual petition.
- **European Convention on Action against Trafficking in Human Beings 2005**—the convention includes measures to prevent trafficking and protect victims and establishes a group of experts to monitor compliance. There is no individual petition.
- **European Convention on Preventing and Combating Violence against Women and Domestic Violence 2011** (not yet in force)—the convention includes measures to prevent violence and to protect victims. It has a group of experts to monitor compliance. There is no individual petition.

The Convention rights

The European Convention for the protection of human rights and fundamental freedoms 1950 (with protocols)

- Article 2—right to life
- Article 3—prohibition on torture, inhuman or degrading treatment
- Article 4—prohibition of slavery
- Article 5—not to be arbitrarily detained,
- Article 6—fair trial
- Article 7—retroactivity of criminal law
- Article 8—family, private life, home and correspondence
- Article 9—freedom of thought, conscience, and religion
- Article 10—freedom of expression
- Article 11—freedom of assembly and association
- Article 12—the right to marry and have a family
- Article 13—access to domestic remedies
- Article 14—non-discrimination

Protocol 1
- Article 1—right to property
- Article 2—not be denied education
- Article 3—right to free elections

Protocol 4
- Article 1—no imprisonment for debt
- Article 2—freedom of movement and choice of residence
- Article 3—freedom from exile and to enter country of which national

- Article 4—prohibition of collective expulsion of aliens

Protocol 6
- Prohibition of the death penalty

Protocol 7
- Article 1—right of non-expulsion of alien without due process
- Article 2—right of appeal in criminal cases
- Article 3—compensation for miscarriage of justice
- Article 4—immunity from being prosecuted twice for same offence
- Article 5—equality of spouses re private law between them and children

Protocol 12
- Non-discrimination as a free standing right

Protocol 13
- Abolition of the death penalty in all circumstances

The European Court of Human Rights (ECtHR)

The European Court of Human Rights is the most developed regional international court for human rights. The Court can examine inter-state complaints (**Article 33 of the ECHR**) and applications from individuals (**Article 34 of the ECHR**).

Revision tip

Concentrate on the major changes to the complaints system outlined below and the main reasons for these as well as the arguments for and against these reforms.

Reform of the complaints system: Protocol 14

The ECtHR has been a success in that it has adjudicated on a large volume of cases covering important issues relating to the Convention rights. However, one of the drawbacks of being accessible to all individuals within the Council of Europe states is the number of cases that come before the Court creating a large backlog of cases. This problem was exacerbated in the 1990s with the entry of the newly independent states after the end of the Cold War and the break-up of states such as Yugoslavia. There have been several attempts to reform the system. **Protocol 11** was an important reform which has now been built upon by **Protocol 14**, which came into force in 2010.

The complaints system that existed before **Protocol 11** came into force in 1998 had several bodies involved in decision-making. The European Commission of Human Rights decided on admissibility. If the case was held inadmissible then the decision was final. If admissible, the Commission made a decision on the merits and it could then be passed to the Committee of

The European Court of Human Rights (ECtHR)

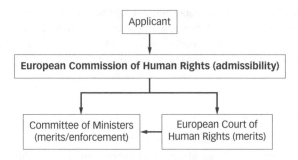

Fig 2.1 Structure of complaint system before Protocol 11

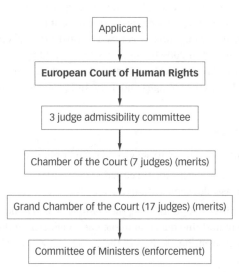

Fig 2.2 Structure of complaints system as amended by Protocol 11 (before Protocol 14)

Ministers for resolutions such as a friendly settlement if a violation occurred or it could be referred to the Court by the Committee or the parties. The Court then delivered a judgment on the merits of the case. The Committee of Ministers then monitored the enforcement of the compliance with the judgments. The ultimate sanction for failure to comply with Court judgments is the suspension of a state from the Council of Europe. (This has not been used as yet.)

Protocol 11 reformed the system in order to speed up the processing of applications. The Commission was abolished and replaced with a full-time Court. It introduced a three-tier court system: a three-judge committee for admissibility decisions, a Chamber that would hear cases held to be admissible, and a Grand Chamber. A case could be referred to the Grand Chamber if parties requested and a panel of five judges accepted the case raised a serious issue of interpretation and importance (**Article 43**) or if jurisdiction was relinquished by the Chamber for similar reasons (**Article 30**). If a violation was found then the Committee of Ministers would be responsible for monitoring compliance with the judgment.

Current structure

In the years following the reform, it became clear that it had not removed the backlog and delay from the system. (As of March 2011 there were 149,900 cases pending before the Court). It has been estimated that the number of cases will continue to grow between 12%–15% per year. The delay undermines the work of the Court and access to justice for individuals who may be suffering rights violations in their states. It is estimated that only about 6% of cases are held admissible. Therefore, change was targeted at the admissibility stage in order to speed up the majority of cases. However, it took some years to get **Protocol 14** enforced. For political reasons, Russia refused to ratify the protocol. A protocol known as **Protocol 14bis** was agreed in 2009 by 46 states that would apply some of **Protocol 14** in signatory states until the full protocol was ratified by Russia. However, Russia agreed in 2010 to ratify **Protocol 14** and the changes under the full protocol are now in force. (**Protocol 14bis** ceased to apply).

Protocol 14: major changes

- Changes to election of judges: will serve one term of nine years.

- A single judge formation replaces three-judge committee for admissibility decision to speed up the process—decision is final (**Article 27**).

- Three-judge committee—if admissible, the committee can make a decision on the merits of a case if the underlying question in the case, concerning the interpretation or the application of the Convention, is already the subject of well-established case law of the Court (**Article 28**).

- Infringement proceedings: if the Committee Minister (by a two-thirds majority) finds a state is refusing to abide by a Court judgment, it can be referred back to the Grand Chamber for an infringement finding which will then be referred back to the Committee to take action (**Article 45**).

- A new admissibility criterion has been added to **Article 35**—the application is not admissible if the applicant has not suffered a significant disadvantage.

It is hoped that these reforms and other minor changes will make the system more efficient. However, discussions on further reform are taking place within the Council of Europe (for example, the Izmir Declaration on the Future of the European Court of Human Rights, April 2011).

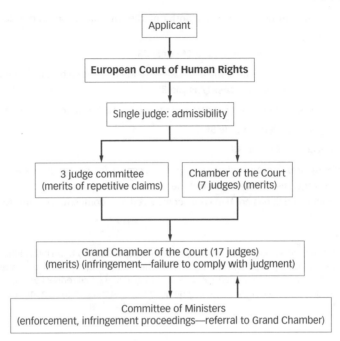

Fig 2.3 Current structure post Protocol 14

✅ Looking for extra marks?

One of the general issues that the Court reform highlights is the effectiveness of a judicial system for the protection of human rights (compare and contrast with reporting mechanisms—see Chapter 1, 'Enforcing the UN treaties?' p 7). See academic commentary and criticisms of the Court; see also Council of Europe Committee reports and reports by non-governmental organisations such as Amnesty International on the changes. Also note that discussions on further reform are ongoing.

Admissibility criteria

As noted (see p 26 above), an applicant has to get through the admissibility stage before the merits of the case are heard by the Court and only 6% of cases manage to do so. The admissibility criteria are set out in the ECHR, as amended by **Protocol 14**:

- Victim—an individual (which includes legal persons such as companies) has to be a victim, meaning he or she must be directly affected by the act complained of (*rationae personae*) (**Article 34**).
- Domestic remedies have to be exhausted (**Article 35**).

****

- Application has to be within six months of the final decision of the domestic court (**Article 35**).

- Cannot be an anonymous complaint (**Article 35**).

- Cannot be substantially the same as a case already examined by the Court or submitted to another international process (**Article 35**).

- Incompatible with Convention (*rationae materiae, rationae loci*) (**Article 35**).

- Manifestly ill-founded (**Article 35**).

- Abuse of process (**Article 35**).

- Not suffered significant disadvantage, unless respect for human rights as defined in the Convention requires an examination of the merits and provided that no case may be rejected on this ground which has not been duly considered by a domestic tribunal (**Article 35**).

Exam tip

An exam question may ask if the admissibility criteria limits the ability of an individual to get redress before the ECtHR, given only 6% of cases are held admissible. This raises a question about the role of an international human rights court—is it to give individual redress or is it to deal with the most serious or important cases that can be used to set standards throughout the Council of Europe area?

Interpreting the Convention rights

It is the ECtHR's role to interpret the Convention rights and this application should be followed by the 47 member states. It has developed important principles that it applies when deciding on alleged violations of the Convention.

Evolutive interpretation: the 'living instrument principle'

The Court is not bound by precedent and is open to a dynamic interpretation which allows the Court to develop human rights protection against the background of changes in society and social attitudes. The ECHR has been described by the Court as a 'living instrument which…must be interpreted in the light of present day conditions' (*Tyrer v UK* (**1978**)). The Court has been prepared to change its findings on many issues, including sexuality, prisoners' rights, and the death penalty. The principle has also allowed the Court to adjudicate on issues, which are not mentioned explicitly in the Convention, such as children's rights and the rights of the disabled.

One factor that heavily influences (but is not always conclusive of) the Court's decision to review and change previous decisions or recognise new areas is the practice of states. If there is a consensus amongst states as to the law or issue in contention then there is a much greater likelihood of a violation being found.

Example: transgender cases

Rees v UK (1981) (Application No 9532/81)

The applicant was a transsexual who wanted to change his name on his birth certificate. Without being able to do so, he did not have legal recognition of his change of gender and so argued this violated his right to private life.

The Court noted a lack of common ground between the member states on transsexual recognition. It varied from state to state and so the margin of appreciation (discretion) given to the state would be applied widely (see p 34 below).

The Court found that there was no violation given this lack of consensus but also noted that the UK should review its position in the light of future scientific and societal developments (decided by 12 to 3).

Ten year later, a similar case came before the ECtHR:

Cossey v UK (1991) (Application No 10843/84)

The applicant was a transsexual who could not change her sex on her birth certificate or contract a valid marriage with a man. She claimed that this violated **Article 8** and **Article 12**.

The Court was asked to reconsider the ***Rees*** decision on the basis of the living instrument principle. However, the Court noted that although there had been developments there was still not enough common ground to reconsider the Rees position under **Article 8**. Therefore, there was no violation of the Convention.

However the decision was a majority of 10 to 8. The dissenting judges argued the Court should be much more progressive in recognising the rights of transsexuals given a growing consensus in Europe.

Goodwin v UK (2002) 35 EHRR 447

The applicant was a transsexual. She claimed a violation of the right to private life. In the UK, her changed gender was not recognised. She could not change her birth certificate, her national insurance number, and was still treated as male for pension purposes. She also claimed that her inability to change her gender on official documents led to discrimination in employment as employers could find out her previous gender.

The Court noted that is not formally bound to follow its previous judgments, although it is in the interests of legal certainty that it should not depart from previous decisions without cogent reasons. However, the Court underlined the living instrument principle: '...since the Convention is first and foremost a system for the protection of human rights, the Court must have regard to the changing conditions within the respondent State and within Contracting States generally and respond, for example, to any evolving convergence as to the standards to be achieved.' The Court considered scientific and social developments in the UK and Europe and the growing legal consensus with regard to recognition meant that there was a violation of **Article 8** on private life and **Article 12** on the right to marry.

Revision tip

This principle is important for the substantive rights that will be discussed, especially when examining why the Court is more willing to find violations in some areas rather than others.

Effectiveness

The Court has often stated that the Convention is intended to guarantee rights are 'practical and effective' and not 'theoretical and illusory'. In other words, it is important that individuals are able to access the Convention rights and they should be enforceable. For example in *Golder v UK* **(1978)**, the applicant was denied access to a solicitor whilst in prison. The Court held that **Article 6** must be read to include access to a court. Without this, the protection under **Article 6** and **Article 5** would become superfluous. The principle has also been used to justify the use of positive obligations (see 'Positive obligations').

Autonomy

The ECtHR can give an **autonomous meaning** to legal terms; meanings that are different from how they are construed in national law. It can construe terms such as 'criminal charge' and 'civil obligations' under **Article 6** differently from the states. This is to prevent a state avoiding its obligations under the Convention by construing terms narrowly and it also provides a common interpretation across the member states when the Court interprets the rights. (See *Engel v Netherlands* **(1976)**.)

Positive obligations

The rights in the Convention are civil and political rights. These are negative rights, in that they obligate the state to refrain from acting in a way that violates the right. (See also Chapter 1, 'First generation rights: civil and political rights', p 12.) However, the ECtHR has interpreted the Convention in a way that places obligations on member states to take positive steps to prevent violations of the Convention.

Revision tip

Positive obligations are important in the interpretation of Convention rights and will be discussed when examining the substantive rights. The general discussion below can be applied to many of the rights.

Article 1 of the ECHR confirms the **subsidiarity** of the Convention by stating that the contracting state must ensure that Convention rights are protected for all people within their jurisdiction. The Court has used **Article 1** when explaining the use of positive obligations. Positive obligations help to ensure the effectiveness of the Convention and are also used to ensure the protection of rights that have evolved under the living instrument principle. The general duty to protect has been developed in such cases as *Osman v UK* **(1998)**. The case considered the right to life under **Article 2** and noted that **Article 2** not only obligates the state to refrain from taking life but also to take appropriate steps to safeguard lives within its jurisdiction. It sets out the test to be applied when deciding if there is a duty on the state to protect, which applies where the state:

- knows or ought to have known at the time
- of the existence of a real and immediate risk (to life) of identified individual(s) and
- failed to take reasonable measures to avoid the risk.

From this principle, the Court has developed positive obligations in situations where the state should reasonably be expected to protect. Examples of these will be highlighted when discussing the substantive rights but some general obligations are:

- When individuals are in custody (see Chapter 4, 'When individuals are in custody', p 64).
- Establishing a legal framework (see Chapter 4, 'Establishing a legal framework', p 64).
- Giving information (see Chapter 4, 'Giving information', p 64).
- Removal of persons from the state (see Chapter 4, 'Removal of persons from state', p 71).
- Investigating alleged violations (see Chapter 4, 'Investigating alleged violations', p 65—this is also a procedural obligation, where the state must put procedures in place to protect rights such as **Article 2** and **Article 3**).

Effect of positive obligations

It should be noted that the use of positive obligations has an impact on the application of the ECHR and can be said to have expanded protection:

- **Blurring the line with social and economic rights?** Positive obligations may place a burden on the state in terms of economic or social policy in order to meet its obligations (*Airey v Ireland* **(1979)**).
- **Horizontality**—the ECHR contains a vertical relationship between the Convention and the individual. An individual can only bring a case against a state (so the violation has to involve the state or state agent) and not if the alleged violation is carried out by a private person. However, when the state is under a positive obligation it may be required to regulate private parties (such as under criminal law) or take steps to protect individuals

from others as in *Osman*. (See Chapter 3, 'Horizontal effect?', pp 41–43 for the vertical/ indirect horizontal effect under the **Human Rights Act 1998**.)

• Putting burdens on a state? As positive obligations put a burden on the state, the ECtHR has been careful not to place excessive obligations on states. As noted in *Osman*, the Court will consider what reasonable steps to be taken so as not to place a disproportionate or impossible burden on the state.

✅ *Looking for extra marks?*

There is academic opinion and comment on the use of positive obligations that you may find useful to read—see the chapters on substantive rights.

Nature of Convention rights

The rights in the ECHR are predominantly civil and political rights (see Chapter 1, 'First generation rights: civil and political rights', p 12). There can also be divided into absolute, limited, and qualified rights.

Absolute rights

Some of the rights under the ECHR are categorised as 'absolute'; the state cannot justify an interference with the rights. These rights are **Articles 2, 3, 4, and 7**. They cannot be derogated from (see 'Derogation', p 33 below).

Limited rights

Articles 5 and 6 are generally considered 'limited' rights. **Article 5** prohibits arbitrary detention. Accordingly, there is an absolute prohibition on detentions which are outside the scope of **Article 5(1)**. Likewise under **Article 6** there is an absolute right to a fair hearing if a case falls within the requirements of **Article 6(1)**. However the Court has found 'inherent' limitations when applied by the state and they can be derogated from (see 'Derogation', p 33).

Qualified rights

These are rights, the enjoyment of which requires a balance to be struck between the rights of the individual and those of the community. These include **Articles 8, 9, 10, and 11**. The state can justify a limitation of these rights and the ECtHR uses proportionality and the margin of appreciation to determine if a state is justified in interfering with a qualified right (see 'Proportionality and margin of appreciation', p 33, below). Any measure taken by a state must be in accordance with law and meet a legitimate aim.

ABSOLUTE	LIMITED	QUALIFIED
Art 2—life	Art 5—detention	Art 8—family, private life
Art 3—torture, inhuman and degrading treatment	Art 6—fair trial	Art 9—conscience, religion
Art 4—slavery		Art 10—expression
Art 7—retrospectivity		Art 11—assembly

Fig 2.4 Nature of ECHR rights

Derogation

Article 15 of the ECHR allows states to derogate from their obligations under the Convention in time of war or other public emergency threatening the life of the nation. States are *not permitted* to derogate from **Articles 3, 4(1), and** 7. Under **Article 2**, derogation is not permitted except in respect of deaths resulting from the lawful acts of war. Under **Article 15**, the state can only derogate if:

1. there must be a war or other public emergency threatening the life of the nation; and
2. the derogation is no more than strictly required by the exigencies of the situation; and
3. it must not be inconsistent with its other obligations under international law; and
4. the state must communicate the derogation to the Council of Europe.

States have used derogations mainly under **Article 5** and **Article 6** in cases such as *A and others v UK* **(2009)**,where the court held that the UK's derogation from **Article 5** satisfied the requirements of **Article 15** (see Chapter 10, 'Limited rights', p 178).

Exam tip

Derogation is usually important when a question arises on terrorism.

Proportionality and margin of appreciation

Proportionality

Proportionality is used by ECtHR as a tool to find the balance between the rights of the individual and the community when deciding upon qualified rights. It is now also used in the

Proportionality and margin of appreciation

✳✳✳✳✳✳✳✳✳✳

UK when courts are adjudicating cases under the **Human Rights Act 1998** (see Chapter 3, 'Proportionality', p 50).

The criteria the Court will examine when looking at the act or measure of the state in question include:

- Is it effective? Does the act/measure meet the legitimate aim? Is there a link between the measure and what the state argues it is meant to be achieving?
- Is it the least intrusive possible? Could other less intrusive measures have been taken?
- Does it deprive the 'very essence of the right'? Does the act/measure take away all of the protection of the right (which it cannot do) or merely limit the right?
- Is it balanced? This applies to both negative and positive obligations. Has a fair balance been struck between the competing interests of the individual and of the community as a whole? Is the individual's right of such importance that only the most compelling reasons would justify any interference?

Case law examples of the use of proportionality will be discussed when examining the substantive qualified rights (Chapters 6–9).

✅ Looking for extra marks?

Many cases are decided on proportionality grounds and there is literature on its use by the ECtHR and by the UK courts (see Chapter 3, 'Proportionality', p 50).

Margin of appreciation

The margin of appreciation doctrine considers the amount of discretion given to the state by the ECtHR when adjudicating on alleged violations of qualified rights.

Revision tip

Similarly to proportionality, the margin of appreciation influences decisions in the qualified rights discussed in Chapters 6–9.

The doctrine is premised on the fact that the state is primarily responsible for upholding Convention rights (**Article 1 ECHR** and subsidiarity) and that there may be variations in tolerance of measures in states. It was outlined in the **Article 10** case of:

. . . .

Handyside v UK (1976) 1 EHRR 737

The applicant distributed a book aimed at school children which contained sexual content. The book was banned in England and Wales and the applicant claimed that this was a violation of **Article 10**.

The Court held that there was no violation of **Article 10**. The limitation on the right was justified and proportionate as it was within the margin of appreciation of the state: 'By reason of their direct and continuous contact with the vital forces of their countries, State authorities are in principle in a better position than the international judge to give an opinion on the exact content of these requirements.'

The concept is controversial and it is not always easy to predict how the Court will use it. A wide margin of appreciation means it is more likely to find no violation whereas a narrow margin means a violation is more likely. However, this is not always the case. Even in cases where traditionally a wide margin of appreciation is usually given, there may still be a violation given the importance of the right in question.

However several factors will influence whether the margin of appreciation is wide or narrow:

- Nature/importance of the right/issue in question: ***Dudgeon v UK* (1981)**—sexual privacy, so narrow margin and violation.
- Nature/importance of general interest/aim: ***Laskey, Jaggard and Brown v UK* (1997)**—criminal law/health re harm; ***Klass v Germany* (1978)**—national security. In both cases, a wide margin and no violation.
- Lack of European consensus or standard (see p 28—importance of the living instrument principle): ***Goodwin v UK* (2002)**—transsexuals; narrowed over time, so violation.
- Areas where judges give wider margin because difficult to judge/resources: ***Buckley v UK* (1996)**—planning, no violation; ***Hatton v UK* (2003)**—economic factors, no violation.

✅ *Looking for extra marks?*

There are criticisms of the use of the margin of appreciation in cases such as ***Hatton*** and in a case such as ***Hirst v UK*** (2005) (a right to vote case), where the Court found that the margin of appreciation was narrow despite a lack of common standards and the state could not rely on it where it had not given proper consideration to the measure rather than relying on tradition. See, for example, dissenting opinions in ***Hatton*** and note academic opinions.

✳ *Key cases*

Case	Facts	Principle
***Goodwin v UK* (2002) 35 EHRR 447**	The applicant was a transsexual. She claimed a violation of the right to private life. In the UK, her changed gender was given legal recognition.	The ECtHR underlined the living instrument principle: '... the Court must have regard to the changing conditions within the respondent State and within Contracting States generally and respond, for example, to any evolving convergence as to the standards to be achieved.'

Key debates

✳✳✳✳✳✳✳✳✳✳✳

Case	Facts	Principle
Handyside v UK (1976) 1 EHRR 737	The applicant distributed a book aimed at school children which contained sexual content. The book was banned in England and Wales and the applicant claimed that this was a violation of Article 10.	The Court held that there was no violation. The limitation on the right was within the margin of appreciation of the state: 'By reason of their direct and continuous contact with the vital forces of their countries, State authorities are in principle in a better position than the international judge to give an opinion on the exact content of these requirements.'
Osman v UK (1998) 29 EHRR 245)	The applicants were attacked and one of them was killed by a stalker. They claimed a violation of Article 2, right to life as the police had failed to act despite knowing the stalking was taking place.	The state should take appropriate steps to protect (positive obligation) when it: knows or ought to have known at the time of the existence of a real and immediate risk (of life) to identified individual(s) and failed to take reasonable measures to avoid the risk.

⁹⁹ Key debates

Topic	'The Interlaken Declaration: the beginning of a new era for the European Court of Human Rights?'
Author	Alastair Mowbray
Viewpoint	Examines the latest discussion on further reform of the ECtHR following entry of **Protocol 14**.
Source	(2010) *Human Rights Law Review* 10(3), pp 519–528

Topic	'What not to wear: Religious rights, the European Court, and the Margin of appreciation'
Author	T Lewis
Viewpoint	Article discusses recent case law on religious rights involving wearing of religious symbols in public life and criticises the Court's approach to the use of margin of appreciation.
Source	(2007) 56 *International & Comparative Law Quarterly* 395

(?) Exam question

Essay question

Explain and analyse the reforms of the complaint system under the European Convention on Human Rights.

Scan here

Scan this QR code image with your mobile device to see an outline answer to this question or log onto www.oxfordtextbooks.co.uk/orc/concentrate/

#3
The Human Rights Act 1998 (HRA)

Key Facts

- The **HRA 1998** was introduced to allow individuals to argue cases involving rights contained in the ECHR directly before a UK court.

- Before the HRA came into force in 2000, individuals could not rely directly on Convention rights before a UK court. Judges could only use the Convention to aid interpretation in cases where the law was ambiguous.

- The **HRA** allows any person within the UK to bring a case against a public body including the courts for breach of a Convention right.

- In theory, the **HRA** has not changed the constitutional arrangements in the UK (Chapter 1, 'Constitutional settlement and rights', p 14). Judges cannot overturn a law that is in breach of the ECHR. They can reinterpret legislation to make it compatible or if this is not possible, they can make a declaration of incompatibility. It is then for Parliament to decide whether to change or repeal legislation. **Parliamentary supremacy** remains intact. (See 'Section 3: interpretation clause', p 44, below for further debate on this issue.)

- The **HRA** has been controversial. It has been criticised for having the effect in practice of undermining parliamentary supremacy. There is also an ongoing debate about whether the Act should be retained or replaced with a 'British Bill of Rights'.

Chapter overview

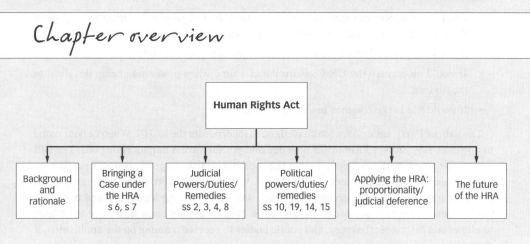

Background: rationale and the rights

Why have a HRA?

Prior to 1998, there had been much debate about the need to 'bring rights home' by making the rights in the European Convention on Human Rights (ECHR) enforceable in the UK courts.

Arguments against a Human Rights Act

- Individuals had already the freedom to do what they liked as long as not forbidden by the common law or statute. This argument defines human rights as essentially negative in nature, ie the non-interference of the state with a person's daily life (see Chapter 1, 'First generation rights: civil and political rights', p 12).

- Rights were already protected by common law and specific statutes.

- A HRA would create an overly litigious society and a charter for 'scroungers' and criminals.

- A HRA would give too much power to a conservative judiciary which would have a negative impact on protection for the poor and excluded.

Arguments for a Human Rights Act

- The negative idea of rights protection was no longer enough in an age of increasing state intervention in daily life.

- The UK increasingly lost cases before the European Court of Human Rights (ECtHR).

Background: rationale and the rights

✳✳✳✳✳✳✳✳✳✳

- The lack of access to Convention rights within the UK resulted in lengthy and costly litigation. A HRA would remove the barrier to arguing rights directly in the UK.
- In the long term, a HRA would create a culture of respect of rights.
- It would modernise the UK Constitution at a time when power was being devolved to the regions.
- It would add to the common law already in place.

The Labour Party under John Smith pledged to incorporate the ECHR. When Labour came to power in 1997, it kept its manifesto pledge and put forward a human rights bill. The Bill limited the power of the judiciary so that the constitutional arrangements under parliamentary supremacy remained intact (see Chapter 1, 'Constitutional settlement and rights', p 14) but it did give the judiciary greater discretion when interpreting legislation and bound all public bodies. The Act received Royal Assent in 1998. It did not come into force until 2000 to allow time for judges, lawyers, and public bodies to receive training on the application of the Act.

> ### Revision tip
>
> To examine the impact of the **HRA** you may need to be able to explain how it changed the law and the powers of the judiciary. To do this, explain briefly the constitutional settlement in the UK (Chapter 1, 'Constitutional settlement and rights', p 14), the position before the Act, and briefly outline why the Act was seen as necessary.

Which rights are covered by the HRA?

These are referred to in **Schedule 1 of the HRA**.

Articles 2–12; **Article 14**; **Protocol 1, Articles 1–3**; **Protocol 13** (as read with **Articles 16 and 18** dealing with interpretation of the rights (see Chapter 2, 'The Convention rights', p 23)).

Rights not covered by HRA

Article 13—access to domestic remedies (it was argued that the **HRA** itself provided a domestic remedy); **Protocols 4, 7, and 12** which are not ratified by the UK.

It should be noted that there are specific provisions dealing with **Article 9** (freedom of religion) and **Article 10** (freedom of expression). **Section 12 HRA** (expression) and **s 13 HRA** (religion) allow the court to give special regard to these rights when making decisions. This can be important when the court is asked to decide on whether to prevent the publication of a newspaper article that may affect the right to private life of a litigant or where a body's religious precepts may limit services provided by them (for discussion of the balance of **Article 8 and Article 10** rights see Chapters 6 ('Right to family and private life' and 7 ('Freedom of religion and expression', p 113 and p 132 respectively).

Sections 6 and 7: bringing a case

Section 7: Who can bring a case?

A person claiming under the **HRA** can bring proceedings in a court or tribunal or rely on Convention rights in any legal proceedings if:

- he or she is (or would be) a *victim* of the unlawful act.

'Victim''' has the same meaning as **Article 34 ECHR** (see Chapter 2, 'Admissibility criteria', p 27): A person has to be directly affected by an act or measure of a public body before they can have 'standing' in legal proceedings using the HRA.

Section 6: Against whom can a case be brought?

Section 6 HRA sets out which bodies are bound by the Act. Like the ECHR, the Act only applies directly to public bodies carrying out public functions (**s 6 (1)**). This is often described as the *vertical* relationship between the individual and the state. Relations between private groups and individuals are described as *horizontal*. The **HRA** has only a *direct vertical effect*. This has made the definition of a public authority under the Act crucial as an application can only be made against these bodies.

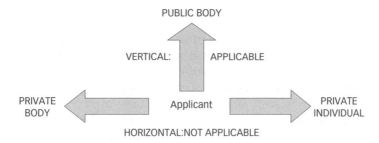

Fig 3.1 Vertical and horizontal effect

Sections 6 and 7: bringing a case

✱✱✱✱✱✱✱✱✱✱✱

Defining a public authority

Section 6 does not set out a clear definition of a public authority under the Act except to state that it is a body carrying out a public function and the act must not be of a private nature (**s 6(3) and s 6(5)**). There are two types of authorities:

- *'core' public authorities*. Established purely to perform public functions and are easily identifiable (eg police forces, local councils, etc). This includes the courts/tribunals but excludes Parliament (**s 6(3)**); and

- *'hybrid' public authorities*. Bodies that may be private in nature but carry out public functions. Services that traditionally were provided by a public authority, such as residential care homes and social housing have increasingly been contracted out to private bodies. Despite calls for further legislation to define a public authority more clearly, it has been left to the courts to decide when the **HRA** applies and this has caused difficulty. In some cases, a narrow interpretation is given which restricts the application of the **HRA** while other cases take a wider approach, looking at several factors to determine whether a body was public under the Act. The issue has still not been satisfactorily resolved.

. . . .

Donoghue v Poplar Housing & Regeneration Community Association & Sec State DETR [2001] 4 All ER 604

When deciding whether a housing association was a hybrid public authority, the court used an 'institutional approach', examining how the body itself related to the state rather than what it actually did in relation to its functions. (This approach was followed by the Court of Appeal in **Heather v Leonard Cheshire Foundation CA (2002).**)

. . . .

Even though it was decided on the facts that Poplar was a public body, the institutional test has been criticised for limiting the application of the **HRA**. The House of Lords took a different approach in:

. . . .

Parish of Aston Cantlow v Wallbank [2003] 3 All ER 1213

The House of Lords considered the issue of whether a Parochial Parish Council was a public authority. The majority of the Lords considered that in relation to repair liability, the Parish Council was not discharging functions of a public nature. It examined several factors including the function in question to see if it was linked to the state's responsibilities.

. . . .

Unlike *Poplar*, *Cantlow* applied a wider function test when examining the nature of the body. This was followed in **YL v Birmingham City Council and others (2007)**. The *Cantlow* test was elaborated on and followed by the court (but it did not overturn *Poplar*). The applicant was in a private care home but her fees etc were paid by the Council. She was told she had to leave the care home even though she was subsidised by the state. She argued her **Article 8** right to private life was violated because the care home was carrying out a public function.

Factors that were relevant when deciding on whether a body was carrying out a public function included:

- work and structures delegated/contracted out from the state;
- public powers assigned to it by statute;
- state supervision;
- public funding;
- public interest in functions; and
- serving public interest rather than profit.

Despite this, the majority found the care home in question was not a public authority due to its contractual relationship with the Council. However, Baroness Hale and Lord Bingham dissented, arguing that a narrow application of the function test can undermine the purpose of the Act which is to protect the vulnerable in society.

In response to **YL**, the Government legislated specifically for care homes. **Section 145 Health and Social Care Act 2008** states that a care home that is accommodating an adult whose placement is supported by a social services authority under **s 21 National Assistance Act 1948** (but not under other provisions) will be deemed to be a 'public authority' under the **HRA**.

The function test has since been applied in several cases including:

....

(Weaver) v London & Quadrant Housing Trust [2009] EWCA Civ 587

The Court of Appeal used the *Cantlow/YL* test and held that most housing associations (registered social landlords) will be hybrid public authorities and carrying out a public function when terminating tenancies.

....

☑ *Looking for extra marks?*

It is worth reading the dissenting judgement in **YL**, which reflects criticism by the Parliamentary Joint Committee on Human Rights. It has been argued that restrictive interpretations of **s 6** have left gaps in protection for the most vulnerable in society and undermine **HRA** protection. See 'The Meaning of Public Authority under the Human Rights Act' (2004) HL 39/HC v382. For further criticism there are numerous articles on this area.

Horizontal effect?

The **HRA** has direct vertical effect in its application. A case can only be brought against a public body. However, there is a debate about how far the **HRA** creates an indirect horizontal effect, where the **HRA** indirectly influences decisions made in a court/tribunal between private parties (for similar debates about the ECHR see Chapter 2, 'Effect of positive obligations', p 31). The court/tribunal is bound by the **HRA** so it must not make a decision that is incompatible with the ECHR. Therefore the **HRA** has indirectly affected cases between private parties. In cases such as *Campbell v Mirror Group Newspapers* **(2004)**, *Douglas v Hello! Ltd (No 6)* **(2005), and** *Mosley v News Group Newspapers Ltd* **(2008)**, the court had to decide on private law issues surrounding breach of confidence. Although the parties could not argue a breach of Convention rights before the court, the court was bound by the **HRA**. It had to consider the competing weight to be given to **Article 8** privacy rights and the **Article 10** expression rights of the publishers involved (see Chapter 6, 'Balancing rights: privacy and expression', p 113 and Chapter 7, 'Balancing rights: expression and privacy', p 132).

Revision tip

An exam question on the right to private life may include a question about how this has been interpreted in the UK. Horizontal effect is an issue that is important to include in any argument surrounding privacy in the UK.

Judicial powers/duties and remedies

Section 2: ECtHR case law

Under **s 2**, a court/tribunal determining cases under the **HRA** must take into account the judgments, decisions, declarations, or opinions of the ECtHR (and the European Commission of Human Rights prior to 1998). There has been debate about how far the domestic court should follow a decision of the ECtHR. In *R v Special Adjudicator, ex p Ullah* **(2004)**, Lord Bingham stated: 'The duty of national courts is to keep pace with the Strasbourg jurisprudence as it evolves over time: no more, but certainly no less.' However, there have been circumstances where the courts have gone further than the ECtHR may be willing to go, such as in *Napier v Scottish Minister* **(2002)**, where slopping out in prison was held to be a violation of **Article 3**. On rare occasions, the court has departed from the ECtHR, such as in *R v Horncastle* **(2009)**. If the court is faced with a conflicting domestic precedent and an ECtHR decision, the court should follow the domestic precedent and refer the case to appeal (*Kay v Lambeth LBC* **(2006)**).

✅ *Looking for extra marks?*

It would be worth reading academic opinion on how far the domestic court should go when considering ECtHR decisions.

Section 3: Interpretation clause

Under **s 3**, **primary and subordinate legislation** 'so far as it is possible to do so' must be read and given effect to a way which is compatible with Convention rights. This gives the courts greater **powers of interpretation** than existed prior to the **HRA**, when the courts could only interpret legislation if the meaning of legislation was 'ambiguous'. **Section 3** allows the courts to go further even where the meaning of the wording of the Act in question may be clear.

However, any reinterpretation of legislation must not create new law. In other words, judges can reinterpret the legislation as long as this does not change the meaning of the law beyond what Parliament intended (as Parliament remains the only body that can make primary legislation). The use of **s 3** has been controversial. The case law suggests that the judiciary have taken a purposive approach to ensure legislation complies with the Convention. However in some cases, they have been criticised for going too far.

. . . .

R v A (No 2) [2001] 3 All ER 1

The case concerned the admissibility of evidence of previous sexual relationships between the defendant and victim in a rape trial. The **Youth, Justice and Criminal Evidence Act 1999** expressly stated that such evidence be excluded.

The House of Lords held that this may violate a defendant's rights under **Article 6 ECHR**. The court used **s 3** to reinterpret the legislation by adding that evidence should only be excluded where the judge was satisfied that the defendant would receive a fair trial.

Lord Hope dissented, arguing that the majority of the House of Lords had gone too far as it was clear what the intention of Parliament was. If the legislation was held to be incompatible with the ECHR, **s 4** should have been used.

. . . .

Similar issues arose in:

. . . .

Ghaidan v Mendoza [2004] 3 All ER 411

Provisions of the **Rent Act 1977** allowed only heterosexual partners to succeed to a tenancy after the death of one of the partners.

The House of Lords held that this was incompatible with **Article 8 and Article 14 of the ECHR** when applied to homosexual couples and chose to use **s 3** to reinterpret the section in the Act so that it included homosexual partners.

Lord Millett dissented in this case. He argued that the intention of Parliament when it made the **Rent Act** was clear and that the interpretation used by the majority went beyond merely interpreting legislation and had changed the law itself. He agreed the Act was incompatible with the ECHR, but he argued **s 4** should have been used. By changing the law, the majority was undermining parliamentary supremacy.

. . . .

However in contrast, other judgments have held that the lower court went too far in trying to reinterpret the law and had in effect created new law: In *Re S (children: case plan)* **(2002)**, the House of Lords held that the Court of Appeal had gone beyond the scope of its powers. By using **s 3** to reinterpret sections of the **Children Act 1989** that allowed the courts to impose obligations on local authorities, the Court of Appeal had contradicted the statute. Instead, it should have made a **s 4** declaration of incompatibility.

Similarly in *R (on the application of Anderson)* **(2002)**, the House of Lords held that the use of **s 3** to reinterpret legislation concerning the power of the Secretary of State to set life sentence tariffs would not be 'judicial interpretation but judicial vandalism'. In other words, the Court of Appeal had gone too far.

Revision tip

The use of **s 3** is one of the key debates surrounding the **HRA** and is linked with the use of **s 4** and with the debate about the role of the judiciary in a democracy. A question on **s 3** may be linked to these areas and so it will be important to have some knowledge and understanding of the constitutional arrangements in the UK and the traditional role of the judiciary (see Chapter 1, 'Constitutional settlement and rights', p 14).

Section 4: declaration of incompatibility

Under **s 4**, if a court finds that a provision of primary legislation (or subordinate legislation which is inextricably linked to the primary provision, **s 4(3)**) is incompatible with the Convention rights, a court *may* (unlike **s 3**, it does not have to use **s 4**), make a declaration of incompatibility. A declaration does not affect the validity of the legislation (**s 4(6)**). In other words, the provision continues to apply and does not bind the parties. Parliamentary supremacy remains intact as the courts cannot declare an Act of Parliament invalid. **Section 4** has been described as a weapon of last resort. It should only be used where **s 3** cannot be used to interpret existing legislation as compatible. When a declaration is made, it is then for Parliament to decide whether to repeal or amend legislation to remove the incompatibility or it can choose to ignore the judgment. To date, Parliament has responded by changing the law or is in consultation on responses to declarations.

Exam tip

As noted with regard to **s 3**, a question on the **HRA** may ask about the relationship between **s 3** *and* **s 4** and how these provisions have affected, if at all, the constitutional arrangements in the UK.

Some examples of **s 4** declarations are:

R (on the application of Anderson) v Secretary of State for the Home Department [2002] UKHL 46

The Secretary of State's power to set sentencing tariffs under the **Crime (Sentences) Act 1997** was held to be incompatible with **Article 6 ECHR**. Finding it impossible to reinterpret the legislation to be compatible, the House of Lords made a declaration of incompatibility which led to Parliament amending the legislation (**Criminal Justice Act 2003**).

Bellinger v Bellinger [2003] 2 AC 467

The case dealt with the rights of transsexuals under the **Matrimonial Causes Act 1973**. Following ECHR cases such as *Goodwin v UK* **(2002)**, the legislation was held incompatible with the applicant's **Article 8** rights. The House of Lords decided to issue a declaration of incompatibility under **s 4**. The Lords noted that it would be difficult to reinterpret the legislation without the decision affecting many fields of law and that Parliament had already begun the process of amending the law to recognise the rights of transsexuals. The law was subsequently amended by Parliament (**Gender Recognition Act 2004**).

....

....

A and Others v Secretary of State for the Home Department [2005] 2 WLR 87

This is one of the most important cases concerning human rights since the **HRA** came into force (see Chapter 10, 'Key Cases', p 188). The **Anti-Terrorism, Crime and Security Act 2001, s 23** allowed the Secretary of State to issue a certificate which could detain indefinitely non-nationals under suspicion of being international terrorists. This was held to be incompatible with **Article 5 and Article 14 of the ECHR** (after they found that a derogation order made under the **HRA** was invalid) and so made a declaration of incompatibility. In response, Parliament allowed the provision to lapse (as it had to be renewed each year by Parliament) and replaced it with the control order scheme under the **Prevention of Terrorism Act 2005**.

....

It is important to note that whilst **s 4** cannot invalidate primary legislation, it can declare subordinate legislation invalid (unless the subordinate legislation in question is inextricably linked to the primary provision). For example, the House of Lords in *A* (2005) was able to able to find the derogation order made under the **HRA** that applied to the **Anti-terrorism, Crime and Security Act 2001, s 23** was invalid (as it would under traditional judicial review). It could therefore strike down the order.

Revision tip

These are only a few of the cases. It would be worthwhile to read these judgments on the use of **s 4** to get a flavour of when and why **s 4** has been used. There are other cases where **s 4** has been used such as the case of *R (F) v Secretary of State Home Dept* (2010) concerning the indefinite registration of sex offenders without being able to challenge the registration.

✔ Looking for extra marks?

There has been much academic writing on this area and a good answer should incorporate the academic opinions on the use of **s 3 and s 4**. Also, it is important to note the debate surrounding the role of the judiciary in the UK and to put the debate about the use of **s 3 and s 4** in this context. This is linked to the discussion below on judicial deference.

Section 8: remedies

Under **s 8**, if a court finds that an act by a public authority is unlawful, it may grant such relief or remedy, or make such order, within its powers as it considers just and appropriate.

Judicial powers/duties and remedies
****

This can include damages. If the court does decide to award damages, it must not do so unless it is satisfied the award is necessary to afford just satisfaction (**s 8(3)**) and it must consider the principles of the ECtHR when doing so (**s 8(4)**). The implication of **s 8** is that damages would be a remedy of 'last resort' and only granted after other forms of remedy had been considered. In the early cases under the **HRA**, it seemed that the courts were taking a liberal approach to the award of damages. In cases such as *R (Bernard) v London Borough of Enfield* (2002), and *R v MHRT & SS Health, ex p KB* (2003), the court compared damages given for comparable torts under English law and found damages under the **HRA** should reflect this. However case law since then has restricted the award of damages in such cases.

....

Anufrijeva & others v Southwark LBC & others [2004] 1 All ER 833

The Court of Appeal stated that compensation was of secondary importance to bringing any infringement of rights to an end and there would need to be a degree of culpability and foresee-able harm before damages should be considered.

....

This restrictive position was also followed in:

....

R (Greenfield) v Secretary of State for the Home Department [2005] UKHL 14

The House of Lords held that damages should not be routinely awarded. However, in cases where a court was satisfied that it was necessary to award damages, the court should examine what the ECtHR would have awarded. It was not appropriate to compare just satisfaction in such cases to tort damages.

....

This restrictive position was also taken in:

....

Dobson v Thames Water Utilities Ltd [2009] EWCA Civ 28

The Court of Appeal considered the relationship between damages for nuisance, personal injuries, and **HRA** infringements. The court suggested that damages under the **HRA** would be very rare in such cases and that the award of common law damages 'normally constitute just satisfaction for the purposes of s 8(3) of the Act'.

....

However, this restrictive approach has not prevented the courts from awarding damages where the victim of a violation of a Convention right has suffered significant detriment or harm; see for example *R (Mohammed) v Chief Constable of West Midlands* (2010) where the court awarded damages (£500) where the effect of a police caution given without sufficient evidence and where the victim had no lawyer or interpreter, was to require the victim to register as a sex offender.

⚫ Looking for extra marks?

The issue of damages under the **HRA** and the relationship of human rights litigation with civil law remedies has increasingly become an issue for debate.

Political powers/duties

Section 10: remedial action

Section 10 gives the power to the relevant minister to amend primary legislation which is the subject of a declaration of incompatibility without going through the full parliamentary procedure including committee scrutiny etc. There are two ways to put through a remedial order. The minister can lay a draft of the remedial order before Parliament, which is then subject to a positive resolution of both Houses. Alternatively, in cases of urgency, the minister can table the order with immediate effect, which ceases to be law if within the following 120 days it fails to be approved by positive resolution of both Houses. A remedial order has rarely been used as it should only be used if 'compelling reasons' exist. In *R v MHRT, North & East London Region & the Secretary of State for Health, ex p H* (2001) a declaration of incompatibility was made concerning a violation of Convention rights where the **Mental Health Act 1983** placed the burden on the patient to establish grounds for discharge. As this involved continuing detention that violated the Convention, the Government tabled a remedial order using the urgency procedure.

Section 19: statement of compatibility

Section 19 states that a minister in charge of a bill before Parliament must, before the second reading of the bill, make either:

- a statement of compatibility, stating that the bill is compatible with Convention rights; or

- a statement of incompatibility, setting out why the bill is not compatible with Convention rights and why the Government wishes Parliament to proceed with the bill.

Parliament can pass an Act which may be incompatible with Convention rights. The statement is designed to ensure proper human rights scrutiny of a Bill.

⚫ Looking for extra marks?

Find out if the minister has ever made a statement on incompatibility with respect to proposed legislation and why this was the case (see **Communications Act 2003** and subsequent case law: *R (Animal Defenders International) v Secretary of State for Culture, Media and Sport* (2008).

Sections 14 and 15: powers of derogation and reservation

Sections 14 and 15 of the HRA give the state the power to derogate (**s 14**) from the relevant Convention rights and the power to add reservations (**s 15**) to the relevant Convention rights (see Chapter 2, 'Derogation', p 33 on the ECHR and Chapters 5 and 10 ('Right to liberty and right to fair trial', p 77 and 'Terrorism', p 178 respectively) on the use of derogations and **s 14** in the UK).

Applying the HRA: proportionality and judicial deference

Proportionality

When deciding whether an act by a public authority is incompatible with a Convention right, one of the principles used by the courts is proportionality: whether the interference with a qualified right is proportionate to the aim sought by the public authority. (For meaning of a qualified right and how the principle is used by the ECtHR see Chapter 2, 'Qualified rights', p 33 and Chapters 6–9). Prior to the **HRA**, judicial review cases were decided by examining the *reasonableness* of a public authority act. This test still applies to cases that do not raise human rights issues. But where a human rights claim is made, the proportionality test should be used. In the early cases, the courts set out a test for proportionality similar to that which is used by the ECtHR. In *R (Daly) v Secretary of State for the Home Department* **(2001)**, the court approved of *De Freitas v Permanent Secretary of Ministry of Agriculture, Fisheries, Land and Housing* **(1999)**, which stated that an act or measure by a public authority would be proportionate and therefore not an interference if:

- the legislative objective is sufficiently important to justify the limitation of the right;
- the measures taken to meet the objective are connected to it; and
- the means used to meet the objective are no more than is necessary to meet the objective.

There has been some debate about how this test is applied in certain areas such as immigration. In *Huang v Home Secretary for the Home Department* **(2007)**, the House of Lords held that there was no need to demonstrate 'exceptionality' for a measure to be disproportionate. The courts must strike a fair balance between the rights of the individual and the needs of the community.

✅ Looking for extra marks?

There are many cases using proportionality under the **HRA**. It would be useful to read some of these and some of the academic writings on the use of proportionality by the courts.

Judicial deference

The concept of 'judicial deference' or a 'discretionary area of judgment' is similar to the principle of margin of appreciation used by the ECtHR(see Chapter 2, 'Margin of appreciation', p 34). When examining decisions by a public authority, the courts recognise that there may be some areas where the public body is best placed to make a judgment. For example, when examining the compatibility of primary legislation in certain areas such as security or social policy, the courts may be reluctant to intervene in an area where Parliament is best placed to make that decision. This may be because the court is not an expert in economic policy or national security, or because it is an issue that should be a matter for the democratically elected legislature.

The issue of when to defer to the public body has been controversial and has led to further debate concerning the role the judiciary should play in a democracy (this is linked to the use of **s 3 and s 4**—the court may choose to use **s 4** rather than reinterpret legislation if it feels Parliament is best placed to decide how to make legislation compatible if it chooses to do so). There have been several controversial cases in the courts that have involved the use of the concept of 'judicial deference':

. . . .

R (on the application of Pro Life Alliance) v BBC [2003] 2 All ER 977

Before a general election, Pro Life Alliance wished to broadcast a party political broadcast which included material on the termination of a pregnancy. The BBC refused to broadcast it, citing its obligations regarding decency in broadcasting legislation. The Court of Appeal gave weight to the importance of the right to freedom of expression and found an interference with the right. However, the House of Lords chose to defer to the judgment of the public bodies and of Parliament on an issue of public morals. It found that there was no interference with expression in this case.

. . . .

Deference was also discussed in:

. . . .

Belfast City Council v Miss behaving Ltd (Northern Ireland) [2008] HRLR 11

The House of Lords held that in some cases, it would be appropriate for the court to find that the legislation had struck a fair balance between the individual and community without having to look at individual cases. However, where the court had to strike the balance itself, it would give due weight to the judgments of those in greater proximity to the issues in question.

. . . .

Terrorism legislation has been a controversial area of litigation before the courts. It is an issue which has led to public criticism of the judiciary by the executive (see Chapter 10, 'Key debates', p 188).

. . . .

A and Others v Secretary of State for the Home Department [2005] 2 All ER 169

The House of Lords had to examine the indefinite detention of non-national terrorist suspects. The UK had derogated from **Article 5 ECHR** in order to detain the suspects. The Government argued that the court should defer to Parliament on a national security issue as it was best placed to decide on the need for the derogation. A majority of the House of Lords agreed that when deciding if there was 'a public emergency threatening the life of the nation', the Government was best placed to make this decision. However, the House of Lords went on to state that as the guardians of the rule of law, the judiciary were best placed to examine the necessity of the measures taken even in a state of emergency.

This tension between the judiciary and the executive and Parliament has been highlighted in cases concerning areas such as security and social policy.

Revision tip

When revising **s 3 and s 4 of the HRA**, issues of proportionality and deference are important when examining why the courts make decisions in a particular case. Keep this in mind when reading cases for revision.

✅ Looking for extra marks?

The tension between the judiciary and Parliament has been one of the features of debates about the **HRA**. This links into general debates about democracy and the rule of law. There has been public criticism of the judiciary by politicians and retired judges have criticised the executive's approach to the **HRA**. There has also been much academic debate on the use of judicial deference.

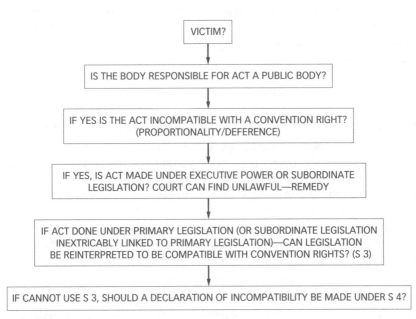

VICTIM?

↓

IS THE BODY RESPONSIBLE FOR ACT A PUBLIC BODY?

↓

IF YES IS THE ACT INCOMPATIBLE WITH A CONVENTION RIGHT?
(PROPORTIONALITY/DEFERENCE)

↓

IF YES, IS ACT MADE UNDER EXECUTIVE POWER OR SUBORDINATE
LEGISLATION? COURT CAN FIND UNLAWFUL—REMEDY

↓

IF ACT DONE UNDER PRIMARY LEGISLATION (OR SUBORDINATE LEGISLATION
INEXTRICABLY LINKED TO PRIMARY LEGISLATION)—CAN LEGISLATION
BE REINTERPRETED TO BE COMPATIBLE WITH CONVENTION RIGHTS? (S 3)

↓

IF CANNOT USE S 3, SHOULD A DECLARATION OF INCOMPATIBILITY BE MADE UNDER S 4?

Fig 3.2 Applying the HRA

The future of the HRA

Since the **HRA** came into force, there has been much debate and criticism of its use. Popular media have criticised the **HRA** with myths arising about its use (Department of Constitutional Affairs review of the HRA, 2006). There have been calls for a 'British Bill of Rights' to replace the **HRA** which may be more restrictive in application than the present Act. Others have called for any new Bill of Rights to be more expansive and include economic and social rights (see Chapter 1, 'Introduction', pp 6–14).

✅ Looking for extra marks?

It may be useful to read some of the debates and reports on this topic. For example, 'A Bill of Rights for the UK?', Joint Committee on Human Rights Twenty-ninth Report Aug 2008 HL165-1/HC 150-1, 'A Bill of Rights for the UK? Government response to the Committee's Twenty-ninth report of Session 2007–2008', Joint Committee on Human Rights Third report Jan 2009 HL 15/HC 145. Also see academic debates.

✳ Key cases

Case	Facts	Principle
***A and Others v Secretary of State for the Home Department* [2005] 2 WLR 87**	Indefinite detention of non-nationals suspected of terrorism, derogation from Article 5 ECHR	Court deferred to Parliament on question of 'emergency' but not on necessity of derogation; derogation not necessary as disproportionate—s 4 used
***Douglas v Hello! Ltd(No 6)* [2005] EWCA Civ 595**	A magazine wanted to publish wedding photographs of the applicants, the rights to which had been sold to a rival magazine.	When deciding a private law matter, the court is bound to act compatibly with the ECHR so has to weigh up competing rights. Laid down principles for use of s 12 HRA.
***Ghaidan v Mendoza* [2004] 3 All ER 411**	Applicant refused succession to tenancy under the Rent Acts as law only applicable to heterosexual partners.	Where legislation is incompatible the court can use s 3 purposively to reinterpret legislation as compatible. Dissent: the court cannot change law beyond parliamentary intention.
***R (Greenfield) v Secretary of State for the Home Department* [2005] UKHL 14**	Prisoner's disciplinary hearing not compatible with Article 6.	Damages should not be routinely awarded in HRA cases. Where necessary, the court should use ECtHR principles and not compare to tort damages.

Key debates

✱✱✱✱✱✱✱✱✱✱✱✱

Case	Facts	Principle
YL v Birmingham City Council and others [2007] UKHL 27	Applicant told to leave private care home. Her fees etc were met by the local authority.	When deciding on the definition of a public authority under the HRA a 'functional test' should be applied. Dissent: majority applied test too narrowly.

⟨⟩ Key debates

Topic	'Weaver: a step too far?'
Authors	Robert Brown and David Cowan
Viewpoint	Analyses the recent **Weaver** judgment on the definition of a public authority under the **HRA**. Although welcoming the outcome of the case for tenants, the authors are critical of the continuing uncertainty surrounding the application of **s 6 HRA** and reiterate the need for a more principled approach.
Source	(2009) *Journal of Housing Law* 12(6) 105–107

Topic	'Judging the judges under the Human Rights Act: deference, disillusionment and the "war on terror"'
Author	Aileen Kavanagh
Viewpoint	The article is a response to Ewing and de Than's criticism of **HRA** and the judiciary for failing to protect human rights by giving too much deference to the executive. It discusses the constraints placed upon the judiciary when implementing the **HRA**.
Source	(2009) *Public Law* 287–304

Topic	'A Bill of Rights: Do we need one or do we already have one?'
Author	Francesca Klug
Viewpoint	Sets out the arguments for replacing the **HRA** with a Bill of Rights and questions the necessity for change.
Source	(2007) *Public Law* 701

? Exam question

Essay question

'Sections 3 and 4 of the 1998 Act were carefully crafted to preserve the existing constitutional doctrine.'

Explain and critically analyse this statement concerning the operation of the Human Rights Act 1998. Illustrate your answer with reference to relevant case law.

 Scan here

Scan this QR code image with your mobile device to see an outline answer to this question or log onto www.oxfordtextbooks.co.uk/orc/concentrate/

#4

Right to life and freedom from ill treatment

Key Facts

- The right to life and freedom from ill treatment are absolute rights and non-derogable.

- **Article 2** has exceptions which allow the state to use lethal force but only when strictly necessary.

- **Article 2** jurisprudence raises controversial issues concerning the beginning and the end of life: abortion, right to die, and the death penalty.

- **Article 3** is absolute even where there may be a threat to the life of others that can be averted by using ill treatment on a suspect.

- The Court has developed positive obligations under **Article 2 and 3**, which have expanded protection.

Chapter overview

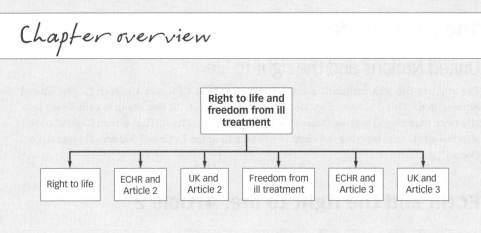

Introduction

The right to life and freedom from ill treatment are often described as the two most fundamental human rights without which all other rights become redundant. The importance of both rights is linked to the idea of the inherent dignity of human beings (see Chapter 1, 'Natural rights and dignity', p 2).

Absolute rights

Both the right to life and the right not to be ill treated are classed as absolute rights: rights that cannot be derogated from (see Chapter 2, 'Absolute rights', p 32). Freedom from torture, inhuman, or degrading treatment has been accepted by commentators and by international and domestic courts as being *jus cogens;* this means it cannot be violated by any state for any reason even in times of war or emergency or terrorist threat. States cannot agree to allow ill treatment through a treaty. The right to life has also been described as a norm of **customary international law** and the *arbitrary* taking of life is seen as *jus cogens*. Though the right to life cannot be derogated from generally, there is a caveat with regard to wartime and the death penalty as well as the taking of life in exceptional circumstances. There are very clear restrictions on the use of lethal force.

The right to life

United Nations and the right to life

The right to life was included in the UDHR and the ICCPR (see Chapter 1, 'The United Nations', p 6). There is also an optional protocol to the ICCPR that abolishes the death penalty (with exceptions) in those states that have chosen to ratify it. The Human Rights Council also has a role in protecting the right to life (see Chapter 1, 'United Nations Human Rights Council', p 8).

ECHR and the right to life: Article 2

Article 2

1 Everyone's right to life shall be protected by law. No one shall be deprived of his life intentionally save in the execution of a sentence of a court following his conviction of a crime for which this penalty is provided by law.

2 Deprivation of life shall not be regarded as inflicted in contravention of this article when it results from the use of force which is no more than absolutely necessary:

   a in defence of any person from unlawful violence;

   b in order to effect a lawful arrest or to prevent the escape of a person lawfully detained;

   c in action lawfully taken for the purpose of quelling a riot or insurrection.

Article 2 prohibits the state from the arbitrary taking of life but recognises exceptional circumstances when the taking of life may be absolutely necessary. **Article 2(1)** also allows for the use of the death penalty. The Court has also recognised that **Article 2** may still be applicable even where no-one dies. In *Makaratzis v Greece* **(2004)**, it was a matter of luck that the applicant had not been killed when his car had been fired at by state agents after he had driven through a red light.

Burden of proof

As in many of the rights in the ECHR, the burden of proof is on the applicant. In *Yasa v Turkey* **(1998)**, the Court held that it will have to be satisfied that there is sufficient evidence to enable it to conclude *beyond reasonable doubt* that the state was responsible for the victim's death before it can hold the state liable.

However, there are circumstances where the burden of proof shifts to the state. If the victim dies whilst in state custody then the state has to provide a satisfactory explanation for the death. The events leading to death in custody are usually within the exclusive knowledge of the state authorities. This may also apply where a victim disappears after being taken into custody (see *Timurtas v Turkey* **(2000)**).

Article 2(2) exceptions

The exceptions under **Article 2(2)** are exclusive. The state can only justify the taking of life by state agents if it is for a reason stated and it is absolutely necessary to do so; meaning the means used has to be strictly proportionate to the legitimate aim under **(a)–(c)**. The European Court of Human Rights (ECtHR) has applied the test for necessity strictly:

a) In defence of any person from unlawful violence;

The ECtHR has found that that a killing in these circumstances has to be strictly necessary and that this includes procedural obligations such as planning a course of action to avoid the taking of life if possible:

McCann, Farrell & Savage v UK (1995) 31 EHRR 97

Three suspected terrorists were killed by the British security forces whilst driving towards Gibraltar to plant a bomb at a British Army base. The security forces shot the suspects rather than arrest them as they believed they might detonate the bomb.

The Court accepted that those who carried out the shootings honestly and reasonably believed it was necessary but that the lack of proper planning before the shootings meant the action was a violation of **Article 2**. The Court said that it 'must,...subject deprivations of life to the most careful scrutiny, particularly where deliberate lethal force is used, taking into consideration not only the actions of the agents of the State who actually administer the force but also all the surrounding circumstances including such matters as the planning and control of the actions...'.

The Court stated that mistakes will not necessarily give rise to a breach of **Article 2** as long as these mistakes are honest *and* reasonable.

b) In order to effect a lawful arrest or to prevent the escape of a person lawfully detained;

The Court has reiterated the need for the state to take life only where there is no alternative and there should be a threat from those escaping of being arrested.

Nachova v Bulgaria (2005) 42 EHRR 933

Two young, unarmed Roma men were shot when running away from security forces who had tried to arrest them for a minor offence. The ECtHR stated that 'in principle there can be no such necessity where it is known that the person to be arrested poses no threat...and is not suspected of having committed a violent offence, even if a failure to use lethal force may result in the opportunity to arrest the fugitive being lost'.

....

c) In action lawfully taken for the purpose of quelling a riot or insurrection

The case law again demonstrates the ECtHR's approach:

....

Stewart v UK (1984) (Application No 10044/82)

When a child was killed by a plastic bullet during a riot in Northern Ireland, the European Commission of Human Rights held that in the particular circumstances there was no breach of **Article 2** as the state had taken proportionate measures to attempt to prevent loss of life.

....

In contrast:

....

Gulec v Turkey (1998) 28 EHRR 121

Machine gun fire was used to disperse a crowd. A young boy was killed. The Court accepted that some force was necessary in the circumstances, but noted that less lethal weapons such as water cannon could have been used and the gathering took place in a region under a state of emergency where disorder should have been expected and planned for.

....

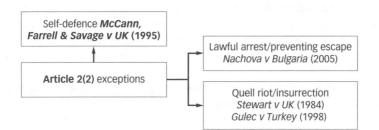

Fig 4.1 Article 2(2) exceptions

Article 2(1): beginning and end of life

The ECtHR has had to adjudicate on controversial issues as to when life begins and ends. These involve issues of morality and state discretion that highlight the difficulties that an international court can face when deciding on such issues.

Abortion

Termination of a foetus is a controversial issue in many jurisdictions. Applicants before the ECtHR have argued that the foetus has a right to life. Other international regional human rights treaties explicitly recognise a foetal right to life. **The Inter-American Convention on Human Rights 1969, Article 4** states that the right to life 'shall be protected by law and, in general, from the moment of conception'. However, the **ECHR** has no such clause. In several cases, the ECtHR has avoided making a definitive statement on when life begins. It has achieved this by arguing there is a lack of consensus amongst states.

In *Paton v UK* **(1979)**, the Commission on Human Rights decided that there cannot be an absolute right to life for the foetus as this would undermine the right to life of the mother. It left open the question of a right to life with certain limitations due to a lack of European consensus on the issue. In *H v Norway* **(1992)**, it was decided that given the wide divergence of views on this issue, the state had acted within the margin of appreciation in allowing an abortion at 14 weeks on social grounds.

In *Vo v France* **(2004)**, the ECtHR found that there was no violation of **Article 2**, as in the light of a lack of consensus on the legal definition of when life begins, it was within the discretion of the state to decide on this issue. Similarly, in a case involving the use of frozen embryos without the consent of the 'father', the ECtHR found that it was within the margin of appreciation of the state to regulate the use of embryos and so it did not fall within **Article 2** (*Evans v UK* **(2006)**). Interestingly, the Court has recognised an increasing consensus reflected in abortion laws in the member states. In *A, B, and C v Ireland* **(2010)**, the ECtHR accepted that only a few states in the Council of Europe had very restrictive abortion laws. However, despite an increasing consensus, states still have a margin of appreciation when balancing the rights of the foetus and the mother.

Exam Tip

It is necessary to be aware of how the EtCHR approaches controversial issues through examining state consensus and the use of margin of appreciation (see Chapter 2, 'Margin of appreciation', p 34).

Right to die

The right to die is another controversial area of debate involving moral and ethical considerations. There is a lack of consensus as to whether a state should allow assisted dying. Only a small number of states (eg Switzerland and the Netherlands) allow forms of assisted dying under their domestic law.

....

Pretty v UK (2002) 35 EHRR 1

The applicant was severely disabled and terminally ill. As she could not take her own life, she wanted her husband to help her. However under English law, assisted suicide is a criminal offence and the Director of Public Prosecutions could not guarantee that he would not be prosecuted. The applicant argued that her right to life included her right to choose when to end it. However the Court found that 'article 2 cannot, without a distortion of language, be interpreted as conferring the diametrically opposite right, namely a right to die'. The Court found that **Article 2** does not include issues regarding the quality of life. Instead this falls under **Article 8**.

....

ECHR and the right to life: Article 2

✱✱✱✱✱✱✱✱✱✱✱

This issue continues to be controversial. In January 2011, the ECtHR decided that a law preventing a person obtaining a drug without prescription in order to end his life was not a violation of **Article 8** (*Haas v Switzerland* **(2011)**). In June 2011, it held that a complaint concerning the refusal to grant permission to the applicant's wife to obtain a drug to commit suicide, which forced the applicant to travel with his wife to Switzerland to end her life, was admissible (*Koch v Germany* **(2011)**).

✅ Looking for extra marks?

In the UK, the House of Lords (now the Supreme Court) has deferred to Parliament on this issue but in *Purdy v DPP* **(2009)**, the House of Lords decided that the Director of Public Prosecutions had to issue clear guidelines setting out in what circumstances a person will be prosecuted for assisting a suicide. Does this demonstrate a step towards acceptance of assisted dying? If the consensus changes in Europe, would the ECtHR come to a different decision?

Death penalty

Although the death penalty is allowed under **Article 2(1)**, two protocols are in force, which abolish the use of the death penalty:

Protocol 6

The death penalty is abolished apart from certain acts during war or in cases where war is imminent.

Protocol 13

The death penalty is abolished in all circumstances.

The death penalty is no longer in use in any Council of Europe state and most states have signed and ratified the protocols (all have signed/ratified **Protocol 6** and all but two have signed/ratified **Protocol 13**). The UK has signed and ratified both protocols and so abolished the death penalty under all circumstances. However, a question arose concerning state practice. If most of the member states recognise abolition, then does this mean **Article 2(1)** is **abrogated**, ie state practice amends the Convention to remove the death penalty?

....

Soering v UK (1989) 11 EHRR 439

The US wanted to extradite the applicant for an alleged murder. He could have faced the death penalty if extradited. One of the arguments put forward by the applicant was that the death penalty was a violation of **Article 3** (see pp 69–72 below). The Court rejected this argument as it would undermine **Article 2** which explicitly allowed the death penalty.

....

The issue of the death penalty came before the ECtHR again in:

Ocalan v Turkey (2005) 41 EHRR 985

The applicant was found guilty of terrorist crimes and was sentenced to death. At the time of sentence, Turkey had not ratified **Protocol 6** though it did so later. A violation was found of **Article 3 and Article 6** as the applicant did not receive a fair trial. However, it was argued that as most member states had signed **Protocol 6** and some had signed **Protocol 13**, then state practice meant that **Article 2(1)** should no longer be recognised as including the death penalty. The ECtHR noted that in practice the death penalty had become unacceptable in peacetime due to the consensus amongst member states. However, it did not make a definitive finding on **Article 2** as it was not necessary in the case. It was reluctant to explicitly amend the Convention. It also rejected the argument that the death penalty was a violation of **Article 3**.

However, the ECtHR has reflected a growing consensus in member states by changing its decision on **Article 3** and the death penalty:

Al Saadoon and Mufdhi v UK (2010) (Application No 61498/08)

The applicants were two Iraqi men accused of murder. They were in British custody in Iraq but were handed over to the Iraqi authorities to be tried for the alleged murder. Iraq had introduced the death penalty for murder and war crimes. The applicants argued that the death penalty violated **Article 3**.

Overturning **Soering and Ocalan**, the Court noted that since **Ocalan** all states had signed **Protocol 6** and all but two states had signed **Protocol 13**. This signalled that **Article 2** had been amended so as to prohibit the death penalty in all circumstances. The Court concluded therefore that the death penalty caused physical and psychological suffering as a result of the foreknowledge of death and, as such, was contrary to **Article 3 of the Convention**.

Exam tip
All three areas discussed above demonstrate the use of consensus and margin of appreciation as a tool for adjudicating controversial issues within the Council of Europe.

Article 2 and positive obligations

Positive obligations help to ensure the effectiveness of the ECHR and have expanded its protection (Chapter 2, 'Positive obligations', pp 30–32). This includes protection from private parties as well as state officials. However, the Court is aware that it cannot put unrealistic burdens onto states where they are not directly responsible for taking life. The jurisprudence reflects this.

ECHR and the right to life: Article 2

✳✳✳✳✳✳✳✳✳✳✳✳

Duty to protect—safeguard life

The general duty to protect has been developed in such cases as *Osman v UK* (1998). Article 2 not only obligates the state to refrain from taking life but the state also has to take appropriate steps to safeguard lives within its jurisdiction. It sets out the test to be applied when deciding if there is a duty on the state to protect, which applies where the state:

- knows or ought to have known at the time
- of the existence of a real and immediate risk (to life) of identified individual(s), and
- failed to take reasonable measures to avoid the risk.

From this principle, the ECtHR has developed further positive obligations in situations where the state should be reasonable expected to protect.

Domestic violence

Applying the *Osman* principle, the ECtHR has recognised an obligation to protect victims of domestic violence if the state is aware of incidents and fails to take reasonable action (*Opuz v Turkey* (2009)).

When individuals are in custody

As noted, the burden of proof shifts if a person dies in custody or disappears (*KhamilaIsayeva v Russia* (2007)). The state has also the duty to protect, where reasonable, those in its care or control (*Edwards v UK* (2002)).

Establishing a legal framework

The state is expected to provide a legal framework to protect those in its jurisdiction from the risk of death (*A v UK* (1998) (Article 3 case)).

Giving information

In certain circumstances, information may be available to the state that should be given to persons in danger that would prevent death (*Öneryildiz v Turkey* (2004)).

Removal of persons from state

See below on **Article 3**, 'Removal of persons from the state', p 71—the ECtHR has held that the state has an obligation not to remove a person to a state where they may be subject to a real risk of ill treatment and this is applicable where the person faces a real risk of the death penalty (*Al Saadoon and Mufdhi v UK* (2010).

Investigating alleged violations

The ECtHR has set out the procedural obligation on a state to investigate deaths. The burden of proof shifts to the state to demonstrate that there has been an effective investigation. Without this, it would be difficult to hold a state accountable. A series of cases before the ECtHR outlined what is necessary for an effective investigation (for example *Jordan v UK* **(2001)**, *Kaya v Turkey* **(1998)**):

- independent;
- prompt;
- should be capable of determining if force was justified and lead to identification/punishment—not necessarily lead to conviction but there should be proper evidence-gathering, where appropriate an autopsy, and an objective analysis of findings;
- open to scrutiny: should include the relatives of the deceased; and
- the state should investigate if a question is raised regarding racial motives for killing (*Nachova v Bulgaria* **(2005)**).

✅ *Looking for extra marks?*

There is a debate about how far **Article 2** protects the right to health. Should the state pay for treatment that could prolong life? Generally there is no right to health if the state would be excessively burdened; however, a state may be liable if the state was responsible for putting the applicant in danger, eg in *Oyal v Turkey* **(2010)**, the state authorities were negligently liable for giving HIV-infected blood to the victim. The Court ordered that the state should pay the cost of medication and health care during the lifetime of the victim.

UK and the right to life

Article 2 has influenced the common law approach to the accountability of state agents for the use of lethal force and where death has occurred.

Osman *test in the UK courts*

Under common law, the courts had found that the police could not be sued for negligence due to failure to protect. However, the House of Lords reconsidered this position in the light of **Article 2** and the *Osman* test.

Examples:

....

Van Colle v Chief Constable of Hertfordshire [2008] UKHL 50

A prosecution witness in a theft case had been murdered by the defendant in the case. There had been threats made against the victim. It was alleged that the investigating police officer should have been aware of these threats and taken steps to protect the victim.

The House of Lords held that there was no violation of **Article 2** on the facts. However, the Court did apply the ***Osman*** test and examined whether the police should have known about the threats and, if so, should have taken reasonable steps to protect where a real risk existed.

....

....

Mitchell v Glasgow City Council [2009] UKHL 11

The victim lived in local authority housing. He was killed by a neighbour after complaints about the neighbour to the local authority. The local authority had met with the assailant and warned him about his behaviour. It was alleged that the authority knew about the danger posed to the victim and took no action under **Article 2** to prevent it.

The House of Lords held on the facts, there had been no violation of **Article 2**. Applying the ***Osman*** test, it was held that there was nothing in the assailant's behaviour to suggest a real and immediate threat to the life of the victim.

....

....

Savage v South Essex Partnership NHS Foundation Trust [2008] UKHL 74

The victim had absconded from a mental hospital she was being held in under mental health legislation and committed suicide. An inquest held that the precautions taken by the hospital to prevent the patient from absconding were inadequate.

The House of Lords held that as well as requiring a health authority to employ competent staff and to adopt systems which protect patients' lives, **Article 2** imposed an 'operational' obligation on health authorities to do what would be reasonably expected to prevent a patient committing suicide, if they knew, or ought to have known, that a particular patient presented a real and immediate risk of suicide.

....

Investigations

The procedural obligation under **Article 2** to hold an investigation has also been applied in the UK courts:

Example:

....

Re McCaughey's Application for Judicial Review [2011] UKSC 20

The appellants were the next of kin of two men shot by the British army in 1990. A coroner had been appointed to conduct an inquest. The applicants wanted the inquest to examine the planning of the operation that led to the deaths and argued **Article 2** was applicable. Previous case law in the UK had found that the **Human Rights Act** was not applicable before 1998.

The Supreme Court held that although the **HRA** did not apply retrospectively in relation to a state's obligation to investigate a death which occurred before it came into force, if a state decides to hold an inquest in relation to such a death, then in certain circumstances, it is under a freestanding obligation to ensure that it complied with the procedural obligation arising under **Article 2**.

· ·

· ·

R (on the application of Amin (Imtiaz)) v Secretary of State for the Home Department [2003] UKHL 51

An Asian prisoner had been killed by his cellmate in prison. The cellmate was found guilty of murder but there had been no full inquest into the killing.

The House of Lords held that there had been a violation of **Article 2**. An inquiry had been held but not in public and the independence of the internal inquiry was questioned. The Court held that an appropriate level of publicity and participation by the deceased's next of kin was required where the state investigated a death in custody.

· ·

✅ *Looking for extra marks?*

There have been numerous cases in the UK courts that involve **Article 2**. There have also been several cases involving extra-territorial protection for the armed forces and whether deaths on the battlefield are covered by **Article 2**. See *R (on the application of Smith) v Oxfordshire Assistant Deputy Coroner* **(2010)** (but see also *Al-Skeini v UK* **(2011)** where the ECtHR disagreed with the UK Supreme Court and found that the applicants fell within the jurisdiction of the UK when claiming procedural violations of **Article 2** against the UK during the occupation of Iraq).

Freedom from ill treatment: torture, inhuman, and degrading treatment

Absolute nature of Article 3

Unlike **Article 2**, there are no exceptions allowed under **Article 3** in time of war or emergency or to protect others. This has led to a debate on whether **Article 3** protection should maintain this absolute nature. The 'ticking bomb' scenario is often used to illustrate the argument:

A bomb is about to go off in the middle of a busy shopping area. The police have a suspect who they believe knows the whereabouts of the bomb. Should they be allowed to torture the suspect to prevent the loss of life that will be caused by the explosion?

Recent allegations about the state use of torture in the 'war on terror' have highlighted this debate. Those who advocate natural rights or Kant's moral imperative (see Chapter 1,

Freedom from ill treatment: torture, inhuman, and degrading treatment
✱✱✱✱✱✱✱✱✱✱✱

'Natural rights and dignity, p 2) argue that even if such a circumstance arose, which is seen as unlikely, the suspect should still not be tortured. Utilitarians would argue that if the suffering of one person saved the lives of many then it may be justified to use torture in limited circumstances. These arguments have been reflected in some of the European case law discussed below.

Revision tip

Note the case of *Gafgen v Germany* **(2010)** which discusses the absolute nature of **Article 3** and is controversial in its approach to the use of evidence adduced through ill treatment.

✔ Looking for extra marks?

There is a lot of literature on this subject and an awareness of the theory that is used in this debate is necessary. It would be useful to note the use of ill treatment by state forces in Abu Ghraib prison in Iraq and the US Government's arguments for using certain interrogation methods in centres such as Guantanamo Bay.

United Nations

Freedom from ill treatment was included in the UDHR and the International Covenant on Civil and Political Rights (ICCPR) (Chapter 1, 'The United Nations (UN)', p 6). The United Nations has a Rapporteur on Torture who reports to the Human Rights Council (Chapter 1, 'United Nations Human Rights Council', p 9). The UN has also developed a specific treaty on torture in 1984. This established a Committee on Torture to monitor and investigate allegations of torture. The treaty also defines torture and inhuman and degrading treatment separately.

UN Convention against Torture and Other Cruel, Inhuman or Degrading Treatment or Punishment 1984

Article 1

...the term "torture" means any act by which severe pain or suffering, whether physical or mental, is intentionally inflicted on a person for such purposes as obtaining from him or a third person information or a confession, punishing him for an act he or a third person has committed or is suspected of having committed, or intimidating or coercing him or a third person, or for any reason based on discrimination of any kind, when such pain or suffering is inflicted by or at the instigation of or with the consent or acquiescence of a public official or other person acting in an official capacity. It does not include pain or suffering arising only from, inherent in or incidental to lawful sanctions.

Article 16

Each State Party shall undertake to prevent in any territory under its jurisdiction other acts of cruel, inhuman or degrading treatment or punishment which do not amount to torture as defined in

article 1, when such acts are committed by or at the instigation of or with the consent or acquiescence of a public official or other person acting in an official capacity

ECHR and freedom from ill treatment: Article 3

Article 3

No one shall be subjected to torture or to inhuman or degrading treatment or punishment

It should be noted that the Council of Europe also has a specific convention on torture. This established a European Committee for the Prevention of Torture which monitors and investigates member states. The ECHR contains the prohibition on ill treatment. Unlike the UN, it does not define the terms used to describe ill treatment. It has been left to the ECtHR to interpret these terms.

The scope of Article 3: defining the terms

The ECtHR has not clearly differentiated between the terms torture, inhuman, and degrading treatment. Instead it decides which form of ill treatment it is by using a sliding scale of seriousness. What is torture or another form of treatment can change over time. It first attempted to define the terms in *The Greek Case* **(1969)**,which was further clarified in *Ireland v UK* **(1978)**.

Torture

The *Greek Case* stated:

> The word 'torture' is often used to describe inhuman treatment, which has a purpose, such as the obtaining of information or confessions, or the infliction of punishment, and it is generally an aggravated form of inhuman treatment.

Ireland v UK added that torture carries a 'special stigma' which attaches to states.

Inhuman treatment

The *Greek Case* stated:

> The notion of inhuman treatment covers at least such treatment as deliberately causes severe suffering, mental of physical,....

Ireland v UK clarified this by stating it need not be deliberate.

✳✳✳✳✳✳✳✳✳✳

Degrading treatment

The *Greek Case* stated that an act is degrading:

> if it grossly humiliates him before others or drives him to act against his will or conscience

The case law illustrates how these definitions are fluid and have changed over time:

Example: torture

....

Ireland v UK (1978) 2 EHRR 25

The UK security forces in Northern Ireland used 'five' techniques to interrogate suspected terrorists. The Court found that together these techniques amounted to inhuman treatment and not torture even though they were deliberate and caused physical and mental suffering.

....

However, what amounts to torture was redefined in later cases:

....

Selmouni v France (1999) 29 EHRR 403

The interrogation techniques used by the French authorities were held to amount to torture. The Court recognised that attitudes towards such interrogation techniques had changed since ***Ireland v UK***: 'the Court considers that certain acts which were classified in the past as "inhuman and degrading treatment"' as opposed to "torture" could be classified differently in the future.'

....

The ECtHR has further developed what acts are covered by torture by recognising the growing international consensus that rape can be a form of torture (***Ayadin v Turkey (1997)***).

Example: discrimination as degrading treatment

The Commission on Human Rights and the ECtHR have developed degrading treatment to include severe discrimination. In the ***East African Asians case (Patel v UK) (1993)***, East African Asians expelled from their states were refused residence in the UK despite having had a previous right of residence. The Commission found that 'a special importance should be attached to discrimination based on race; that publicly to single out a group of persons for different treatment...might in certain circumstances constitute a special form of affront to human dignity,....'.

The ECtHR confirmed that severe discrimination can amount to degrading treatment in ***Moldovan v Romania* (2005)**, where the treatment of Roma by the state was held to amount to racial discrimination severe enough to be degrading under **Article 3**.

Meeting the threshold: when does Article 3 apply?

Article 3 only becomes applicable if the act meets the threshold of severity of treatment or punishment (treatment or punishment is not defined by the Court). The state can punish but the punishment cannot go beyond what is proportionate to the crime etc *(Peers v Greece (2001))*.

The threshold is not static and is dependent on several factors. *Ireland v UK* laid out the factors that may be taken into account. These include:

- duration and scope of treatment/punishment;
- physical and mental effects on the victim;
- sex, age, and state of health of the victim.

It is only when the threshold is met that **Article 3** is applicable. Once the threshold of at least degrading treatment is met then the state cannot justify the treatment/punishment.

Article 3 and positive obligations

The same principles apply to **Article 3** as set out above under **Article 2** (p 63).

The general duty to protect that has been developed in *Osman v UK* **(1998)** applies to **Article 3** (see *Z & others v UK* **(2002)** where the failure of the local authority to remove children into care when they were aware of severe child abuse was held to violate **Article 3**).

When individuals are in custody

(Price v UK **(2001)**, *Keenan v UK* **(2001)**.)

Establishing a legal framework

(A v UK **(1998)** where the ECtHR held that the defence of reasonable chastisement where a stepfather quite severely beat his stepchild did not provide enough legal protection against an assault on a child.)

Giving information

The principle established in *Öneryildiz v Turkey* **(2004)** is also applicable to **Article 3**.

Removal of persons from state

In a series of cases the ECtHR has established that the removal of a person from the state may violate **Article 3** if the applicant can 'establish substantial grounds have been shown for believing that the person concerned, if extradited, faces a real risk of being subjected to torture or to inhuman or degrading treatment or punishment in the requesting country' *(Soering v UK)*.

The conduct of the applicant is irrelevant. As **Article 3** is absolute, suspected or even convicted terrorists or criminals cannot be sent back to where there is a real risk of ill treatment. States have attempted to argue this obligation is less than the obligation for the expelling state not to ill treat those within its jurisdiction and so risk of expulsion can be balanced against the risk to the state from the applicant. The Court has rejected this, emphasising the absolute nature of Article 3 (see *Chahal v UK* **(1996)**, *Saadi v Italy* **(2008)**).

However, the Court has been less stringent when the expulsion involves applicants who may suffer because of a lack of medical treatment in the receiving state. In *D v UK* **(1997)**, the Court found the expulsion of a dying AIDS victim was a violation of **Article 3** as the applicant would get no treatment in the receiving state. However, this is an exceptional case. In contrast, the Court held in *N v UK* **(2008)** that the applicant, who suffered from HIV, would possibly get some treatment in her receiving state. The threshold was lowered in this case.

Investigating alleged violations

The same principles apply as for Article 2 (see p 65), see for example *Assenov v Bulgaria* **(1998)**.

Exam tip

If a question arises on positive obligations, similar principles apply to both **Article 2** and **Article 3** (and other articles in the ECHR) and so be aware of case examples and of criticisms of the use of positive obligations by the Court.

UK and freedom from ill treatment

Similarly to **Article 2**, **Article 3** has influenced UK domestic law. For example, in *A and others v Secretary of State for the Home Department (No 2)* **(2005)** decided evidence that may be gathered through torture in another state is not admissible in a UK court.

Other examples

....

R v Secretary of State Home Department, ex p Adam and Limbuela [2005] UKHL 66

The applicants challenged the provisions of asylum legislation which removed state provision for asylum seekers who did not claim asylum promptly on arrival in the UK. The lack of any state support (they were also not allowed to work), meant the applicants were left destitute.

The House of Lords held that there was a duty on the Secretary of the State to avoid the breach of **Article 3** which was applicable if the threshold of severity was met. Destitution did not generally give rise to a violation of **Article 3**. However, if the state is responsible for placing a person in destitution then the state could be held liable. The threshold of severity depended on all the circumstances of the case.

....

....

R (on the application of Mousa) v Secretary of State for Defence [2010] EWHC 3304 (Admin)

The applicants argued that the Secretary of State should hold a public inquiry into allegations of ill treatment of detainees by British forces in Iraq. A failure to do so arguably breached the procedural obligation under **Article 3**.

The Divisional Court held that there was no violation of **Article 3** as the state had already set up two inquiries. The investigation team was sufficiently independent and the state had not ruled out a further inquiry. It had fulfilled its obligation under **Article 3**.

Revision tip

As under **Article 2**, there are a variety of cases that can be used as examples of **Article 3** adjudication in the UK courts.

(✻) **Key cases**

Case	Facts	Principle
Ireland v UK **(1978) 2 EHRR 25**	The UK security forces in Northern Ireland used 'five techniques' to interrogate suspected terrorists.	The Court found that these techniques amounted to inhuman treatment and not torture even though they were deliberate and caused physical and mental suffering.
McCann, Farrell & Savage v UK **(1995) 31 EHRR 97**	Suspected terrorists were killed by British security forces who believed they were about to deliver a bomb.	The ECtHR will place any state killing under careful scrutiny, including all the surrounding circumstances. Violation of Article 2
Osman v UK **(1998) 29 EHRR 245)**	A pupil was stalked by his teacher who attacked and killed the pupil's father. The police were aware of the stalking.	Article 2 obligates the state to take appropriate steps to safeguard lives within its jurisdiction—test: knows or ought to have known at the time of the existence of a real and immediate risk (of life) of identified individual(s) and failed to take reasonable measures to avoid the risk. On facts, no violation.
Pretty v UK **(2002) 35 EHRR 1**	The applicant was terminally ill. As she could not take her own life, she wanted her husband to help her to commit suicide. However, under English law, assisted suicide is a criminal offence and the Director of Public Prosecutions could not guarantee that he would not be prosecuted.	Article 2 cannot be interpreted as conferring the right to die. Article 2 does not include quality of life. Instead this falls under Article 8. No violation of Articles 2 or 8.

Key debates

✶✶✶✶✶✶✶✶✶✶✶

Case	Facts	Principle
R v Secretary of State for the Home Department, ex p Adam and Limbuela [2005] UKHL 66	Asylum seekers were left with no state support as it was decided they did not apply promptly for asylum	The House of Lords held that there was a duty on the Secretary of State to avoid the breach of Article 3 which was applicable if the threshold of severity was met. Destitution did not generally give rise to a violation of Article 3. However, if the state is responsible for placing a person in destitution then the state could be held liable.
Van Colle v Chief Constable of Hertfordshire [2008] UKHL 50	A prosecution witness in a theft case was murdered by the defendant in the case. It was argued the police should have protected the victim.	There was no violation of Article 2 on the facts. However, the court did apply the *Osman* test and examined whether the police should have known about the threats and, if so, should have taken reasonable steps to protect where a real risk existed.

⑨⑨ Key debates

Topic	**'R. (Purdy) v DPP and the case for wilful blindness'**
Author	Kate Greasley
Viewpoint	The author discusses *Pretty* and *Purdy* and the wider issues surrounding assisted suicide. She argues that the *Purdy* decision is unsatisfactory.
Source	(2010) *Oxford Journal of Legal Studies* 30(2), 301–326

Topic	**'Should police threats to torture suspects always be severely punished? Reflections on the *Gafgen* case' (case comment)**
Author	Steven Greer
Viewpoint	The author discusses the *Gafgen* case and the legal and moral issues surrounding the absolute nature of **Article 3**, comparing the case to the ticking bomb scenario.
Source	(2011) *Human Rights Law Review* 11(1), 67–89

⑦ Exam questions

Problem question

Adam legally enters the UK from the USA. He is detained pending extradition to the USA. He has been indicted in the USA, accused of murder. The authorities claim that he is part of a terrorist organisation that was responsible for the bombing of a government office, killing six people including a child. It is claimed that he made the bomb. If extradited, Adam may face the death penalty in the state where the bombing took place. The court decides to allow the extradition of Adam to the USA.

Whilst in detention, Adam was threatened by other prisoners for being a 'baby killer'. He told the prison governor and asked to be segregated but nothing was done. He was later attacked by a prisoner and was severely injured. Adam wishes to sue the prison for damages but his claim is dismissed by the court.

He appeals both decisions but the Court of Appeal dismisses his claims and refuses an appeal to the Supreme Court in April 2011. He applies to the European Court of Human Rights in July 2011.

Advise Adam as to what human rights claims could be made against the state.

An outline answer is included at the end of the book.

Essay question

Explain and analyse how the European Court of Human Rights has expanded the protection of Articles 2 and 3 through the use of positive obligations.

 Scan here

Scan this QR code image with your mobile device to see an outline answer to this question or log onto www.oxfordtextbooks.co.uk/orc/concentrate/

#5

Right to liberty and right to fair trial

Key Facts

- Right to liberty and fair trial are due process rights and essential to rights protection in a democratic society.

- They are not qualified rights but they can be derogated from in times of war and emergency.

- **Articles 5 and 6** are the most commonly argued rights before the ECtHR.

- **Article 5** protects individuals from unlawful and arbitrary detention for specified reasons in the article. Detention must be within the limitations of the article unless derogated from.

- **Article 6** protects the rights to fair trial in both criminal and civil cases (with added protection in criminal cases). The ECtHR has expanded protection of **Article 6** through its interpretation of 'fair' hearing and 'civil' rights and obligations.

- Due process rights have been part of UK law since **Magna Carta**. **Article 5 and Article 6** have developed the protections under the **HRA**.

Chapter overview

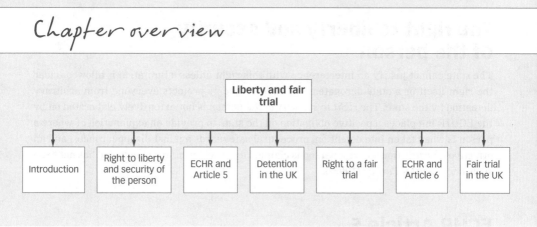

Introduction

The right to liberty and the right to a fair trial guarantee the right to due process in law. The right to due process is one of the essential protections under democratic government and has been integral to human rights instruments since the **Magna Carta**. Without these rights the essence of rights protection would be undermined.

Revision tip

The chapter will only cover some of the main areas as the rights are wide-ranging. It may not cover all areas covered on the human rights course being taught so be clear what is being covered in the course.

The rights are not qualified but neither are they absolute. They can be derogated from in times of war and emergency (see p 78 below and Chapter 10, 'Derogation: Article 15 ECHR', p 178: there is a debate in international law that liberty and fair trial rights should be *jus cogens* and so should be non-derogable). They also have **inherent limitations**. The UNDHR and the ICCPR both contain due process rights. There have been many communications brought before the Human Rights Committee at the UN. However the chapter will focus mainly on the ECHR. Both liberty and fair trial protections have had extensive jurisprudence before the European Court of Human Rights (ECtHR).

Exam tip

Some courses focus on domestic legislation in the UK such as **Police and Criminal Evidence Act 1984** (as amended). If so, be aware of the case law and statutes that are applicable and how the **ECHR/HRA** has affected UK law.

The right to liberty and security of the person

The state cannot justify an interference with this right unless a limitation is allowed under the right itself or a state derogates. *The right to liberty* protects everyone from arbitrary detention by the state. The *right to security of the person* is not extensively elaborated on by the ECtHR but places a positive obligation on the state to provide an explanation of where a person is when taken into detention, procedural safeguards against disappearances, and an effective investigation where a person is claimed to be held in state custody and has not been seen since (***Kurt v Turkey* (1998)**).

ECHR Article 5

Article 5

1. Everyone has the right to liberty and security of person. No one shall be deprived of his liberty save in the following cases and in accordance with a procedure prescribed by law:
   a the lawful detention of a person after conviction by a competent court;
   b the lawful arrest or detention of a person for non-compliance with the lawful order of a court or in order to secure the fulfilment of any obligation prescribed by law;
   c the lawful arrest or detention of a person effected for the purpose of bringing him before the competent legal authority on reasonable suspicion of having committed an offence or when it is reasonably considered necessary to prevent his committing an offence or fleeing after having done so;
   d the detention of a minor by lawful order for the purpose of educational supervision or his lawful detention for the purpose of bringing him before the competent legal authority;
   e the lawful detention of persons for the prevention of the spreading of infectious diseases, of persons of unsound mind, alcoholics or drug addicts or vagrants;
   f the lawful arrest or detention of a person to prevent his effecting an unauthorised entry into the country or of a person against whom action is being taken with a view to deportation or extradition.
2 Everyone who is arrested shall be informed promptly, in a language which he understands, of the reasons for his arrest and of any charge against him.
3 Everyone arrested or detained in accordance with the provisions of paragraph 1.c of this article shall be brought promptly before a judge or other officer authorised by law to exercise judicial power and shall be entitled to trial within a reasonable time or to release pending trial. Release may be conditioned by guarantees to appear for trial.

4   Everyone who is deprived of his liberty by arrest or detention shall be entitled to take proceedings by which the lawfulness of his detention shall be decided speedily by a court and his release ordered if the detention is not lawful.

5   Everyone who has been the victim of arrest or detention in contravention of the provisions of this article shall have an enforceable right to compensation.

Deprivation of liberty

For **Article 5** to be applicable, a person must be deprived of their liberty. Not all restrictions on liberty will amount to a deprivation. It is clear in some cases, such as prison, that a person is deprived of their liberty. However, the ECtHR has had to interpret what is meant by deprivation in cases where the state has interfered with a person's liberty outside of these scenarios.

The ECtHR found that deprivation depends on the circumstance in each case:

....

Guzzardi v Italy (1980) 3 EHRR 333

The applicant was suspected of Mafia activities and was subjected to an order to live in a small area of an island and under curfew, in poor conditions and with limited contact with others.

The ECtHR held on the facts, that there was a deprivation of liberty and not just a restriction. The distinction between a restriction and deprivation is one of 'degree or intensity' and 'not of nature and substance'. When assessing the degree or intensity, the Court will consider criteria such as 'the type, duration, effects and manner of implementation of the measure in question'.

....

(See also **Engel v Netherlands (1976)**).

Deprivation and mentally ill patients

In cases where the applicant is a patient, the ECtHR will examine how much control the state has over the patient in terms of treatment, supervision, etc.

....

H.M. v Switzerland (2004) 38 EHRR 314

An elderly woman was placed in residential accommodation. She was in an open ward and was able to contact friends. The ECtHR held in these circumstances she was not deprived of her liberty.

....

In contrast:

....

H.L. v UK (2004) 40 EHRR 761

A young incapacitated patient was held informally in a hospital ward outside of compulsory detention procedures. The ECtHR held that in this case, the patient was under continuous supervision and control and was not free to leave the hospital. There was a deprivation of liberty and violation.

....

✳✳✳✳✳✳✳✳✳✳

See p 84 below for UK case on the application of deprivation of liberty.

Exam tip

In a problem question involving **Article 5**, the answer should address whether a deprivation has taken place. If it hasn't then **Article 5** is not applicable (using relevant case law).

In accordance with procedure prescribed by law

Conformity with domestic law

Conformity with the relevant domestic law is primarily a question for the state but the ECtHR will scrutinise the measure to be certain that this is the case (*Winterwerp v Netherlands* (1979)). The Court will then evaluate the quality of the domestic law to consider if it is arbitrary.

Is the measure arbitrary?

Legal basis for measure

The measure must have some basis in domestic law. See *Baranowski v Poland* (2000), where detention on remand was a practice that had not been based on any legal regulation in the state.

Link between detention and reasons

The ECtHR has determined that a measure is arbitrary if there is no link between the detention and the reason given for it. For example, the ECtHR has consistently held that detaining prisoners under sentencing rules that allow for indeterminate sentencing are compatible with **Article 5** as long as there is a link between the sentence passed by the court and the reason for continuing detention (*Stafford v UK* (2002)).

Revision tip

There are examples that can be found for all the reasons for detention listed under **Article 5(1)**, for example *Brand v Netherlands* (2004), where it was held that the detention of a person as a mental health patient will only be 'lawful' for the purposes of **Article 5(1)(e)** if the applicant is detained in a hospital, clinic, or other appropriate institution.

Legal certainty

Any measure should be based on domestic law and should not be vague, unclear, or unpredictable. A person should be able to reasonably foresee what action may be taken by the state and when detention may occur. For example:

....

H.L. v UK (2004) 40 EHRR 761

The applicant was held for mental health reasons but not under the statutory provisions that allowed non-consensual detention as the applicant lacked the capacity to refuse or grant consent. He was held under the common law of necessity. The ECtHR held that this legal basis for detention was arbitrary as there were no clear rules in place to provide safeguards for the applicant.

. . . .

(See also *Storck v Germany* **(2005)**.)

Detention under Article 5(1)(a)–(f)

Crime: Article 5(1)(a), (c)

Article 5(1)(a) allows detention after conviction. However, continuing detention after conviction cannot be arbitrary and must be linked to conviction (*Stafford v UK* **(2002)**) and any conviction must be established by a competent court, meaning it should be independent and impartial (*Engel v Netherlands* **(1976)**).

Article 5(1)(c) allows detention where a person is arrested on reasonable suspicion of committing a criminal offence. In *Fox, Campbell and Hartley v UK* **(1990)** the applicants were arrested under a law which required the officer to 'genuinely and honestly' suspect the person of being a terrorist. The question was whether this was enough to amount to 'reasonable', which meant that it would 'satisfy an objective observer' and would depend on the circumstances of the case. There was not enough evidence that the honest belief of the officer could be sustained as reasonable on the facts. (In contrast see *Murray v UK* **(1994)** where a suspected terrorist was held on 'honest suspicion based on reasonable grounds' and so there was not a violation.)

Other reasons for detention

Non-compliance with court order or non-fulfilment of legal obligation: Article 5(1)(b)

This covers measures taken where a court order has already been made and may include civil orders such as matrimonial orders or psychiatric confinement (*X v FRG* **(1975)**). 'Legal obligation' allows the police to detain for the administration of criminal law, eg tests for drink-driving etc. The ECtHR has developed strict limitations. The measure taken should be necessary and used as a last resort, and the obligation must be 'specific and concrete' so that the detention is not based on vague grounds. (*McVeigh, O'Neill and Evans v UK* **(1981)**).

Detention of a minor: Article 5(1)(d)

Educational supervision is given a wide meaning by the ECtHR and covers the detention of minors in residential facilities where teaching may be part of what is provided (*Koniarska v UK* **(2000)**).

Disease, unsound mind, etc: Article 5(1)(e)

Most cases under **Article 5(1)(e)** deal with unsound mind and the ECtHR has laid down general principles that should be followed in order for detention on this ground to be lawful (see *Winterwerp v Netherlands* **(1979)**):

- The mental disorder must be reliably established by objective medical expertise.
- The nature/degree of the disorder must be sufficient to justify the detention.
- The detention should only last as long as the medical disorder persists.
- If the detention is potentially indefinite, then detention should be periodically reviewed.
- The detention must be in a hospital, clinic, or other appropriate institution authorised for the detention of such persons.

Immigration, deportation, extradition: Article 5(1)(f)

The ECtHR has established that detention for unlawful entry or removal should be necessary for reasons of immigration control, should be proportionate in that the length of detention should be no more than necessary, and conditions of detention should be appropriate to the reasons for detention. These principles were applied in *Saadi v UK* **(2008)**, where the ECtHR found that the detention of an alien for unauthorised entry was lawful in the circumstances given the legitimate aim and 'good faith' of state action.

✅ *Looking for extra marks?*

Note: the Grand Chamber decision in *Saadi v UK* was a majority decision and the dissent criticised the majority for giving too much weight to the state's administrative problems. The applicant had not tried to evade immigration control and had been given temporary admission, which was still held to be 'unauthorised'.

Article 5(2): promptly given reasons

In *Fox, Campbell and Hartley v UK* **(1990)**, the ECtHR found a delay of seven hours was acceptable. A few hours seems to be the acceptable length of time to be 'prompt'. The Court is also flexible on the details that have to be given to the detainee, as long as reasons for arrest or charge are clear from the circumstances.

Article 5(3): brought promptly before judicial officer (Article 5(1)(c)) and trial within reasonable time

The length of time between detention and being brought before a judicial officer is important. The longer detention is before charge without some form of judicial oversight, the more likely detention will be arbitrary.

Promptly

The ECtHR has interpreted promptly on a case-by-case basis. In *Brogan v UK* (**1988**), the Court held that four days and six hours between arrest and being brought before a judge was too long. In *McKay v UK* (**2006**), the Court held four days may be the maximum.

Judicial officer—independent and impartial

The judicial officer must be independent; he or she cannot be part of the criminal investigation (*Hood v UK* (**1999**)).The officer must also be able to make a binding decision which cannot be overturned by the executive (*Schiesser v Switzerland* (**1979**)).

Reasonable time and bail

The state must show due diligence in expediting the determination of a charge. The Court will consider the conduct of proceedings and the complexity of the case. It will also examine if continuing detention is necessary before trial or if a person can be released on bail. The Court has found that there should be a presumption of bail (which gets stronger the longer detention exists (*Labita v Italy* (**2000**)) unless there are convincing reasons for continuing detention. The state must demonstrate that the public interest outweighs personal liberty even where serious offences are involved. Refusal of bail may be justified if there is a substantial risk of absconding (*Barfuss v Czech Republic* (**2000**)), witness interference (*Wemhoff v FRG* (**1968**)), or substantial risk of further offences (*Matznetter v Austria* (**1969**)).

Article 5(4): detention 'speedily' reviewed by a court

Anyone detained under **Article 5(1)** is entitled to a review of detention before an independent and impartial court. The judicial body must have the power to order release. 'Speedily' will depend on the reasons for detention and circumstances of each case. If a person is in continual detention then it should be reviewed periodically (*Stafford v UK* (**2002**)). A detainee should also have procedural protections such as legal representation and the right to be heard (*Shtukaturov v Russia* (**2008**)).

Article 5(5): right to compensation

Where there has been violation of **Article 5**, an applicant has an enforceable right of compensation which will be dependent on the circumstances of the case. See Fig. 5.1 overleaf.

Detention in the UK

The protection of the right to liberty (habeas corpus) has been a part of English law since Magna Carta (see Chapter 1, 'Constitutional settlement and rights', p 15). The **Human Rights Act 1998** has further expanded protection. Some examples of recent case law involving the principles discussed above are set out below:

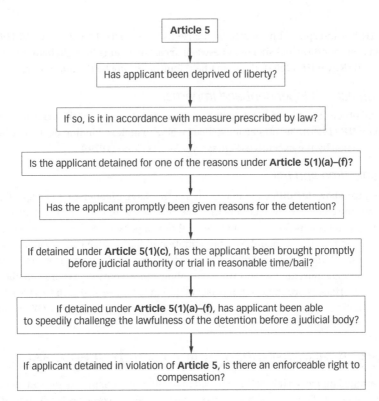

Fig. 5.1 Bringing a case under Article 5

Deprivation of liberty

. . . .

Secretary of State for the Home Department v JJ and Others [2007] All ER (D) 489;
Secretary of State for the Home Department v E [2007] All ER (D) 27

In both cases, the applicants were controlees held under the control order regime as suspected terrorists. The control orders involved restrictions on liberty. The controlees argued that
the restrictions amounted to a 'deprivation' and so **Article 5** was applicable. If so, the control
order used should have derogated from **Article 5** (see Chapter 10, 'Derogation: Article 15 ECHR',
p 178).

The House of Lords applied *Guzzardi v Italy*. Each case had to be decided on its facts, given the
circumstances of the measures taken. On the facts, JJ's restrictions amounted to a deprivation
whilst E's did not.

. . . .

Decision in *JJ* and *E* cases based on different facts

JJ and Others	*E*
• 18-hour curfews;	• 12-hour curfew;
• vetted communication;	• vetted communication;
• tagging;	• tagging;
• lived in flat chosen by security services;	• lived in own home;
• not live with family;	• lived with family;
• severe limits on movement outside curfew hours;	• no geographical restrictions in non-curfew hours;
• restrictions on mosque etc;	• attend mosque of his choice;
• Held (majority (3:2)): amounted to deprivation of liberty	• Held (unanimous): did not amount to a deprivation of liberty

Detention in prison

Impartial and independent judicial body under Article 5(4)

R (Brooke and another) v Parole Board and another [2008] EWCA Civ 29

The respondents were prisoners who were before the Parole Board. They argued the Board was insufficiently independent from the executive to meet the requirements of **Article 5(4)**.

The Court of Appeal dismissed the appeal from Secretary of State. The Home Office was the sponsoring department for the Parole Board and was responsible, inter alia, for appointments to the Board. As the Parole Board was a 'court' for the purposes of **Article 5**, it was not sufficiently independent from the influence of the executive and so did not meet requirements of **Article 5(4)**.

Inability to challenge detention

Wells v Secretary of State for Justice (Parole Board Intervening) [2009] UKHL 22

The prisoners were being held under indeterminate sentences. Once the determinate part of the sentence was finished, they could be held indefinitely, subject to review. Implicit in the scheme was that the claimants were provided with a means to demonstrate they no longer posed a risk and so should be released. The lower courts held there has been a breach of a public law duty. The claimants argued that the delay in providing a means to demonstrate they were not a risk violated **Article 5(1) and (4)**.

The House of Lords held no violation of **Article 5**. The causal link between the reason for detention and continuing detention might be broken by a prolonged failure to enable the prisoner to demonstrate that he was safe for release and so have an effective review, but such failure would have to be for a period of years rather than months.

Mental illness

Burden of proof

R v MHRT, North & East London Region & the Secretary of State for Health, ex p H [2001] EWCA Civ 415

The claimant was detained under mental health provisions. To gain release the burden of proof was on the claimant to show the conditions were met for release.

The Court of Appeal held the law governing release was incompatible with **Article 5**. In cases concerning 'unsound mind', the burden is on the authorities to demonstrate on objective medical evidence that the detention is justified (following *Winterwerp* (see p 82, above)). The court made a declaration of incompatibility.

Public order

There have been a series of cases on the limiting of liberty for public order (see also Chapter 8 on **Article 11**, 'Criminal offences', pp 147–149). For example:

Austin v Commissioner of Police of the Metropolis [2009] UKHL 5

During a demonstration in London which had partially been violent, the police decided to cordon off protestors and release them over a number of hours (known as 'kettling'). The applicant argued that **Article 5** had been violated.

The House of Lords held there was no violation of **Article 5**. There had not been a 'deprivation' of liberty considering all the factors, one of which was the necessity of the measure, which had to be taken in good faith and be proportionate to the situation. In this case, the police decision was taken to maintain the cordon only as long as necessary and was proportionate.

Applying *Austin* in *R (on the application of Moos) v Commissioner of Police of the Metropolis* (2011), the court decided that the police containment of a relatively peaceful demonstration to protect it from being hijacked by violent protesters was not lawful because there had been no risk of an 'imminent' breach of the peace. Imminence was an essential condition of preventative action, which had to be necessary and a measure of 'last resort'. The test of necessity is only met in extreme circumstances.

✅ Looking for extra marks?

The debates over the use of cordons by police during protest marches or 'kettling' as it is commonly referred to have been given heightened scrutiny in recent years. Case law may continue to develop in this area and it is worth finding academic and other articles on this subject (which overlaps with **Article 11**).

The right to a fair trial

Like liberty, the right to fair trial is a fundamental right. The right to fair trial is a limited right. The state cannot justify an interference with the right unless any limitation is allowed under the right itself or a state derogates.

Revision tip

Article 6 is the most frequently argued right before the ECtHR and it can be procedurally complex. The chapter will only focus on some of the main issues so it is essential that module textbooks and readings are covered. Also, be aware that a module may focus on UK law.

ECHR Article 6

Article 6

1   In the determination of his civil rights and obligations or of any criminal charge against him, everyone is entitled to a fair and public hearing within a reasonable time by an independent and impartial tribunal established by law. Judgment shall be pronounced publicly but the press and public may be excluded from all or part of the trial in the interests of morals, public order or national security in a democratic society, where the interests of juveniles or the protection of the private life of the parties so require, or to the extent strictly necessary in the opinion of the court in special circumstances where publicity would prejudice the interests of justice.

2   Everyone charged with a criminal offence shall be presumed innocent until proved guilty according to law.

3   Everyone charged with a criminal offence has the following minimum rights:

   a   to be informed promptly, in a language which he understands and in detail, of the nature and cause of the accusation against him;

   b   to have adequate time and facilities for the preparation of his defence;

   c   to defend himself in person or through legal assistance of his own choosing or, if he has not sufficient means to pay for legal assistance, to be given it free when the interests of justice so require;

   d   to examine or have examined witnesses against him and to obtain the attendance and examination of witnesses on his behalf under the same conditions as witnesses against him;

e to have the free assistance of an interpreter if he cannot understand or speak the language used in court.

Article 6(1) guarantees the right to a fair hearing covering both criminal and civil issues. Criminal proceedings are given greater protection by the guarantees in **Article 6(2) and (3)**.

Article 6(1)

This protects the right to a fair hearing which is:

- a determination of criminal charge or civil right/obligation;
- before an independent and impartial tribunal or court;
- within a reasonable period of time;
- in public; and
- 'fair'.

Determination

This covers the proceedings in general. It may not cover all preliminary proceedings, though it can include the enforcement of any judgment (*Hornsby v Greece* (1997)).

Criminal charge

The meaning of 'criminal charge' can vary between states: the ECtHR examines the measure in question and gives it an autonomous meaning so that states cannot avoid their obligations under **Article 6**. The ECtHR will examine criteria such as the classification of the offence by the state in question, the nature of the offence, and the potential punishment (*Engel v Netherlands* (1976)). If the state describes the offence as criminal then that is accepted by the ECtHR. If not, the Court will examine the other criteria and apply them to the facts of each case. For example, if a measure described as 'disciplinary' applies to a specific group then it may fall outside **Article 6** but if applied generally, then it may fall under Article 6; for example, *Weber v Switzerland* (1990), where the applicant was held liable for releasing confidential information about a judicial process. It was held to be a 'criminal' charge because it applied to all and not just to the legal profession, where it would have been a disciplinary matter.

Civil right/obligation

The ECtHR has also interpreted what is meant by a civil right. The Court has to interpret 'civil' against a background of European diversity in legal systems. In general, it differentiates between 'private' rights which are 'civil', and public/administrative rights that are not covered by **Article 6**. 'Civil' private rights include areas where financial interests are involved in proceedings such as employment, personal injury, reputation, property, or are seen as proximate to private rights such as child custody (*Olsson v Sweden* (1992)).

Difficulties have arisen concerning public employment cases and public authority complaint procedures. The ECtHR has expanded **Article 6** protection where the proceedings may be directly decisive with regard to private rights such as employment or property rights (*Le Compte, Van Leuven and De Meyerev Belgium* (1981)). The ECtHR has also expanded the applicability of **Article 6** by including social security claims (*Schuler-Zgraggen v Switzerland* (1993). However **Article 6** has not yet been held to apply to taxation, immigration matters, certain parts of public employment, and political matters such as voting.

Revision tip

There is a large amount of case law developing the meaning of civil rights and obligations. For more detail on this, it is strongly advised to consult the module reading and textbook.

Independent tribunal/court

The legal proceedings must be held by an independent and impartial tribunal or court. To establish independence, the ECtHR will examine the appointment and tenure of the decision-makers, the relationship with the executive and parties, the ability to make a binding decision, and the general 'appearance of independence' (*Campbell and Fell v UK* (1984). In *Bryan v UK* (1995), the ECtHR found the planning system in the UK was not independent as the executive could revoke the authority of planning inspectors to hold appeals. However, there was no violation because the applicant had redress by being able to apply for judicial review on the point of law being argued. In contrast in *Kingsley v UK* (2002), the court found that the lack of independence of the Gaming Board was not solved by judicial review owing to the restrictiveness of review (could not revoke Gaming Board's decision).

The tribunal or court must also be impartial; there must be no prejudice or bias. The ECtHR applies a two-part test (*Piersack v Belgium* (1982)):

1. Subjective:

Can it be shown that a member of court had personal bias against the applicant?

2. Objective:

Can any doubts as to impartiality be objectively justified? Even where no subjective bias can be established, the appearance of bias may be enough to call into question the impartiality of the proceedings.

Reasonable time

When determining what is 'reasonable', the ECtHR will consider several factors, such as the complexity of the case, the applicant's conduct, and the conduct of the state (*Konig v FRG* (1978)).

ECHR Article 6

✳✳✳✳✳✳✳✳✳✳

Revision tip

There are a large number of cases that examine delay before the courts; many of these cases are against Italy due to its legal system. See the module textbook and readings for detail on this.

Public

The right to a public hearing includes the right to an oral hearing and pronouncements of decisions. However, these can be limited in certain circumstances such as in the best interests of children (*B and P v UK* (**2002**)) and national security (*A v UK* (**2009**)), as long as procedural safeguards are in place.

Fair?—implied obligations

The right to a fair hearing has been interpreted to include several principles. The ECtHR has determined the principles to be *implied obligations* of states, without which the right would not be effective. These include:

Access to a court

Article 6 is ineffective if an applicant cannot gain access to legal proceedings.

. . . .

Golder v UK (1975) 1 EHRR 524

The applicant prisoner wished to sue the prison for negligence but was denied access to a solicitor. The ECtHR held that this meant his right to a fair hearing was 'illusory' as he had no way of making a claim of negligence against the prison. There was a violation of **Article 6**.

. . . .

A denial of access may also include a denial of legal aid in civil law cases where this leads to a denial of effective legal proceedings (*Steel and Morris v UK* (**2005**)). However, a state may limit access to proceedings in certain circumstances as long as the right is not removed completely.

Attendance at hearing and the right to participate

There is a general expectation that an applicant should be present at a hearing though this can be limited. If present, the applicant should be able to participate and be able to understand the proceedings (*V and T v UK* (**1999**)).

Equality of arms

One party to a case should not suffer a significant disadvantage compared to the other party. There should be a 'fair balance' in proceedings (*Steel and Morris v UK* (**2005**)).

Right to adversarial trial

This includes the right of a defendant to see the evidence against him or her (*Edwards v UK* (**1992**)).

Evidential rules

As evidential rules differ between member states the Court has a supervisory role to determine if the use of inadmissible evidence would render any trial unfair (see the controversial decision in *Gafgen v Germany* **(2010)**: the general principle is that evidence gained through ill treatment renders a trial unfair. However, in this case, the ECtHR held that evidence obtained following degrading treatment had no effect on the outcome of the trial so there was no violation of **Article 6**. (See dissent in this case.)).

Presumption of innocence, self-incrimination

See the discussion of **Article (6)(2)** below; however, this principle applies to **Article 6** generally where a criminal charge may not be at issue (*Phillips v UK* **(2001)**). An applicant also has a right not to be compelled to give evidence that might incriminate him or her. This is not absolute as the state may compel evidence in some circumstances but this must not be improper. Safeguards should be in place. In *Murray v UK* **(1996)**, restrictions on the right to silence were not a violation of **Article 6** owing to the safeguards in place.

Legal representation

See the discussion of **Article 6(3)** below; also applies to non-criminal cases through the right of access to a court.

Reasoned and final judgement

This applies to criminal and civil cases; the decision should be made with sufficient clarity depending on the circumstances of the case. Any final judgment made in a case should be irreversible (*Brumarescu v Romania* **(1999)**).

✅ *Looking for extra marks?*

There are many cases on these issues and several UK cases dealing with implied obligations. It may be useful to read UK human rights texts if the module studied focuses on UK law.

Article 6(2): criminal offence 'presumed innocent'

Article 6(2) provides explicit protection for the presumption of innocence. This raises the issue of the burden and standard of proof in criminal cases. These may differ amongst states but the Court will scrutinise the circumstances of each case to determine the fairness of the burden and standard of proof under **Article 6(2)**. For example, in *Salabiaku v France* **(1988)**, strict liability for a drug smuggling offence was held not to violate the ECHR as a defence was available to the applicant. It may violate **Article 6(2)** if a court expresses a view of the guilt of an applicant where he or she has not been tried and found guilty (*Minelli v Switzerland* **(1983)**).

Article 6(3): minimum guarantees re criminal charge

Article **6(3)** guarantees explicit minimum rights for anyone charged with a criminal offence:

Article 6(3)

a   to be informed promptly, in a language which he understands and in detail, of the nature and cause of the accusation against him;

b   to have adequate time and facilities for the preparation of his defence;

c   to defend himself in person or through legal assistance of his own choosing or, if he has not sufficient means to pay for legal assistance, to be given it free when the interests of justice so require;

d   to examine or have examined witnesses against him and to obtain the attendance and examination of witnesses on his behalf under the same conditions as witnesses against him;

e   to have the free assistance of an interpreter if he cannot understand or speak the language used in court.

Revision tip

Some of these overlap with the implied obligations in **Article 6(1)**. Be aware of the case law on these specific rights.

See Fig. 5.2 on p 93.

Fair trial in the UK

The right to fair trial has been a part of English common law since **Magna Carta** and has also been guaranteed in statute (eg **Police and Criminal Evidence Act 1984**). The **Human Rights Act 1998** has added to the legal protection in the UK. The following cases are just a few examples of **Article 6** cases before the UK courts:

The court examined the issue of self-incrimination in:

....

Brown v Stott [2001] 2 WLR 817

The respondent was found guilty of drink-driving. She was under a compulsion to answer police questions as to whether she was driving the car when stopped. She argued that this amounted to self-incrimination. The lower court had found that there was a violation of **Article 6**.

The Privy Council held that the compulsion was compatible with **Article 6**. The right to self-incrimination was not absolute and could be limited in the public interest. The regime was a proportionate response to the need to maintain road safety and did not completely undermine the right to fair trial as other evidence was needed to corroborate any admission made. (Appeal allowed.)

....

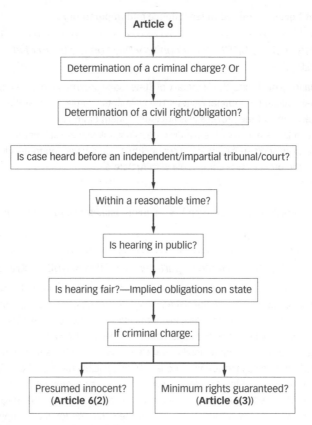

Fig. 5.2 Bringing a case under Article 6

Admissibility of evidence was the issue in:

Cadder v HM Advocate [2010] UKSC 43

The claimant was interviewed by the police and made admissions without access to legal advice which later secured a guilty verdict against him. The HM Advocate argued that guarantees within the system as a whole meant the trial was fair.

The Supreme Court held following the ECtHR decision in **Salduz v Turkey (2009)** on access to legal advice under **Article 6(1) and Article 6(3)(c)**, a detainee should have access to legal advice from the first interrogation, unless there were compelling reasons that made the presence of a lawyer impracticable. The safeguards elsewhere in procedures did not remove the disadvantage suffered by the claimant. The procedures were incompatible with **Article 6**.

Fair trial in the UK

✳✳✳✳✳✳✳✳✳✳

The House of Lords examined independence and impartiality in:

. . . .

R v Secretary of State DETR, ex p Alconbury Developments Ltd et al [2001] 2 WLR 1389

In several planning decisions, the Secretary of State made determinations on the decisions. These decisions were subject to **judicial review**. The claimants complained that the executive's role in decision-making meant the process was not independent or impartial.

The House of Lords held that the planning decisions taken were subject to judicial review. The judicial review provided an independent tribunal that had jurisdiction to decide on the nature of the decision. The process was compatible with **Article 6**.

. . . .

The House of Lords examined equality of arms issues arising from the use of special advocates in:

. . . .

Secretary of State for the Home Department v AF (No 3) [2009] UKHL 28

Controlees under the control order regime had their case held in closed hearing and could not hear the evidence against them. Special advocates were appointed to represent them. Special advocates could not tell the controlees any of the closed evidence against them. The controlees argued they were unable to defend themselves and so violated **Article 6**.

The House of Lords held that (following ***A v UK* (2009)**), a person should have sufficient information to be able to give instructions. There is an 'irreducible minimum' of information needed to allow a fair hearing under **Article 6**. In *AF*, there was not enough open material to meet this minimum. Using **s 3 HRA**, the legislation was read down to give the judge discretion as to whether there was enough information given to the controlee for the hearing to be fair under **Article 6**.

. . . .

✔ Looking for extra marks?

It may be useful to read articles on the role of judicial review to providing an independent tribunal for administrative decisions and the controversy surrounding the use of closed hearings for terrorist suspects.

Key cases

Case	Facts	Principle
Austin v Commissioner of Police of the Metropolis [2009] UKHL 5	During a demonstration, the police cordoned off protestors and released them over a number of hours.	.There had not been a 'deprivation' of liberty considering all the factors, one of which was the necessity of the measure, which had to be taken in good faith and be proportionate to the situation. Appeal dismissed.
Brown v Stott [2001] 2 WLR 817	Defendant asked to name driver when stopped for drink-driving	The right to self-incrimination is not absolute and can be limited in the public interest if a proportionate response did not completely undermine the right to fair trial. Appeal allowed.
Golder v UK (1975) 1 EHRR 524	Prisoner who wanted to sue prison was denied access to a solicitor.	Right to fair trial includes access to a court, without which the right would not be effective. Violation
Guzzardi v Italy (1980) 3 EHRR 333	The applicant was suspected of Mafia activities and was subjected to an order to live in a small area of an island under curfew.	Violation. The distinction between a restriction and deprivation is one of 'degree or intensity' and 'not of nature and substance'. The Court will consider criteria such as 'the type, duration, effects, and manner of implementation of the measure in question'.
Secretary of State for the Home Department v AF (No 3) [2009] UKHL 28	Under control order regime, controlees had special advocates who could not inform client of closed evidence against them.	A person should have sufficient information to be able to give instructions. There is an 'irreducible minimum' of information needed to allow a fair hearing under Article 6. Appeal allowed
Secretary of State for the Home Department v JJ and Others [2007] All ER (D) 489	Controlees were suspected terrorists under control orders, which included curfews and other restrictions.	What amounts to 'deprivation' has to be decided on its facts, given the circumstances of the measures taken—*Guzzardi* applied and appeal allowed.

Key debates

✱✱✱✱✱✱✱✱✱✱

〉〉 Key debates

Topic	'Derogation from the European Convention on Human Rights in the light of "Other Obligations under International Law"'
Author	Jean Allain
Viewpoint	The article argues that detention and fair trial should be non-derogable under international law
Source	(2005) *European Human Rights Law* Vol 5 pp 480–498

Topic	'Marginalising human rights: breach of the peace, "kettling", the Human Rights Act, and public protest'
Author	Helen Fenwick
Viewpoint	The article discusses the decision in ***Austin***, criticising the use of 'kettling' re **Article 5** and the House of Lords decision
Source	(2009) *Public Law*, Oct, pp 737–765

? Exam questions

Problem question

Andrew is a lecturer who attended a demonstration outside his university, protesting about government policy. The protest, which included lecturers and students, marched to the town centre. A few of the students were seen attacking a government office. However, the main demonstration was not near the government office and was peaceful. As the protest ended, the police forced the students onto a bridge and cordoned off both sides. The protesters, including Andrew, were kept on the bridge for several hours. The police claimed this was to avoid a breach of the peace.

After being released from the bridge, Andrew was arrested on his way home. He was taken to a local police station, where he was questioned on suspicion of criminal damage. He was initially questioned for one hour without a solicitor present. He was charged with criminal damage. At his bail hearing, he was refused bail on the grounds he may have reoffended. He spent several weeks in prison on remand before being released when the charges were dropped.

After returning to work at the university, Andrew was suspended from his job for a month for bringing the university into disrepute. He appealed against the decision but there was no oral hearing. The appeal panel was made of up three members, one of which made the original decision to suspend. Andrew received a letter, dismissing his appeal. No reasons were given.

Advise Andrew as to what human rights claims can be made against the state and examine the likely outcome of the case.

An outline answer is included at the end of the book.

Essay question

'Due process rights concerning liberty and fair trial are too important to allow a state to limit protection.'

Explain and analyse this statement, with particular reference to the jurisprudence of the European Court of Human Rights.

 Scan here
Scan this QR code image with your mobile device to see an outline answer to this question or log onto www.oxfordtextbooks.co.uk/orc/concentrate/

#6
Right to family and private life

Key Facts

- The right to family and private life is a qualified right.

- **Article 8** has been developed to expand protection of the ECHR through wide definitions and use of positive obligations.

- The Court has defined private life widely and used the living instrument principle to include areas such as sexuality and the environment.

- When examining the justification of an interference with the right, proportionality and margin of appreciation are decisive in many cases.

- The right to family and private life may need to be balanced against other rights.

- The **HRA** has developed the right to privacy in the UK.

Chapter overview

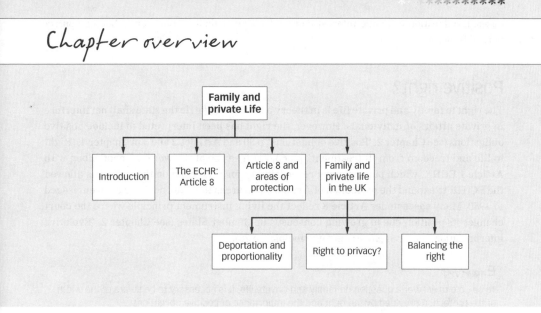

Introduction

The right to family and private life is a-wide ranging right that encompasses many aspects of a person's life. The United Nations include the right to family and private life in the UDHR and ICCPR (Chapter 1, 'The United Nations', p 6). However this chapter will focus on the ECHR. The ECHR and the **Human Rights Act** have heavily influenced how privacy has been adjudicated in the UK.

The right to family and private life is a qualified right (see Chapter 2, 'Qualified rights', p 52). This means that a state can justify an interference of the right under certain conditions. The width of protection under the right has meant that a court often finds an interference, so that many cases are decided on whether the state's interference is justified. The principles of proportionality and margin of appreciation (see Chapter 2, 'Proportionality and margin of appreciation', pp 33–35) are important in the decision-making process.

Balancing rights: privacy and expression

The right to family and private life is a qualified right as it often clashes with the rights of others. The case law will highlight where the right to family and private life may interfere with another's freedom of expression. Much of the UK case law on this issue has involved newspapers who wish to print stories about individuals and their private lives. In these cases, the question of public interest can be decisive. This has consistently been a controversial issue.

Positive right?

The right to family and private life is in theory a negative right, ie the state shall not interfere in private affairs of individuals. However, the right has been interpreted to include positive obligations (see Chapter 2, 'Positive obligations', p 30 and **Articles 2 and 3** in Chapter 4, 'Right to life and freedom from ill treatment', pp 63, 71). The use of the word 'respect' along with **Article 1 ECHR**, which puts primary responsibility for protection on the state, has allowed the ECtHR to expand the protection of **Article 8** into areas that may not have been envisaged in 1950. Many cases under **Article 8** reflect the living instrument principle where the court changes its position due to growing consensus in Member States (see Chapter 2, 'Evolutive interpretation: the 'living instrument principle'', p 28).

Exam tip

To be able to answer a question on family and private life, it is necessary to be aware of the width of the protection provided by the right and the importance of positive obligations.

ECHR Article 8

Article 8

1) Everyone has the right to respect for his private and family life, his home and his correspondence.
2) There shall be no interference by a public authority with the exercise of this right except such as is in accordance with the law and is necessary in a democratic society in the interests of national security, public safety or the economic well-being of the country, for the prevention of disorder or crime, for the protection of health or morals, or for the protection of the rights and freedoms of others.

Article 8 of the ECHR includes four protected interests:
The right to respect for:

- family life;
- private life;
- home; and
- correspondence.

Article 8(1)

Family life

The ECtHR has found that family life encompasses children and grandchildren (***Marckx v Belgium* (1979)**). It also includes adoptive relationships (***Pini and others v Romania* (2005)**). The Court has also found that a family relationship continues after divorce (***Berrehab v Netherlands* (1989).**)

The ECtHR has found other relationships are part of family life. The applicants will have to demonstrate close family ties and this is a matter of fact and degree depending on the circumstances (***Lebbink v Netherlands* (2004)**). The Court has found that cohabiting heterosexual couples may fall under family life (***Kamal v United Kingdom,* DR 20/168**) and similarly, foster relationships (***X v Switzerland,* DR 13/248**). Until recently the Court had found that homosexual relationships fell under private life rather than family life. Reflecting the living instrument principle, the ECtHR in *Schalk and another v Austria* (2010) has now recognised that a same sex relationship may fall under family life. If a relationship does not fall under family life, it may fall under private life.

Private life

Private life has been given a wide meaning by the ECtHR. The Court has expanded the meaning over time and has stated that it is not capable of 'exhaustive definition' (***Peck v UK* (2003)**). However, it includes a 'person's physical and psychological integrity' for which respect is due in order to 'ensure the development, without outside interference, of the personality of each individual in his relations with other human beings' (***Botta v Italy* (1998)**). In *Pretty v UK* (2002), the ECtHR noted that 'the very essence of the Convention is respect for human dignity and human freedom'. It stated that private life encompasses 'quality of life' issues. In *S and Marper v UK* (2009), the ECtHR noted that private life encompasses 'multiple aspects of a person's physical and social identity'.

Home

The meaning of 'home' includes a person's existing home but does not guarantee a right to a home (***Novoseletskiy v Ukraine* (2005)**). The state is not under a general obligation to provide accommodation. However, there may be limited circumstances where **Article 8** may be infringed such as *Marzari v Italy* (1999), where the failure to provide alternative accommodation to an applicant with a severe disease may fall under **Article 8**. It was held in *Cyprus v Turkey* (2001) that preventing applicants returning to their homes fell under **Article 8**.

'Home' can also cover houses that have not been lived in continuously (***Gillow v UK* (1986)**). In ***Connors v UK* (2004)**, the Court held that land occupied by caravans could constitute a home under **Article 8**. The ECtHR has also expanded the meaning of 'home' to include business premises (***Niemietz v Germany* (1993)**).

Correspondence

'Correspondence' covers all forms of communication including letters, telephone, fax, and emails. Any state interference (other than due to Post Office inefficiencies) interferes with **Article 8(1)** and requires justification under **Article 8(2)**. This includes correspondence from those held in state custody (***Golder v UK* (1975)**).

Article 8(2)

If it is established that there is an interference with **Article 8(1)**, the state has to justify the interference with the right. Any interference has to be:

- in accordance with law;
- meet a legitimate aim; and
- necessary in a democratic society.

In accordance with law

Any act by the state that interferes with **Article 8(1)** must be in accordance with law. This means that there must be some legal basis for the action and that this has to be clear, precise, and predictable. For example, in ***Copland v UK* (2007)** it was held that surveillance of a staff member's college email account was not justified as there was no clear basis in law that allowed the college to monitor email (see also ***Gillan and Quinton v UK* (2010)**).

Legitimate aim

Article 8(2) sets out the reasons why a state can interfere with the right to family and private life. These are quite wide:

- national security;
- public safety;
- the economic well-being of the country;
- for the prevention of disorder or crime;
- for the protection of health or morals; and
- for the protection of the rights and freedoms of others.

The state does not usually have a problem demonstrating a legitimate aim as they are quite wide-ranging. Which legitimate aim is argued may be important as it can influence the margin of appreciation given to the state and the proportionality of a measure.

Necessary in a democratic society

Many cases are decided on whether a measure is necessary in a democratic society. To adjudicate on this question the ECtHR (and the UK courts), uses the concept of proportionality and will apply a margin of appreciation (see Chapter 2, 'Margin of appreciation', p 34 and Chapter 3, 'Applying the HRA: Proportionality and judicial deference', pp 50–52).

Proportionality

Article 8 is a qualified right as the right may conflict with the needs of the community or the rights of others. Proportionality aims to find a balance between the individual right and the community. The criteria the ECtHR will examine when looking at the act of the state include:

- Is it effective? Does the act/measure meet the legitimate aim? Is there a link between the measure and what the state argues it is meant to be achieving?
- Is it the least intrusive measure possible?
- Does it deprive the 'very essence of the right'? Does the act/measure take away all of the protection of the right?
- Is it balanced? This applies to both negative and positive obligations. Has a fair balance been struck between the competing interests of the individual and of the community as a whole? Is the individual's right of such importance that only the most compelling reasons would justify any interference?

The cases below examining the different areas of protection, illustrate some examples of the use of proportionality in the ECtHR.

✅ *Looking for extra marks?*

Proportionality is widely used by the Court and there has been much academic writing on its use.

Margin of appreciation

The margin of appreciation doctrine considers the amount of discretion given to the state by the ECtHR when adjudicating on alleged violations of qualified rights. The doctrine is premised on the fact that the state is primarily responsible for upholding Convention rights and that there may be variations in tolerance of measures in states. It was outlined in the **Article 10** case of *Handyside v UK* **(1976)** (see Chapter 7, 'Necessary in a democratic society', p 128).

Revision tip

Margin of appreciation is important in all the qualified rights and similar principles apply.

A wide margin of appreciation means that the ECtHR is more likely to find no violation whereas a narrow margin means a violation is more likely. However, this is not always the case. Even in cases where traditionally a wide margin of appreciation is given, there may still be a violation given the importance of the right in question.

Several factors will influence whether the margin of appreciation is wide or narrow:

- The nature/importance of the right/issue in question: *Dudgeon v UK (1981)*—the case involved sexuality which is seen as an intimate part of private life, therefore narrow margin; violation found.

- Nature/importance of general interest/aim: *Laskey, Jaggard and Brown v UK (1997)*—legitimate aim was criminal law/health, so even though involved sexual acts a wide margin given; no violation.

- Lack of European consensus or standard: *Goodwin v UK (2002)*—transsexuals; violation.

- Areas where judges give wider margin because difficult to judge/resources: *Buckley v UK (1996)*—the area of planning involved resources and state knowledge; no violation, *Hatton v UK (2003)*—economic well-being of state so wide margin was given; no violation found.

✅ *Looking for extra marks?*

There are criticisms of the use of the margin of appreciation in cases such as *Hatton* where the dissenting opinion criticised the majority for giving the state too much discretion and argued that the majority failed to examine fully state claims that a violation finding would be detrimental to the economic well-being of the state, while at the same time underestimating the importance of the right.

See Fig. 6.1 on p 105.

Article 8: areas of protection

The expansion of the protected interests along with the use of positive obligations has led to **Article 8** being used in a wide number of cases involving a wide number of different issues.

Revision tip

There is a huge volume of case law from the ECtHR involving **Article 8**. Some of these are outlined below but these are not exhaustive. When revising **Article 8**, it is useful to divide into areas and note a few of the cases to illustrate your answer.

Family proceedings

There have been many cases dealing with family proceedings such as care proceedings and child contact cases. The state can remove children into care and may have a wide margin of appreciation but it must act proportionately. Many of the cases are decided on the proportionality of the measures taken.

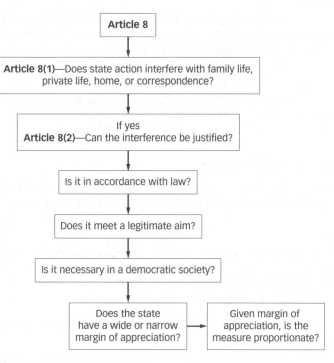

Fig. 6.1 Bringing a case under Article 8

Some examples:

Johansen v Norway (1996) 23 EHRR 33

A child had been in local authority care since the age of two weeks. The state decided to terminate parental contact so that the child could be adopted.

The ECtHR recognised care proceedings may have been necessary in this case but the decision to put the child up for adoption was disproportionate. Adoption completely terminated family life and prevented a reunion of the parent with the child. This could only be done in exceptional circumstances and these were not met in this case. There was a violation of **Article 8**.

Similarly in:

Kutzner v Germany (2002) 35 EHRR 653

The applicants' daughters had been removed from their care. The state argued that the parents' 'impaired mental development' rendered them incapable of bringing up their children. The children were eventually fostered. They had limited contact with their parents.

Article 8: areas of protection

✳✳✳✳✳✳✳✳✳✳✳

> The state has a positive obligation to facilitate family reunion if possible to do so. Where practicable, the state should provide educational support for the family. The measures taken were held to be disproportionate and a violation of **Article 8**.

Also note that in cases involving child contact, the state is under an obligation to facilitate child contact between parents where possible, considering the best interests of the child principle (***Sommerfield v Germany* (2004)**).

Removal from the state

Matters concerning immigration usually involve a wide margin of appreciation. Many of the cases involve convicted criminals or people who pose a danger to the state.

Exam tip

Removal cases involving deportation etc may fall under **Article 3** (see Chapter 4, 'Removal of persons from state', p 71) as well as **Article 8**. **Article 3** may be invoked if the applicant faces a substantial risk of ill treatment in the receiving state. Be aware that an essay or problem involving removal cases may involve several rights.

The principles to be applied were fully outlined in ***Boultif v Switerland* (2001)**. There are several examples including:

Kaya v Germany (2007) (Application No 31753/02)

The state wished to deport a convicted criminal who had committed very serious offences to Turkey for five years.

The ECtHR held that the deportation was justified as it was proportionate. The Court examined the seriousness of the offences, the length of stay of the applicant in Germany, the length of deportation, the length of time since the offences, the applicant's conduct, and his nationality, family, and cultural ties.

Contrast with:

Nasri v France (1996) 21 EHRR 458

The applicant had been convicted of rape and threatened with deportation. He argued that this violated his right to family life as his parents and siblings all lived in France.

It was held that although the state can justify deportation for criminal offences, in this case the applicant was deaf, without speech, and illiterate. He lived with his family and was dependent on them. Deportation could not be justified given the circumstances of the applicant. It would be disproportionate.

Searches and surveillance

If the aim of surveillance or a search is to prevent crime or national security, then the state may be given a wide margin of appreciation. However, any interference still has to have a legal basis and be proportionate:

Some examples:

Niemietz v Germany (1993) 16 EHRR 97

The police searched the business premises of a lawyer to identify a suspect.

It was held that the search was an interference with 'home' even though it was business premises. Due to a lack of safeguards, the minor offence involved, and the importance to the administration of justice of protecting a lawyer's files, the search was disproportionate.

Similarly in:

Gillan and Quinton v UK (2010) (Application No 4158/05)

Using powers under the **Terrorism Act 2000** which allowed the police to stop and search without reasonable suspicion, the police searched the applicants on their way to protest at an arms fair.

The ECtHR held that the stop and search powers were used in a disproportionate manner. Despite a wide margin of appreciation in issues of national security, there still needed to be proper safeguards in place to prevent the misuse of power.

Similarly, when surveillance is used:

Halford v UK (1997) 24 EHRR 523

An assistant police constable's office phone calls were monitored by the police. The police system was not part of the public network.

It was held that the office calls fell under **Article 8**. The surveillance was not in accordance with law as there was no legal basis existing at the time that allowed for the monitoring of police telecommunication systems.

The ECtHR has also examined the taking and use of photographs. It has found that the police may use images in a proportionate manner to investigate crime etc. However, the use of these images may result in a violation of **Article 8** if used in a disproportionate manner. For example, in *Peck v UK (2003)*, it was held that the release of CCTV footage on a national television programme of the applicant attempting to commit suicide in public was disproportionate.

Personal Information

The holding or disclosure of personal information has given rise to much case law. For example in *Z v Finland* **(1997)**, the release of medical records containing information about the applicant's HIV status was held to be disproportionate. In contrast, in *Leander v Sweden* **(1987)** the refusal of the state to disclose records for reasons of national security (information held for security-vetted employment) was held to be proportionate and within the state's margin of appreciation.

S and Marper v UK (2009) 48 EHRR 1169

The applicants had their DNA samples retained on a national police database. They had both been arrested but had not been found guilty of any offence. In order to get removed from the database, there was a very limited procedure involving a discretionary power held by the police. Any person who had their DNA taken by police had their information retained indefinitely whether convicted or not.

The Court held that DNA was a fundamental part of a person's identity. The blanket and indiscriminate nature of the retention on the database and the lack of procedures for review meant that it went beyond what was proportionate when balancing the right of the individual against the needs of the community, even with a wide margin of appreciation given for the prevention of crime.

Protection from harm

The state may have a positive obligation to provide protection for a person's private and family life. This means the state has to have a legal framework in place to prevent harm even where that harm is caused by a private party (applicable to the environment, below).

X and Y v Netherlands (1985) 8 EHRR 235

The applicant was a young woman sexually assaulted by a man. The applicant was mentally disabled. Owing to her disability, the authorities held that she could not give evidence and so no charges were brought.

It was held that the state was under a positive obligation to prevent harm which may interfere with the **Article 8** right of the applicant. The legal framework did not provide adequate safeguards to protect the applicant. There was a violation of **Article 8**.

Sexual identity and activity

The ECtHR has expanded the protection of **Article 8** to include sexual rights. In several cases it has recognised the importance of the right.

Homosexuality

Dudgeon v UK (1981) 4 EHRR 149

Although homosexual acts had been decriminalised in most of the UK, they were still a criminal offence in Northern Ireland. Although the applicant had not been convicted of an offence, he had been investigated and lived under a real threat of conviction.

The Court held that, given the growing consensus in Europe and the intimate nature of the right, the applicant's right outweighed the needs of the community. Criminalisation of homosexuality was a violation of **Article 8**.

Transsexuals (see also Chapter 2, 'Example: transgender cases', p 29)

Goodwin v UK (2002) 35 EHRR 447

The applicant was a transsexual. She claimed a violation of the right to private life. In the UK, her changed gender was not recognised in that she could not change her personal documents such as her birth certificate.

The Court noted the living instrument principle: '..., the Court must have regard to the changing conditions within the respondent State and within Contracting States generally...'. The Court considered scientific and social developments and the growing legal consensus meant that there was a violation of **Article 8**.

But note: The ECtHR has not yet found enough consensus to find that same sex 'marriage' should be treated in the same way as heterosexual marriage. Although recognising a growing consensus on giving legal recognition to same sex couples under 'civil partnerships', there is still no obligation on states to provide the same legal rights that marriage may give. States still have a wide discretion in this area: *Schalk and another v Austria* **(2010)**.

Also, whilst recognising the intimate nature of sexual acts, the state may still justify interference. In *Laskey, Jaggard and Brown v UK* **(1997)**, the applicants were convicted of sadomasochistic acts which took place between consenting adults. The ECtHR held the convictions were justified as the state had a wide a margin of appreciation where the prevention of crime was the legitimate aim.

Reproductive rights

The ECtHR has recognised reproductive rights as being an important part of private life. The state has a margin of appreciation in the regulation of these rights (*Evans v UK* **(2007)**), but must do so in a proportionate manner and the rights of the applicant's partner as well as those of the applicant should be taken into account (*Dickson v UK* **(2007)**).

Article 8: areas of protection
✳✳✳✳✳✳✳✳✳✳

Environment

The right to a healthy environment can be found in human rights treaties such as the African Charter of Human Rights and Peoples Rights 1981. However, it is often described as a third generation right (see Chapter 1, 'Third generation rights', p 12), and the ECHR deals with civil and political rights. There is no explicit right to a healthy environment in the ECHR. However, the ECtHR has expanded the Convention into the area of environmental protection.

Article 8 is not applicable where there is general deterioration of the environment (*Kyrtatos v Greece* **(2003)**). An applicant must show:

- A causal link between pollution and effect (not necessarily health).
- There has to be a minimum level of severity before **Article 8** is engaged.

Examples

....

Fedeyeva v Russia (2005) 49 EHRR 295

The applicant lived inside a sanitary zone around an iron smelter plant. There was evidence of pollution and the state said it would rehouse those living within the zone but this had not happened. The applicant argued her health and quality of life had been affected.

The ECtHR held that the applicant had to demonstrate actual interference with her private life and a minimum level of severity. The ECtHR had doubts with regard to the actual causal link between pollution and health in this case but the pollution had adversely affected her quality of life at home. It was a private factory but there was a positive obligation on the state as a regulator. There was a failure to resettle the inhabitants as promised and to regulate properly. There was a violation.

....

(See also *Lopez Ostra v Spain* **(1994)**, and also *Guerra v Italy* **(1998)**, where is was held that the state had a positive obligation to provide those at risk with information if reasonable to do so.)

....

Hatton v UK (2003) 37 EHRR 611

The applicants complained about night flights into Heathrow airport which caused an interference with aspects of family life. The state argued that night flights were important to the economic well-being of the state.

The **Grand Chamber** overturned the **Chamber**, finding there was no violation. It did not recognise the special nature of environmental rights and found the economic interests of the state outweighed the individual right in this case, given the wide margin of appreciation of the state.

....

Revision tip

The Chamber had found that the Court had developed an important protection from environmental harm and the importance of the right outweighed economic considerations. Note the dissent in the Grand Chamber which criticised the majority for taking a step backwards in the protection from environmental harm.

✅ *Looking for extra marks?*

There is debate on the Court's expansion of environmental protection and the limitations placed on this by *Hatton*. Are human rights a proper vehicle for the protection of the environment?

Balancing rights?

Article 8 often clashes with the right to freedom of expression under **Article 10**. The ECtHR will balance both rights before deciding which right should be given protection.

Example:

....

Von Hannover v Germany (2004) 43 EHRR 2

The applicant, Princess Caroline of Monaco, had photographs taken of her in a cafe with her children that were published in German magazines.

The ECtHR held that the photographs clearly fell within **Article 8**. The ECtHR noted it had to balance the right to private life of the applicant with the right of the magazines to freedom of expression. The court noted that the taking of photographs was particularly intrusive. It held that they made no contribution to a debate of public interest as the applicant was not at an official function.

....

Family and private life in the UK

In the UK, the **Human Rights Act** has influenced the development of the law relating to family and private life. It has been used many of the areas already discussed. There has been a difference of interpretation between the UK courts and the ECtHR on the applicability of **Article 8**. For example, in the *Marper* case (p 108, above) the House of Lords had found that **Article 8** was not applicable to DNA which was in contrast to the decision of the ECtHR. **Article 8** has been raised in prison cases (*Wainwright v Home Office* (2003)) where the ECtHR again disagreed with the UK court (*Wainwright v UK* (2006)). The court did apply the ECtHR principles with regard to the use of photographs in *Wood v Commissioner of Police of the Metropolis* (2009) where the Court of Appeal held that the retention by the police of photographs taken of an arms protester was an interference with **Article 8** and was not justified.

✅ *Looking for extra marks?*

The cases below are a small sample of the case law concerning **Article 8**. It would be worth searching for cases in family proceedings and other such areas.

Deportation and proportionality

Article 8 is frequently argued in the UK courts by persons facing removal or deportation from the state. In *Huang v Secretary of State for the Home Department* **(2006)**, the House of Lords noted 'the main importance of the [Strasbourg] case law is in illuminating the core value which article 8 exists to protect...'. In *Beoku-Betts (FC) v Secretary of State for the Home Department* **(2008)**, the removal of the claimant would separate him from his mother and sisters. The House of Lords found that not only his right but the family life of his relatives should be considered.

Developing the right to privacy?

Under English common law, there traditionally has been no right to privacy that can be argued before a court. The closest form of protection for private information is the tort of **breach of confidence**. This was restricted to confidential information held in a confidential relationship. The **Human Rights Act** has developed the law in this area and there has been debate as to whether there is now a tort of privacy in English law (between private parties). It is important to note that **Article 8** can only be raised directly against a public authority. However, the court is bound to consider **Article 8** (and **Article 10**) even in private claims for breach of confidence as the court must act in a manner compatible with the ECHR. (See Chapter 3, 'Horizontal effect', p 43.)

Development of case law

In *Campbell v MGN Ltd* **(2004)** Lord Nicholls stated that the time had come to recognise that the 'values enshrined in articles 8 and 10 are part of the cause of action for breach of confidence'. The court stated that a breach of confidence occurred where the person has a 'reasonable expectation of privacy'. This is wider than pre **HRA** interpretations.

This has been further developed in cases such as:

....

McKennit v Ash [2007] EWCA Civ 1714

The appellant wanted to publish a book which included details about her relationship with M, a folk artist. This included details about M's personal life. The appellant argued the judge had not properly balanced her right to expression with M's **Article 8** right.

The appeal was dismissed. The information the appellant wanted published did engage the **Article 8** rights of M. M had a reasonable expectation of privacy as the information was private information gained through a close friendship and there was a pre-existing relationship of confidence. M's right to private life outweighed the appellant's right to expression.

The case underlines that a reasonable expectation of privacy is now the ground for a breach of confidence claim and not the limited confidential relationship that existed before the **Human Rights Act**. In *Murray v Big Pictures* **(2008)**, the Court of Appeal found that there was a reasonable expectation of privacy when non-consensual photographs were taken. The Court of Appeal was moving closer to the *Von Hannover* decision and to recognising a right to privacy in private law, although this has not yet been clearly stated by the courts. Privacy protection still falls under an extended breach of confidence.

Balancing rights?

UK courts have had to consider the difficulties that arise when several rights under the ECHR clash. This has arisen when **Article 8** and **Article 10** are in question.

In *Douglas v Hello! Ltd (No 6)* **(2005)**, the court had to balance the right of the claimants to privacy and the right of the magazine to publish photographs of the claimants' wedding. Despite the fact that **s 12 of the Human Rights Act 1998** places a duty on the court to have due regard to freedom of expression, the court found that the claimants had an expectation of privacy. A similar weighing process between **Article 8** and **Article 10** was carried out in *Campbell v MGN Ltd* **(2004)** and in *Mosley v News Group Newspapers Ltd* **(2008)**. In both cases, the court found that the private life of the claimant outweighed the freedom of expression of the newspapers.

Super injunctions?

There has been much debate in the media about the imposition of super injunctions by the courts to stop newspapers printing details of **injunctions** that have been taken out to prevent the publication of private details. The courts have been clear that these injunctions are to protect private individuals where there is no public interest in their private lives and where this might lead to harassment of the litigants where injunctions are sought.

In *TSE v News Group Newspapers Ltd* **(2011)**, the judge made it clear that the principles outlined in cases such as *Campbell* are being applied, taking into consideration the duty under **s 12(3) HRA** to allow injunctions only if a claimant was likely to establish publication should not be allowed.

Revision tip

This area is a fast-moving and changing area of law. The development of privacy rights and the use of super injunctions is a developing topic. Be aware of recent case law and academic writing on this area.

Key cases

✱✱✱✱✱✱✱✱✱✱

(✱) *Key cases*

Case	Facts	Principle
Campbell v MGN Ltd [2004] 2 All ER 192	The claimant had photographs published of her attending a clinic for drug treatment.	Court held claimant had a reasonable expectation of privacy and set out principles for balancing Articles 8 and 10.
Gillan and Quinton v UK (2010) (Application No 4158/05)	Applicants stopped and searched without reasonable suspicion under terrorism legislation.	The state has a wide margin of appreciation re national security but must have procedural safeguards in place to prevent abuse of law. The ECtHR found a violation.
Hatton v UK (2003) 37 EHRR 611	The applicants complained about night flights into Heathrow airport which caused an interference with aspects of family life.	The ECtHR found that the state had wide margin of appreciation given the economic interest involved and there were no special environmental rights under Article 8. No violation.
S and Marper v UK (2009) 48 EHRR 1169	Applicants' DNA held indefinitely on national database with little chance of removal.	The ECtHR underlined wide definition of Article 8 which covers 'social' identity; the state must act in proportionate manner.

(❞) *Key debates*

Topic	'International human rights in an environmental horizon'
Author	Francesco Francioni
Viewpoint	The article examines the use of human rights to protect the environment and argues this is a limited, individualistic approach. A more collective approach is needed
Source	(2010) *European Journal of International Law* 21(1) 41–55

Topic	'Injunctions and the protection of privacy'
Author	David Eady
Viewpoint	Eady LJ gives a judicial view of the use of injunctions and the development of privacy protection in the UK
Source	(2010) *Civil Justice Quarterly* 29(4), 411–427

(?) Exam questions

Problem question

Anne is 17 years old and the daughter of a politician, who is a government minister. Anne is a member of a group called the AWC (Anti-war coalition). A national newspaper, the *Daily News*, contacted Anne for a comment on a story they want to print. The story alleges the AWC has a radical agenda including the use of violence. Alongside detailing Anne's membership of the group, it also plans to print a story about an alleged sexual relationship with her father's assistant, alleges she smokes cannabis regularly, and will print photographs of Anne with her younger sister attending a school function.

Anne asks a court for an injunction, stating that the dissemination of the story would release private information about her into the public domain.

During the Court hearing, it is revealed that Anne's mobile phone messages had been intercepted by the secret service under a regulation which allows them to do so if the person 'is suspected to be a danger to the state'. No warrant is needed.

1. Examine what principles the court would apply when examining the application for an injunction and what the outcome may be, considering the HRA and the jurisprudence of the ECtHR.

2. If Anne were to challenge the lawfulness of the interception of her messages, examine what principles the court would apply and what the outcome would be, considering the HRA and the jurisprudence of the ECtHR.

An outline answer is included at the end of the book.

Essay question

Explain and analyse how the European Court of Human Rights has used the living instrument principle to expand the protection given by Article 8.

 Scan here

Scan this QR code image with your mobile device to see an outline answer to this question or log onto www.oxfordtextbooks.co.uk/orc/concentrate/

#7

Freedom of religion and expression

- Freedom of religion and expression are essential to democratic society.

- They are qualified rights as individual rights may impinge on the rights of others.

- **Article 9 of the ECHR** has been interpreted restrictively by the ECtHR. The right to hold or not hold a belief is absolute; the right to manifest a belief is qualified.

- The ECtHR will first decide if there has been manifestation of belief. It has been restrictive in interpretation, especially in the workplace and education.

- **Article 10** has been interpreted as including views that shock and disturb; however, it has excluded some forms of hate speech.

- State restriction of expression must be justified. This will depend on issues such as the type of expression, source of expression, and who/what the expression is concerned with.

Chapter overview

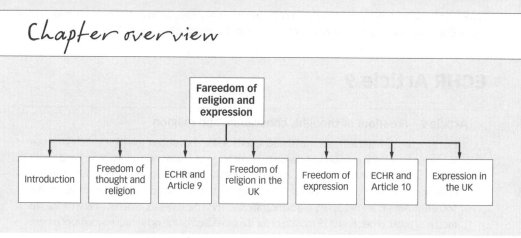

Introduction

Freedom of religion and expression are fundamental rights and are essential components of democracy. This is underlined by J S Mill, who argued that without freedom to express thoughts and beliefs then truth cannot be found or questioned. Without political expression in a pluralist society, democracy becomes meaningless. (*Handyside v UK*) (**1976**). However, it is recognised that freedom of religion and expression are qualified rights (see Chapter 2, 'Qualified rights', p 32) as an idea or belief may encroach on the rights of others. Although the UNDHR and the ICCPR both include these rights, the chapter will concentrate on the ECHR.

✅ Looking for extra marks?

J S Mill's 'On Liberty' should be read to understand the arguments for the importance of freedom of expression and belief as well as justification for limitations on these rights.

Freedom of thought and religion

Freedom of thought and religion is essential to rights protection particularly against the background of the mass religious discrimination in World War Two. However, the protection of individual belief can be controversial as beliefs can clash with the religious and non-religious beliefs of others.

✅ Looking for extra marks?

These difficulties are underlined by problems the UN has faced in getting agreement for a convention guaranteeing protection from discrimination based on religious belief. It has only managed to get agreement on a non-binding declaration: UN Declaration on the Elimination of All Forms of Intolerance and of Discrimination Based on Religion or Belief (General Assembly Resolution 36/55).

ECHR Article 9

Article 9—Freedom of thought, conscience and religion

1 Everyone has the right to freedom of thought, conscience and religion; this right includes freedom to change his religion or belief and freedom, either alone or in community with others and in public or private, to manifest his religion or belief, in worship, teaching, practice and observance.
2 Freedom to manifest one's religion or beliefs shall be subject only to such limitations as are prescribed by law and are necessary in a democratic society in the interests of public safety, for the protection of public order, health or morals, or for the protection of the rights and freedoms of others.

Article 9 protects freedom of thought, conscience, and belief. This covers religion and non-religious beliefs. **Article 9** is a qualified right. The state can justify an interference with the right under **Article 9(2)**.

Article 9(1)

In *Kokkinakis v Greece* **(1993)**, the ECtHR underlined the importance of the protection of religious and non-religious beliefs:

> It is, in its religious dimension, one of the most vital elements that go to make up the identity of believers and their conception of life, but it is also a precious asset for atheists, agnostics, sceptics and the unconcerned. The pluralism indissociable from a democratic society, which has been dearly won over the centuries, depends on it.

Scope of 'thought, conscience and belief'

Religion

The ECtHR has given a wide and flexible interpretation of religion, which includes established religions such as Christianity, Islam, Judaism, Buddhism, Hinduism, etc, and includes more recent religious groups such as Jehovah's Witnesses and the Church of Scientology (*Church of Scientology Moscow v Russia* **(2007)**).

Non-religious beliefs

The ECtHR has also recognised other beliefs as falling under **Article 9**. These include beliefs such as veganism (*H v UK* **(1993)**) and pacifism (*Arrowsmith v UK* **(1978)**).

However, the ECtHR does not recognise all genuinely held beliefs as being protected by **Article 9**. In *Campbell and Cosens v UK* **(1982)**,the ECtHR stated that a belief was covered by the ECHR if it attained a level of:

- cogency;
- seriousness;
- cohesion; and
- importance.

If this threshold for a belief is met, then it will fall under **Article 9**.
Example of not meeting the threshold:

....

Pretty v UK (2002) 35 EHRR 1

The applicant was terminally ill and wished to end her life. However, she was too ill to do so and wanted her husband to help her. Assisted suicide is a criminal offence in the UK. It was argued (along with **Articles 2, 3, 8, 14**) that belief in assisted suicide was covered by **Article 9**.

Not all opinions or convictions meet the threshold for belief under **Article 9(1)**. The ECtHR found that a conviction on the right to assisted suicide did not meet the threshold for belief.

....

Manifestation of belief

If the belief is recognised, the ECtHR differentiates between the right to *hold* that belief and the right to *manifest* it. This has also been described as the difference between the internal and the external dimensions of belief.

Internal dimension: holding a belief

Everyone has the right to hold a belief, which includes the right not to hold a belief (*Darby v Sweden* **(1990)**). This is absolute. There is no justification for interference and the state cannot force a person to adopt a religious belief or deny the right to hold a belief. The ECtHR has stated the need to protect against indoctrination by the state (*Angelini v Sweden* **(1986)**). This also underlines the importance of pluralism and neutrality in a state's dealing with religious organisations. In *Hasan and Chaush v Bulgaria* **(2000)**, the state was held in violation of **Article 9** as it appointed the head of the Bulgarian Muslim community. The ECtHR held that the state favoured one faction over another so did not remain neutral. This does not exclude recognition of a state religion as long as other religious communities are allowed to exist. States may have a positive obligation to ensure pluralism by protecting the religious organisation from violence. In **97** *Members of the Gldani Congregation of Jehovah's Witnesses v Georgia* **(2007)**, the ECtHR held that the state had a positive obligation to protect the Jehovah's Witness group who had been subject to attacks.

ECHR Article 9

✱✱✱✱✱✱✱✱✱✱

External dimension: manifesting a belief

Article 9 protects the right of a person to manifest belief through 'worship, teaching, practice and observance'. Manifestation of belief is not absolute; it is qualified. Manifestation can be carried out alone or in community with others, in public or in private (*Kokkinakis v Greece (1993)*). If the practice interfered with is not defined as a manifestation under **Article 9(1)** then the article is not applicable.

Practice motivated by belief?

The ECtHR will examine whether a practice is 'intimately linked' to the belief in question and whether the practice is necessary in order to manifest the belief. In *Arrowsmith v UK (1978)*, it was held that the distribution of leaflets concerning the removal of troops from Northern Ireland was not a manifestation of belief as it was not necessarily linked to pacifism.

Specific situation

In *Kalac v Turkey* (1997), the ECtHR held that 'in exercising his freedom to manifest his religion, an individual may need to take his specific situation into account'.

The ECtHR has been restrictive when deciding on whether there has been a manifestation of belief in public areas such as education and employment:

Education:

The Commission on Human Rights had found that the wearing of an Islamic head scarf by a student in *Karaduman v Turkey* (1993) was not manifestation of belief as Article 9 'does not in all cases guarantee the right to behave in the public sphere in a way which is dictated by a belief'.

However, in *Leyla Sahin v Turkey* (2005), the ECtHR reinterpreted *Karaduman* and held that the wearing of a head scarf by a student to class did amount to a manifestation and the state had to justify a restriction. This seemed to mark a shift in the Court's approach with regard to religious dress in education.

Employment:

The Commission and the Court have been restrictive when recognising practice in employment as a manifestation of belief. There are numerous examples where it was decided that the applicant's practice was not covered by **Article 9(1)**: the applicants were not forced to take employment that meant they had to work at times of religious practice, they had a choice to leave the employment, and their manifestation was not completely restricted; for examples, see *Kalac v Turkey* (1997), *X (Ahmad) v United Kingdom* (1981), *Konttinen v Finland* (1996), and *Stedman v United Kingdom* (1997).

Exam Tip

In a problem question, it is necessary to establish whether a practice is a manifestation of belief, before examining whether there has been interference, and then discussing whether an interference is justified under **Article 9(2)**.

✅ *Looking for extra marks?*

There is some debate and criticism of the Court's approach to manifestation of belief and the lack of clarity in the jurisprudence.

Article 9(2): limitations to manifestation of belief

Article 9 is a qualified right and **Article 9(2)** contains the conditions that must be met for a state to limit the right.

Prescribed by law

Any act by the state that interferes with **Article 9(1)** must be prescribed by law. This means that there must be some legal basis for the action and that this has to be clear, precise, and predictable. In *Hasan and Chaush v Bulgaria* (2000), there was a violation as the state appointment of the Muslim leader was done without any legal basis allowing the state to do so.

Legitimate aim

Article 9(2) sets out the reasons why a state can interfere with **Article 9(1)**:

- interests of public safety;
- the protection of public order;
- health or morals; or
- the protection of the rights and freedoms of others.

These are more limited than under **Article 8** (Chapter 6, 'Legitimate aim', p 102) and **Article 10**. Usually a state can demonstrate a legitimate aim. The legitimate aim may be important as it can influence the margin of appreciation given to the state and the proportionality of a measure.

Necessary in a democratic society

Many cases are decided on whether a measure is necessary in a democratic society. To adjudicate on this question the ECtHR uses the concept of proportionality and will apply a margin of appreciation.

Proportionality

Article 9 is a qualified right as the right may conflict with the needs of the community or the rights of others. Proportionality aims to find a balance between the individual and the community. The criteria the ECtHR will examine when examining the act of the state include:

- Is it effective?
- Is it the least intrusive measure possible?

✳✳✳✳✳✳✳✳✳✳

- Does it deprive the 'very essence of the right'?
- Is it balanced? Has a fair balance been struck between the competing interests of the individual and of the community as a whole?

Revision tip

Proportionality is widely used by the ECtHR and an exam question on proportionality may ask about its use in more than one right. Be aware of examples in all the qualified rights studied (see Chapter 6, 'Right to family and private life', p 105, Chapter 8, 'Freedom of assembly and association', p 143, and Chapter 9, 'Freedom from discrimination', p 161).

Margin of appreciation

A wide margin of appreciation means that the ECtHR is more likely to find no violation whereas a narrow margin means a violation is more likely, though the ECtHR will decide on the facts. Several factors will influence whether the margin of appreciation is wide or narrow:

- The nature/importance of the right/issue in question.
- Lack of European consensus or standard (importance of the living instrument principle).
- Areas where judges give wider margin because difficult to judge/resources.

✅ Looking for extra marks?

There are criticisms of the use of the margin of appreciation by the ECtHR when interpreting **Article 2** and in cases involving the qualified rights (see Chapter 2, 'Qualified rights', p 33 and generally Chapters 4 ('Right to life and freedom from ill treatment', pp 60–63), 6 ('Right to family and private life', p 103), 8 ('Freedom of assembly and association', p 143), and 9 ('Freedom from discrimination', p 161)).

Revision tip

Margin of appreciation is important in all the qualified rights and similar principles apply.

Case examples of Article 9(2)

Religious symbols in the classroom

. . . .

Lautsi v Italy (2011) (Application No 30814/06)

In Italy state schools have a crucifix in the classrooms. The applicants claimed this was a violation of the right to education under **Protocol 1–2** along with **Article 9** as it violated the principle of neutrality expected in education.

The ECtHR decided the case on **Protocol 1–2** but the principles are applicable to **Article 9**. The interference was justified. The state has a wide margin of appreciation in its efforts to reconcile education with respect for the philosophical convictions of the parents, as long as there was no indoctrination. Given this wide margin, the crucifix was not enough to amount to indoctrination as:

- the fact that the school curriculum gave a historically important state religion greater prominence than other religions could not in itself be viewed as indoctrination;
- a crucifix on a wall was an essentially passive symbol whose influence on pupils was not comparable to speech or participation in religious activities; and
- other religions were clearly tolerated.

✔ Looking for extra marks?

Note the concurring opinion, highlighting the difference between maintaining neutrality and imposing secularism on the state. Secularism is itself a belief that should not be imposed on a state whereas neutrality implies tolerance of different beliefs. Also note the Grand Chamber overturned the Chamber, which had found a violation.

Religious dress in education

Leyla Sahin v Turkey (2005) 44 EHRR 99

The applicant was a medical student. She wore an Islamic headscarf to university and was not allowed to sit her exams. Turkey is a secular state and regulations were in place to maintain a secular state so that the headscarf was banned in public buildings such as universities.

The Court held that the wearing of the headscarf was motivated by the applicant's belief and was accepted as a manifestation of her belief. However, the state could justify a ban on the head-scarf given the legitimate aim of maintaining the rights of others. Turkey feared fundamentalists exerting pressure on students. The Court gave a wide margin of appreciation to the state, which argued that the principle of secularism was a prerequisite for a liberal pluralist democracy in the case of Turkey. It accepted that the measure was a legitimate interference with the right to manifest religion.

Revision tip

This is an important case and has been criticised. Note the dissent of Judge Tulkens, criticising the Court for a lack of understanding of Islam and giving too wide a margin to the state.

Religious dress in a public place

Ahmet Arslan and Others v Turkey (2010) (Application No 41135/98)

The applicants belonged to a religious group known as Aczimenditarikatÿ. They had met in Ankara for a religious ceremony at a mosque then toured the city in their distinctive dress. They were prosecuted and convicted for a breach of the law on the wearing of religious garments in public.

The ECtHR accepted it was prescribed by law and it met the legitimate aims of public safety, prevention of disorder, and protection of others. However, the prosecution was not proportionate as the wearing of religious dress was in public areas open to all. This was different from public establishments where religious neutrality may take precedence over the right to manifest religion (*Leyla Sahin*). This was beyond the margin of appreciation given to the state.

✓ *Looking for extra marks?*

The question of religious symbols and dress in public building and places is controversial and will continue to generate case law. France's recent ban on the wearing of the hiqab in public may come under the scrutiny of the Court in the future.

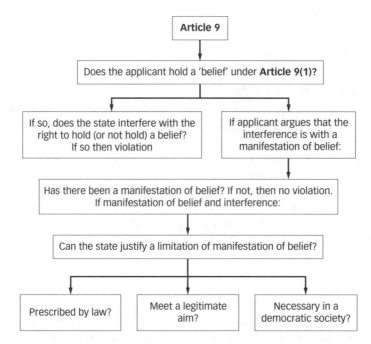

Fig. 7.1 Bringing a case under Article 9

Religion in the UK

In the UK, the established state religion is Church of England. The UK had blasphemy laws which protected Christian belief. However, legislation has been enacted governing incitement to religious hatred which includes other religions as well as Christianity (**Racial and Religious Hatred Act 2006**). Protection from discrimination based on religion is covered by the **Equality Act 2010** (see Chapter 9, 'Equality Act 2010', p 167). The **Human Rights Act 1998** has added to protection and places a duty on the court to have special regard to **Article 9** when making decisions (**s 13 HRA**).

Case law has been raised under **Article 9** concerning religious symbols and dress, and governing religious practices.

Religious dress and symbols in education

. . . .

R (on the application of Begum) v Denbigh High School [2006] UKHL 15

The school appealed against a decision that the respondent had been unlawfully excluded from school. The respondent, a Muslim, wanted to wear the jilbab instead of the shalwar kameeze, which the school had allowed under its uniform policy. She was excluded from school for failure to adhere to the uniform policy.

The House of Lords held the uniform policy of the school was compatible with **Article 9**. The majority of the court found that the wearing of the jilbab was not a manifestation of belief. She could have attended an alternative school. The minority followed *Sahin* and found that the desire to wear the jilbab was something that the respondent found necessary and so was a manifestation.

Unanimously, the court found that the school policy was justified under **Article 9(2)** as proportionate: the respondent could have attended a school in her catchment area where she could wear the jilbab; the uniform policy had been carefully devised to consider the needs of the Muslim community. The school was best placed to devise the policy.

. . . .

In contrast, see ***Watkins-Singh v Aberdare Girls' High School Governors*** (**2008**), where a Sikh schoolgirl wished to wear a Sikh bracelet to school against the school uniform policy and was excluded for wearing it. In contrast to *Begum*, it was held the ban was discriminatory as there was a blanket ban which was disproportionate on the facts. See also, *Playfoot v Millais School Governing Body* (**2007**), where the ban on the wearing of a chastity ring was held not to violate **Article 9**.

Sacred cows

. . . .

R (Suryananda) v Welsh Ministers [2007] EWCA Civ 893

A bullock owned by a Hindu community was suspected of bovine tuberculosis and so would be compulsorily slaughtered. This would violate a tenet of Hindu belief.

The Court of Appeal held that the decision interfered with a manifestation of belief but was not a violation of **Article 9** as the slaughter was justified to meet the legitimate aim of public health and was a proportionate measure.

. . . .

Funeral pyres

....

R (Ghai) v Newcastle City Council and others [2010] EWCA Civ 59

The claimant wanted to be cremated in accordance with Hinduism on a traditional fire. Cremation is governed by legislation, stating cremation has to be in a building.

    The Court of Appeal held that **Article 9** was engaged as it was a manifestation of belief and to not allow the claimant's wish was incompatible. The legislation should be interpreted (using **s 3 HRA**, see Chapter 3, 'Section 3: Interpretation clause', p 44) to include a funeral pyre in a structure that would fit into the definition of a 'building' in order to make the cremation lawful.

....

Revision tip

Employment cases such as ***Eweida v British Airways (2009)*** (wearing of crucifix) and ***Islington LBC v Ladele* (2009)** (refusal to officiate a civil partnership) were argued under anti-discrimination provisions. In both cases, the court took a similar stance to the ECtHR in finding no discrimination.

Freedom of expression

As noted above, freedom of expression is essential to democratic society. However, even in liberal states, there is a recognition that it is a qualified right and there is a need to balance the right against the rights and freedoms of others (such as privacy; see Chapter 6, 'Balancing rights?', p 111). Much of the case law below examines limitations.

✅ *Looking for extra marks?*

The limits on expression have caused academic debate. Much of the debate surrounds how and when expression should be limited.

ECHR Article 10

Article 10

1 Everyone has the right to freedom of expression. This right shall include freedom to hold opinions and to receive and impart information and ideas without interference by public authority and regardless of frontiers. This article shall not prevent States from requiring the licensing of broadcasting, television or cinema enterprises.

2   The exercise of these freedoms, since it carries with it duties and responsibilities, may be subject to such formalities, conditions, restrictions or penalties as are prescribed by law and are necessary in a democratic society, in the interests of national security, territorial integrity or public safety, for the prevention of disorder or crime, for the protection of health or morals, for the protection of the reputation or rights of others, for preventing the disclosure of information received in confidence, or for maintaining the authority and impartiality of the judiciary.

Article 10(1) sets out the meaning of expression. If there is an interference with **Article 10(1)**, the state must justify this under **Article 10(2)**.

Article 10(1)

Article 10(1) contains an explicit limitation on expression with regard to the ability of the state to impose licensing conditions on broadcasting.

Expression can take many forms. Which form of expression is at issue may influence the restrictions allowed under **Article 10(2)**. Some forms of expression can be described as **high value** (constitutional and political expression, some forms of artistic expression, religious expression) whilst others may be **low value** (arguably artistic expression, commercial speech). The higher the value attached to expression, the more difficult it is for a state to restrict it.

The ECtHR has decided that the freedom to receive information does not include a positive obligation on the state to provide information (***Guerra v Italy* (1998)**) (this may fall under **Article 8**). However, the state may have positive obligations such as having a legal framework in place to protect expression.

Article 10(2): limitations on freedom of expression

Article 10 is a qualified right and **Article 9(2)** contains the conditions that must be met for a state to limit the right.

There is considerable debate surrounding the limits on expression. J S Mill argued that expression should only be limited under the harm principle: where there is a direct and clear danger of harm. This principle is reflected in the clear and present danger principle applied under the First Amendment of US law. As noted in ***Handyside***, opinions that shock and disturb should be allowed under **Article 10**. Therefore, how harm is defined and measured is central to limits on expression.

Prescribed by law

As under **Article 9(1)**, any act by the state that interferes with **Article 10(1)** must be in accordance with law. This means that there must be some legal basis for the action and that this has to be clear, precise, and predictable.

✳✳✳✳✳✳✳✳✳✳

Legitimate aim

Article 10(2) sets out the reasons why a state can interfere with **Article 10(1)**:

Article 10(2)

- in the interests of national security,
- territorial integrity or public safety,
- for the prevention of disorder or crime,
- for the protection of health or morals,
- for the protection of the reputation or rights of others,
- for preventing the disclosure of information received in confidence, or
- for maintaining the authority and impartiality of the judiciary.

As under **Article 9(1)**, there is not usually a problem with the state demonstrating a legitimate aim. Which legitimate aim is argued may influence the necessity of a measure. It should be noted that these are arguably wider than contemplated by J S Mill as he did not include immoral expression as necessarily harmful.

Necessary in a democratic society

To adjudicate on this question the ECtHR uses the concept of proportionality and will apply a margin of appreciation. The factors outlined above with regard to **Article 9** and proportionality are equally applicable to **Article 10**. Margin of appreciation was developed under **Article 10** as recognition of the difficulties in framing qualified rights in diverse cultures within states. The concept recognised that the state is best placed to make decisions under the supervision of the ECtHR (*Handyside v UK* (1976)).

As will be illustrated in the case law, different factors will influence the proportionality of a measure which include:

- Type of expression.
- Who/what is the expression about?
- Who is the source of the expression.

Case law examples

Political expression

Political expression is high value expression and so this narrows the margin of appreciation. Political debate and free elections have been described as the 'bedrock of any democratic system' (*Lingens v Austria* (1981)). Government should be exposed to close scrutiny not just by branches of state but by public and media (*Castells v Spain* (**1992**)). The Court has also noted that any state measure that limits expression may have 'a **chilling effect**' on future expression (*Sadik v Greece* (**1996**)). The press provide an important 'public watchdog' role. Journalist sources should be protected to ensure proper press scrutiny (*Goodwin v UK* (**1996**)).

Civil/public interest expression

This type of expression is high value and the margin of appreciation is narrow:

....

Sunday Times v UK (1979) 2 EHRR 245

The newspaper published stories on the Thalidomide litigation (children were born with deformities after their mothers took thalidomide during pregnancy). The Court granted an injunction which included 'prior restraint'; preventing the newspaper publishing a future story on the litigation.

The Court held there was a violation. **Article 10** encompassed 'not only the freedom of the press to inform the public but also the right of the public to be properly informed'. Prior restraint in this case prevented the publication of a matter of political and civil importance and was disproportionate.

....

....

Steel and Morris v UK (2005) 41 EHRR 403

The applicants gave out leaflets, protesting against McDonald's and claiming it exploited children, mistreated workers, etc. McDonald's sued the applicants for defamation. Under English law there was no legal aid for libel so the applicants had to defend themselves and prove their claims. The court found against the applicants. The applicants claimed their **Article 10** (and **Article 6**) rights were violated due to the lack of legal aid.

The Court held there was a violation. The inequality of arms caused by the lack of legal aid meant that the applicants could not mount a proper defence. There was a danger of a chilling effect on protest, which is important to the public interest. The right balance had not been struck between the protection of reputation and the right of the applicants.

....

Revision Tip

There are many case examples of this before the ECtHR. The decision in *Steel and Morris* does not mean the state has to provide legal aid in every case of libel; only where there is a clear inequality between the two parties.

Artistic expression

There has been some debate as to the importance of artistic expression. It may be dependent on the cultural values of the states. The ECtHR has made it clear it considers artistic expression important for democracy (*Alinak v Turkey* (**2005**)). However, it has given states quite a wide margin of appreciation in this area in some cases:

ECHR Article 10
✱✱✱✱✱✱✱✱✱✱✱

Otto-Preminger-Institut v Austria (1994) 19 EHRR 34

The applicant made a film which contained erotic scenes involving Jesus Christ and the Virgin Mary. A local authority banned it in a predominantly Catholic area of the state.

The Court held that there was no violation as the ban was justified given the need to protect the religious beliefs of others where something was gratuitously offensive. A wide margin was given to the state.

Revision tip

See also the similar decision in **Wingrove v UK (1996)**.

The Court has been criticised for giving too much discretion to the state and allowing limitations due to majority religious belief (giving preference to **Article 9**?). However, see the critical minority in *Otto-Preminger* case.

In contrast, the ECtHR has in recent cases been more inclined to protection the right to expression. See *VereinigungBildender Kunstler v Austria* **(2008)**.

Hate speech

The ECtHR has dealt with cases involving expression that may express or incite hatred. The Court's approach has been to distinguish between 'hate speech' and 'incitement to hatred'. The difference between the two types of expression is not clear but:

* 'hate speech': falls outside the scope of **Article 10** by applying **Article 17 ECHR**, which excludes cases that undermine the values of the ECHR;
* if the expression is found to be 'incitement to hatred' the Court will allow it to be argued under **Article 10(1)** and the state may justify restriction under **Article 10(2)**.

Garaudy v France (2003) (Application No 65831/01)

The applicant published a book which denied the Holocaust and criticised Israel and the Jewish community. He was convicted of Holocaust denial and incitement to hatred for statements about Jews.

The Court held there was no violation: the Court separated the two issues of Holocaust denial and incitement:

Holocaust denial: described as hate speech, this was a denial of a crime against humanity. This undermines the values of the Convention and is incompatible with democracy and human rights, so should be excluded under **Article 17**.

Incitement to hatred: this criticism was allowed to come under the scope of **Article 10** as an opinion worthy of protection. However, the conviction was justified under **Article 10(2)** for the legitimate aim of protection of others given the racist content.

See also a series of Turkish cases on incitement to hatred where the court scrutinised the facts to differentiate between legitimate political criticism and incitement to hatred, for example, *Surek v Turkey (No 1)* **(1999)**, *Surek and Ozdemir v Turkey* **(1999)**, and *Zana v Turkey* **(1997)**.

Balancing rights: expression and privacy (see Chapter 6, 'Balancing rights?', pp 111–113)

Von Hannover v Germany (2004) 43 EHRR 2

The applicant, Princess Caroline of Monaco, had photographs taken of her in a cafe with her children that were published in German magazines.

 The ECtHR noted it had to balance the right to private life of the applicant with the right of the magazines to freedom of expression. It held that the photographs made no contribution to a debate of public interest as the applicant was not at an official function. The context was important as to whether it was in the public interest.

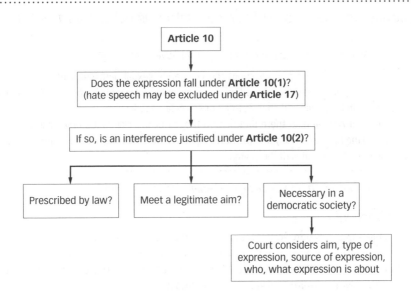

Fig. 7.2 Bringing a case under Article 10

Expression in the UK

Freedom of expression in the UK has historically been held to be the basis for democracy. Receiving information from the state is partially protected by the **Freedom of Information**

Act 2000. However, information from the state is also limited by the **Official Secrets Act 1989** and public interest immunity certificates. Contempt of court, covered by common law and statute (**Contempt of Court Act 1981**), also limits expression in order to protect the right to fair trial. This includes protection of journalist sources except where disclosure is necessary for national security, interests of justice, or prevention of disorder and crime.

Exam tip

Some modules concentrate on UK law. If so, knowledge of case law and criticisms is needed from the relevant textbooks and articles.

The **Human Rights Act 1998** has added to protection but has also raised issues of conflict with other rights such as privacy. **Section 12 of the Human Rights Act 1998** places a duty on the court to have due regard to freedom of expression. Issues have also been raised concerning public order and the right to protect.

Case law examples

Privacy and expression (see Chapter 6, 'Balancing rights?', pp 112–113)

....

Mosley v News Group Newspapers Ltd [2008] EWHC 2341 (QB)

The newspaper published a story about the claimant's sexual activities with prostitutes. The claimant was a public figure but argued there was no public interest in his private life as it was not connected with his public activities as Head of Formula one racing.

    The Court of Appeal held there had been a breach of the claimant's privacy in this case. In weighing up the right to privacy and the newspaper's right to publish, there was little public interest in the sexual proclivities of the claimant.

....

See also ***Douglas v Hello! Ltd (No 6)***, ***Campbell v MGN Ltd (2004)***.

Super injunctions?

There has been much debate in the media about the imposition of super injunctions by the courts to prevent newspapers printing details of injunctions that have been taken out. The courts have explicitly balanced **Article 10** (as required by **s 12 HRA**) with privacy rights, (example: ***TSE v News Group Newspapers Ltd (2011)***).

Revision tip

This area of law is a fast-moving and changing area of law. Be aware of recent case law and academic writing on this area.

Political expression

R (on the application of Pro Life Alliance) v BBC [2003] 2 All ER 977

Before a general election, Pro Life Alliance wished to broadcast a party political broadcast which included material on the termination of a pregnancy. The BBC refused to broadcast it, citing its obligations regarding decency in broadcasting legislation. The Court of Appeal gave weight to the important of the right to freedom of expression and found an interference with the right.

Overturning the Court of Appeal, the House of Lords chose to defer to the judgement of the public bodies and of Parliament on an issue of public morals. It found that there was no interference with expression in this case. The legitimate aim outweighed the right of expression.

Revision Tip

Contrast the Court of Appeal with the House of Lords and research criticisms of this case as a 'bad day for free speech'.

Public order and protest

Public order legislation allows for the conviction of those who express views or insulting behaviour that may cause harassment etc.

Munim Abdul and Others Appellants v Director of Public Prosecutions [2011] EWHC 247 (Admin)

Protestors against the wars in Iraq and Afghanistan protested at a homecoming parade for soldiers fighting in Afghanistan. This included shouts of baby killers etc. The appellants were later charged and found guilty under **s 5 of the Public Order Act**.

The appeal was dismissed. The court considered **Article 10** and whether the actions of the appellants went beyond legitimate protest. It noted that the onus was on the state to convincingly establish the need for limitations for public order. The court noted that the right to expression covers things some may find distasteful. However on the facts, context is of primary importance. It was accepted that the actions of the appellants went beyond what could be considered legitimate protest.

Revision Tip

These are only a sample of some of the cases dealing with expression in the UK. Be aware of articles and criticisms of these issues and what is expected of your module.

Key cases
****

✱ Key cases

Case	Facts	Principle
Leyla Sahin v Turkey (2005) 44 EHRR 99	The applicant was a student. She wore an Islamic headscarf to university and was not allowed to sit her exams.	The wearing of the headscarf was motivated by the applicant's belief and was accepted as a manifestation of her belief. However, the state could justify a ban on the headscarf given the legitimate aim of maintaining the rights of others. No violation.
Mosley v News Group Newspapers Ltd [2008] EWHC 2341 (QB)	The newspaper published a story about the claimant's sexual activities. The claimant was a public figure but argued there was no public interest in his private life.	Appeal dismissed. There had been a breach of the claimant's privacy in this case. In weighing up the right to privacy and the newspaper's right to publish, there was little public interest in the sexual proclivities of the claimant.
R (on the application of Begum) v Denbigh High School [2006] UKHL 15	The respondent wanted to wear the jilbab, which the school did not allow under its uniform policy. She was excluded from school for failure to adhere to the uniform policy.	Appeal allowed—school acted compatibly. It could justify the policy as proportionate as it had taken measures to respect the Muslim faith and the respondent could have gone elsewhere.
R (on the application of Pro Life Alliance) v BBC [2003] 2 All ER 977	Before a general election, Pro Life Alliance wished to broadcast a party political broadcast which included material on the termination of a pregnancy. The BBC refused to broadcast it, citing its obligations regarding decency in broadcasting legislation.	Appeal allowed. The House of Lords deferred to the judgment of the public bodies and of Parliament on an issue of public morals. The legitimate aim outweighed the right of expression..
Steel and Morris v UK (2005) 41 EHRR 403	The applicants gave out leaflets that contained claims against McDonalds. McDonald's sued the applicants for defamation. Under English law there was no legal aid for libel so the applicants had to defend themselves and prove their claims. The applicants claimed violation due to the lack of legal aid.	Violation. The inequality of arms caused by the lack of legal aid in this case meant that the applicants could not mount a proper defence. There was a danger of a chilling effect on protest. The right balance had not been struck between the protection of reputation and the right of the applicants.

Case	Facts	Principle
Sunday Times v UK **(1979) 2 EHRR 245**	The applicant published stories on the Thalidomide litigation. The Court granted an injunction which included 'prior restraint': preventing the newspaper publishing a future story on the litigation.	Violation. Article 10 encompassed 'not only the freedom of the press to inform the public but also the right of the public to be properly informed'. Prior restraint in this case was disproportionate

🗩 Key debates

Topic	'Redefining Manifestation of Belief in Leyla Sahin v Turkey'
Author	H Gilbert
Viewpoint	The article examines the development of 'manifestation of belief' by the ECtHR, comparing **Sahin** with **Begum**, and criticising the approach of the ECtHR as unclear.
Source	(2006) *European Human Rights Law Review* (3) pp 308–326

Topic	'Religious cartoons and human rights—a critical legal analysis of the case law of the European Court of Human Rights on the protection of religious feelings and its implications in the Danish affair concerning cartoons of the Prophet Muhammad'
Author	N Nathwani
Viewpoint	The article criticises the approach of the ECtHR to the protection of religious minorities within Europe.
Source	(2008) *European Human Rights Law Review* pp 488–507

⑦ Exam questions

Problem question

Andrew, his wife Clara, and their son, Brian are members of a religious group called the 'Children of Adam'. The group believes that they are the direct descendants of the biblical Adam and Eve. They believe adultery and homosexuality should be punishable by death. As part of their belief, Monday is a day of rest and silent prayer. The group precepts also state that members should wear a silver pendant around the neck to protect against evil.

Exam questions

✳✳✳✳✳✳✳✳✳✳

Clara is a journalist. She writes a story that a national newspaper plans to publish, alleging a government minister is having an extra-marital affair. The minister gets a court injunction to prevent publication.

She also writes an opinion piece for the newspaper, arguing that homosexuals are a threat to society and good people should remove them 'by any means necessary'. Clara is charged and found guilty under incitement to hatred legislation. She is fined £5,000. She appeals.

Andrew works as a teacher in a primary school. The school has attempted to accommodate Andrew's beliefs by arranging that he only teaches on Monday morning. Although he initially accepted this, he has now told the school that he must have all of Monday free due to his religious beliefs. The school refuses to grant this.

Brian is also told that the pendant he wears to the same school is a breach of school uniform policy that bans the wearing of all jewellery.

Both Andrew and Brian claim that the school is violating their rights and bring a case against the school.

1) Examine what principles the court would apply when examining an application for appeal against the injunction and what the outcome may be, considering the HRA and the ECtHR jurisprudence.

2) Examine what principles the court would apply when considering Clara's appeal and what the outcome would be, considering the HRA and the ECtHR jurisprudence.

3) Examine what principles the court would apply when considering Andrew and Brian's claims and what the outcome would be, considering the HRA and the ECtHR jurisprudence.

An outline answer is included at the end of the book.

Essay question

Critically discuss the extent to which the European Court of Human Rights prioritises freedom of expression and freedom of religion when the rights conflict with the rights of others.

 Scan here

Scan this QR code image with your mobile device to see an outline answer to this question or log onto www.oxfordtextbooks.co.uk/orc/concentrate/

#8

Freedom of assembly and association

Key Facts

- Freedom of assembly and association is linked to freedom of belief and expression.
- The **ICCPR** deals with assembly and association separately, the **ECHR** deals with them together in **Article 11**.
- An assembly can be formed for a range of reasons and can take various forms.
- Association includes political parties, other interest groups, and trade unions.
- The right to form and join a trade union is given explicit protection in **Article 11** although the scope of the protection can be limited.
- A state must justify any restriction on **Article 11(1)**; the margin of appreciation is especially narrow where the restriction is on political parties.
- Public order and protest has led to litigation in England and Wales to define what is meant by imminent breach of the peace, the limits on processions and assembly, and the proportionality of state measures under **Article 11** (with **Article 10** and **Article 5**).

Chapter overview

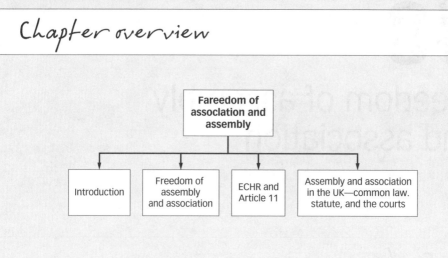

```
                    ┌─────────────────┐
                    │   Fareedom of   │
                    │  association and│
                    │    assembly     │
                    └─────────────────┘
        ┌──────────────┬──────────┴────────┬───────────────────┐
        ▼              ▼                    ▼                   ▼
┌──────────────┐ ┌──────────────┐ ┌──────────────┐ ┌─────────────────────┐
│              │ │  Freedom of  │ │              │ │ Assembly and association│
│ Introduction │ │  assembly    │ │  ECHR and    │ │ in the UK—common law.│
│              │ │and association│ │  Article 11  │ │ statute, and the courts│
└──────────────┘ └──────────────┘ └──────────────┘ └─────────────────────┘
```

Introduction

Freedom of assembly and association is closely related to the freedom of belief and expression. The right to assembly and association is perceived as essential to pluralism and liberty in a democratic society. However, as assembly and association may infringe on the rights of others, it is a qualified right (see Chapter 2, 'Qualified rights', p 32). The state can justify interference with the right. Unlike other civil and political rights, the right to assembly and association is a collective right as it protects the right of individuals to join together in order pursue collective action.

The United Nations includes protection of assembly and association in the **International Covenant on Civil and Political Rights**. It deals with the right to assembly (**Article 21 ICCPR**) and the right to association (**Article 22 ICCPR**) separately. The right to association includes the right to join a trade union. Trade union rights are also covered in international agreements under the International Labour Organisation (ILO). Individual cases have also come before the Human Rights Committee of the ICCPR.

Exam tip

The chapter will concentrate on the ECHR but if your module focuses on the United Nations and other international organisations, be aware of the work of the Human Rights committee and the ILO.

ECHR Article 11

Article 11

1 Everyone has the right to freedom of peaceful assembly and to freedom of association with others, including the right to form and to join trade unions for the protection of his interests.

2 No restrictions shall be placed on the exercise of these rights other than such as are prescribed by law and are necessary in a democratic society in the interests of national security or public safety, for the prevention of disorder or crime, for the protection of health or morals or for the protection of the rights and freedoms of others. This article shall not prevent the imposition of lawful restrictions on the exercise of these rights by members of the armed forces, of the police or of the administration of the State.

Unlike the ICCPR, the ECHR includes assembly and association in the same right, which includes trade union membership. Restrictions on the right are allowed if justified under **Article 11(2)**.

Article 11(1)

Article 11(1) covers both assembly and association and the right to form and join trade unions.

Peaceful assembly

The right to peaceful assembly covers assembly for a range of reasons including political, religious, social, and cultural purposes. This list is not exhaustive. It can cover meetings in public and private and can take various forms such as demonstrations, marches, and even sit-ins (***Cisse v France* (2002)**).

Positive obligation?

Positive obligations are imposed on a state to ensure effective protection of the rights protected by the ECHR. **Article 11** would be ineffective if those who wished to assemble could not do so due to fear of violence from counter-demonstrations. The state is under an obligation to take reasonable steps to prevent violence against demonstrators.

....

Plattform 'Ärzte für das Leben' v Austria (1988) 13 EHRR 204

A march was disrupted by counter-demonstrators despite the prior deployment of police. The marchers did not suffer any physical violence but eggs were thrown. The organisers complained that they had received insufficient police protection.

The ECtHR held that there was a positive obligation upon states to take reasonable and appropriate measures to enable lawful demonstrations to proceed. However this was not an absolute guarantee. The state has a margin of appreciation, and given appropriate steps had been taken there was no violation.

The state may also be under a positive obligation where private parties are engaged.

Appleby v UK (2003) 37 EHRR 38

The applicants were barred from their local shopping centre owing to their disorderly behaviour. They wished to gather a petition in the centre. The centre was owned privately but it was argued the state was engaged as it had privatised the centre. The question raises issues involving a clash of rights between **Articles 10** and **11** and property rights under **Protocol 1, Article 1**.

The ECtHR found no violation, as **Article 11** does not guarantee the type of forum to be used for the exercise of the right. However, it did find that a positive obligation may arise, that limits private interests if the essence of the right is undermined.

Third parties

What if a demonstration encroaches on the third parties who are taking no part in the demonstration?

Ollinger v Austria (2006) 46 EHRR 849

A demonstration in a cemetery was banned by the state as it infringed on the rights of the public who wished to visit the cemetery.

The ECtHR held that the state could consider the rights of others but any restriction had to be proportionate. In this case there was a violation as the ban was disproportionate.

Content

The approach to **Article 11** is similar to **Article 10**: demonstrations etc are allowed to cover subjects that may offend those opposed to their views (***Plattform 'Ärztefür das Leben' v Austria* (1988)**).However, an assembly must be 'peaceful'; it is not covered by the article if the purpose is to cause violence. However, a protest such as a sit-in which violates domestic law can still be 'peaceful' within the article (***Cisse v France* (2002)**).

Where the state requires notification or authorisation for an assembly, this will not necessarily interfere with **Article 11(1)**. However, a refusal to authorise an assembly may be an interference that the state must justify, especially if there are no procedural safeguards in place (such as the right to appeal a ban before the date of the assembly). Widespread bans on assemblies could have a chilling effect (***Baczkowski v Poland* (2009)**).

Association

Freedom of association guarantees the rights of persons to come together and form an association. It also includes the right not to be part of an association and not to be penalised for not joining (*Young, James and Webster v UK* (1981)).

'Association' is given an autonomous meaning by the ECtHR. The Court will examine the existence of an association even if the state has not defined it as such. 'Association' constitutes more than spending time in others' company such as contact with prisoners (*McFeeley v UK* (1980)). An association should be stable and for a purpose. The ECtHR has found that some professional associations may not fall under the scope of **Article 11** (*Le Compte, Van Leuven and De Meyere v Belgium* (1981)).

Political parties have been found to be an association under **Article 11**. In *United Communist Party of Turkey and others v Turkey* (1998), the ECtHR underlined the essential role played by political parties in a functioning democracy. Other associations that may or may not have a political objective and may have a cultural or social objective are also important to democracy (*Gorzelik v Poland* (2004)).

Trade unions

Trade unions are recognised as associations under **Article 11** so the general principles apply. However, they are also explicitly mentioned in **Article 11(1)**; everyone has the right to join and form a trade union.

Trade union protection can be restricted by the state if justified but can include:

- The right to form a trade union and to join the trade union of one's choice (*National Union of Belgian Police v Belgium* (1975)).

- The right not to join a trade union (*Young, James and Webster v UK* (1981)). Although the ECtHR has not found that a '**closed shop**' system (where an employee in a profession must join a particular union) is completely prohibited, recent case law has stated that the growing consensus in European states reflects the opinion that such arrangements are not needed to protect trade union freedoms. (*Sorenson and Rasmussen v Denmark* (2008), where a violation was found when a closed shop agreement would force the applicants to join a trade union.)

- The right to be heard, though this does not include a right to consult or a right to collective bargaining (*Swedish Engine Driver's Union v Sweden* (1976)). However recent case law has noted the importance of collective agreements to trade unions as a means to protect member's interests. In *Demir and Baykara v Turkey* (2009), the ECtHR held that where a collective agreement was the only means to protect members' rights, then they may be an interference with **Article 11(1)**.

- Freedom to protect the occupational interests of trade union members by trade union action, the conduct and development of which the contracting states must both permit and make possible. This implies a positive obligation on the state to make possible trade union protections. In *Wilson v UK* (2002), the state was held to have interfered with

Article 11 as it allowed a private company to offer financial inducements to employees to forfeit trade union rights.

- Right to strike? The ECtHR has recognised that the use of industrial action can be important for the protection of members' interests. (*Wilson v UK* (2002)). However, the ECtHR has held that trade union protection under **Article 11** does not include the right to strike. The state can regulate strike action (*Schmidt and Dahlström v Sweden* (1976)).

- Freedom to choose its own members: this includes the right to expel members as long as the union is not abusing a dominant position and acted reasonably. In *Associated Society of Locomotive Engineers & Firemen (ASLEF) v UK* (2007), the applicant union had expelled a member who was a member of a far right political party, the BNP. The views of the BNP conflicted with that of the union. The state had held that the member had been expelled illegally. The ECtHR disagreed. It held that a union can have partisan political views which reflect those of its membership. The expelled member could still express his views and continue his employment. The state's intervention had failed to strike the right balance between the expelled member's rights and the rights of the union. There was a violation of **Article 11**.

Revision tip

Article 11(1) is linked with **Article 10** and some of the cases argue both rights so they (along with **Article 9**) should be considered together. Much of the ECtHR jurisprudence involves political parties and trade union rights.

Exam tip

Articles 9, 10, and 11 might overlap in an exam or problem question. If a problem question arises under **Article 11**, be sure to identify the applicability of **Article 11** before discussing justifications. Where a demonstration is restricted in its movements a question may arise under **Article 5** (the right to liberty).

Article 11(2)

As a qualified right, an interference with **Article 11(1)** may be qualified but only if it meets certain conditions:

Prescribed by law

Any act by the state that interferes with **Article 11(1)** must be prescribed by law. This means that there must be some legal basis for the action and that this has to be clear, precise, and predictable. In *Galstyan v Armenia* (2007), public order offences which restricted freedom of assembly were not prescribed by law as they were not sufficiently precise and clear.

Legitimate aim

Article 11(2) sets out the reasons why a state can interfere with **Article 11(1)**:

Article 11(2)

- national security or public safety
- for the prevention of disorder or crime
- for the protection of health or morals
- for the protection of the rights and freedoms of others

Usually a state can demonstrate a legitimate aim. The legitimate aim may be important as it can influence the margin of appreciation given to the state and the proportionality of a measure.

Necessary in a democratic society

Many cases are decided on whether a measure is necessary in a democratic society. To adjudicate on this question the ECtHR uses the concept of proportionality and will apply a margin of appreciation.

Proportionality

Article 11 is a qualified right as the right may conflict with the needs of the community or the rights of others. Proportionality aims to find a balance between the individual right and the community. The criteria the ECtHR will examine when looking at the act of the state include:

- Is it effective?
- Is it the least intrusive measure possible?
- Does it deprive the 'very essence of the right'?
- Is it balanced? Has a fair balance been struck between the competing interests of the individual and of the community as a whole?

Revision tip

Proportionality is widely used by the ECtHR and an exam question on proportionality may ask about its use in more than one right. Be aware of examples in all the qualified rights studied (see Chapter 6, 'Right to family and private life', p 105, Chapter 7, 'Freedom of religion and expression', p 122, and Chapter 9, 'Freedom from discrimination', p 161).

Margin of appreciation

A wide margin of appreciation means that the ECtHR is more likely to find no violation whereas a narrow margin means a violation is more likely, though the ECtHR will decide on the facts. Several factors will influence whether the margin of appreciation is wide or narrow:

- The nature/importance of the right/issue in question.
- Lack of European consensus or standard (importance of the living instrument principle).
- Areas where judges give wider margin because difficult to judge/resources

✅ *Looking for extra marks?*

There are academic criticisms of the use of the margin of appreciation in the qualified rights and under **Article 2** (see Chapter 4, 'Right to life and freedom from ill treatment', pp 60–63, Chapter 6, 'Right to family and private life', p 103, and Chapter 7, 'Freedom of religion and expression', p 122).

Revision Tip

Margin of appreciation is important in all the qualified rights and similar principles apply.

Case law examples: assembly

If the assembly intentionally causes disruption, the state may be given a broad margin of appreciation. However, the need to protect political expression and assembly means the ECtHR will closely scrutinise any restriction.

In *Christians against Racism and Fascism v UK* **(1980)**, the Commission on Human Rights found a ban on demonstrations was justified as it was proportionate. The ban was designed to stop marches by the National Front and the applicants could still hold meetings.

In contrast:

....

Stankov and United Macedonian Organisation Ilinden v Bulgaria (2001) (Application No 29221/95)

The state placed total bans on meetings including speeches and banners to be held by the applicants to commemorate historical events important to the Macedonian minority. The state argued that the meetings were banned on public order grounds as they would cause tension with the majority in Bulgaria.

It was held that there was a violation of **Article 11**. The state had a margin of appreciation but any restriction had to be proportionate. **Articles 10** and **11** underline the importance of pluralism and a state had to be vigilant to ensure that the majority opinion is not protected at the expense of minority views. An automatic ban was not proportionate as political ideas in this case were being advocated by peaceful means. There was no foreseeable risk of violence or incitement to violence.

....

Penalties imposed by state?

The state may impose penalties following an assembly but these should not be disproportionate.

....

Ezelin v France (1991) 14 EHRR 362

The applicant was a lawyer who attended a lawful demonstration criticising the courts and judiciary. The demonstration led to violence and the lawyer refused to answer police questions in an inquiry. The applicant was not involved in the violence. He was reprimanded by the French Court of Appeal as a disciplinary matter for not disassociating himself from the march.

The ECtHR held there was a violation of **Article 11** despite the minor sanction as the sanction would discourage people from making peaceful beliefs known.

....

Contrast with *Osmani v FYRM* **(2001)**, where the applicant was mayor of a town that organised a meeting to defend the flying of the Albanian flag, which was banned. The meeting later led to a riot where people were killed and injured. He was convicted and jailed for 15 months. The ECtHR held that the penalty was proportionate as the applicant's actions led to the violence and promoted an action in breach of a constitutional decision.

Case law examples: association

Restrictions on political parties are closely scrutinised as the right to associate as a political party is essential to pluralism and democracy. The margin of appreciation is narrow and restriction has to be convincingly justified:

....

United Communist Party of Turkey and others v Turkey (1998) 26 EHRR 121

The state dissolved the applicant party on the grounds that it espoused separatism and threatened the state.

The Court held that there was a violation of **Article 11**. The only compelling reason for dissolving a political party was a threat to democracy. However the ECtHR noted that restrictions could not be imposed solely because a party sought to have a public debate about the situation of a minority population and strived for democratic solutions for that population. Parties that question the organisation of the state have a right to do so as long as they act within democratic principles.

....

In contrast:

....

Refah Partisi v Turkey (2001) 37 EHRR 1

The state dissolved a party that was part of a coalition government. It claimed the applicant party threatened the principle of secularism and had made statements referring to the possible use of force.

The Court held that there was no violation of **Article 11**. A political party wishing to change the constitutional order should seek to do so by peaceful and democratic means. In deciding the proportionality of the measure the ECtHR examined the evidence that there was an imminent risk to democracy, whether the acts of party members were imputable to the whole party, and whether party policy as a whole was incompatible with a democratic society. On the facts, the state measure was proportionate.

✔ Looking for extra marks?

The decision in **Refah Partisi** is controversial given the Grand Chamber's decision that Sharia law is not compatible with the principle of pluralism. The dissent in the Grand Chamber criticised the decision as the party's constitution supported secularism and the evidence used to ban the party was based on isolated events.

Trade unions

See pp 141–142 for the case law on trade unions. The states have a margin of appreciation when regulating trade unions but the ECtHR will scrutinise for the proportionality of a measure. For example, in **Associated Society of Locomotive Engineers & Firemen (ASLEF) v UK (2007)**, the expulsion of a member of a far right party from the union was held by the state to be illegal. The ECtHR held that this violated the right of association of the union as the law did not strike a proportionate balance between the individual and the right of the union to regulate its members.

Explicit restrictions on members of the armed forces, of the police, or of the administration of the state

The ECtHR applies the same principles to this part of **Article 11(2)** as to the general part. In **Sen and Cinar v Turkey (2006)**, the ECtHR found the dissolution of a civil servants' union was a violation because the absolute ban (whilst it could be allowed in principle) was in this case disproportionate as it posed no threat to the state. (Contrast with the earlier Commission decision in **Council of Civil Service Unions v UK (1987)**, where the ban on employees working for the security services was held to be proportionate due to national security reasons, and **Rekvenyi v Hungary (2000)**, where a ban preventing a police officer joining a political party was held to be proportionate (under **Article 10(2)**) owing to state concerns over a politicised police force.)

✔ Looking for extra marks?

Some of the criticisms of the approach of the ECtHR under **Article 11** are similar to that under **Article 10** so both articles should be studied together. There are other case examples that you may choose to use to illustrate your answer.

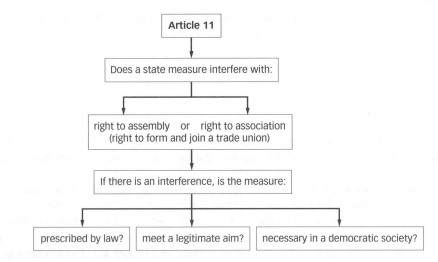

Fig.8.1 Bringing a case under Article 11

Assembly and association in the UK

The right to assembly and association is a negative right in the UK; a person has the right to assembly and to associate unless this is limited by law. It is these legal restraints that have been adjudicated before the courts. The **Human Rights Act 1998** has added to protection by creating an explicit enforceable right to assembly and association.

Revision tip

As case law below illustrates, **Article 11** can overlap with **Articles 5, 9, and 10**.

The right to assembly and association has been limited by:

Common law

Common law offences such as breach of the peace are a restriction on assembly and association. A breach of the peace has been defined as an act which is likely to cause harm to a person or their home or puts a person in fear of such harm (*R v Howell* (1981)). This has been used at gatherings, which the police believe have got out of control. The police should only act if there is a reasonable belief of imminent breach of the peace. The *Laporte* case (below) examined the compatibility of common law breach of the peace with **Article 11** and found its use in this case was disproportionate. See also right to liberty case law in Chapter 5, 'Public order', p 86: *Austin v Commissioner of Police of the Metropolis* (2009) and *R (on* *the application of Moos) v Commissioner of Police of the Metropolis* (2011), where the imminence of a breach of the peace was discussed; imminence had to be necessary, and a matter of 'last resort'.

Statute

Criminal offences

Public Order Act 1986 ss 1–5 cover criminal offences such as riot (**s 1**), violent disorder (**s 2**), affray (**s 3**), fear or provocation of violence (**s 4**), and harassment (**s 4A, s 5**—reasonableness defence).

These offences often involve a gathering of persons which may be a demonstration or protest. The **Human Rights Act 1998** has meant that if argued, **Article 11** (and **Article 10**) will influence the outcome of a case. The state may have to demonstrate not only that the offence is established but that the imposition of the offence is a proportionate response to meet a legitimate aim (see the **Article 10** case of *Munim Abdul and Others Appellants v Director of Public Prosecutions* **(2011)** (Chapter 7, 'Public order and protests', p 133), which involved a demonstration).

Revision tip

Some modules will focus on the English law in this area so be aware of case law before and after the **Human Rights Act 1998**.

Other criminal offences include obstructing the highway (**Highways Act 1980, s 137**) and aggravated trespass under the **Criminal Justice and Public Order Act 1984** (**s 68**). (Note the anti-terrorism offences that list proscribed organisations deemed to be a terrorist group or supporting terrorism (**Terrorism Act 2000**) and limits to demonstrations in the **Serious Organised Crime and Police Act 2005 Part 4**).

Powers to regulate

Public Order Act 1986, ss 11–13 gives powers to ban and regulate public processions. These include the necessity for prior notice (**s 11**) unless the route of the procession is customary or falls into one of the defences (*Kay v Commissioner of Police of Metropolis* **(2008)**). The police also have the power to impose conditions on a march if there is a reasonable belief of serious disorder (**s 12**) and in extreme situations a council can ban all demonstrations for three months in a particular area (**s 13**).

Section 14 of the 1986 Act is similar to **s 12** with regard to the powers to restrict but applies to assemblies (more than two people) rather than processions. In *R (on the application of Brehony) v Chief Constable of Greater Manchester* **(2005)**, the court found that the restriction of a long-running protest outside a shop over the Christmas period was proportionate under **Article 11** as it was one day a week and an alternative site was provided.

Section 14 A–14C covers the banning of trespassory assemblies.

Revision tip

Not all statutory offences and regulations are covered here. If a module focuses on English law then public order offences should be studied in detail and note other restrictions found in statutes such as the **Anti-Social Behaviour Act 2003, s 30**, which gives the police power to disperse individuals or ban a person from an area for 24 hours.

✅ *Looking for extra marks?*

Note that trade union laws in the UK restrict strike action and place conditions on unions with regard to negotiations and strikes.

Case law examples: public order and protest

The use of public order powers to restrict protest has been found to be disproportionate in:

....

R (on the application of Laporte) v Chief Constable of Gloucestershire Constabulary [2006] UKHL 55

The appellant was in a coach taking passengers from London to a RAF base in order to join an anti-war demonstration. The police, believing that the protesters were members of an anarchist group, stopped the coaches and searched them. The chief superintendent had concluded that a breach of the peace was not imminent, but decided to send the coaches back to London with a police escort in order to prevent a breach of the peace occurring at the RAF base.

The House of Lords allowed the appeal (cross appeal by Chief Constable dismissed). The police failed to show that the action taken was the least restriction necessary and so it was disproportionate considering the right to expression and assembly. It was also not reasonable for the police to believe that there would be disorder once the coaches reached the RAF base as extensive precautions had been put in place there.

....

Similarly in:

....

Tabernacle v Secretary of State for Defence [2009] EWCA Civ 23

The applicants were members of a long-established women's protest camp outside an atomic weapons site. The camp had been in place for 23 years and was always peaceful. In 2007, the Secretary of State used a byelaw to ban camping in the controlled area around the site. The applicants claimed this violated their rights under **Article 11** and **Article 10**. The Secretary of State argued that the byelaw only restricted the manner and form of protest and so was proportionate.

The Court of Appeal allowed the appeal. Any distinction between an outright ban and the manner and form of a protest had to be treated with care. Restricting the manner and form may in itself put restrictions on the nature and quality of the protest. The camp was the essence of the protest, therefore the restriction was disproportionate.

....

Key cases

****

✔ *Looking for extra marks?*

Recent demonstrations and protests against government policy may mean more cases coming before the courts. It is worth keeping updated on this area.

✱ *Key cases*

Case	Facts	Principle
Associated Society of Locomotive Engineers & Firemen (ASLEF) v the UK (2007) 45 EHRR 793	The union had expelled a member who was a member of a far right political party, the BNP. The views of the BNP conflicted with that of the union. A court held the expulsion illegal.	The ECtHR held that a union could have partisan political views which reflected those of its membership and do not have a public role beyond union interests. The state interference was a violation of Article 11.
Plattform 'Ärzte für das Leben' v Austria (1988) 13 EHRR 204	A march was disrupted by counter-demonstrators despite the prior deployment of police. The marchers did not suffer any physical violence but eggs were thrown.	The ECtHR held that there was a positive obligation upon states to take reasonable and appropriate measures to enable lawful demonstrations to proceed. However, the state has a margin of appreciation and, given appropriate steps had been taken, there was no violation.
R (on the application of Laporte) v Chief Constable of Gloucestershire Constabulary [2006] UKHL 55	The appellant had been in a coach taking passengers from London to a RAF base in order to join an anti-war demonstration. The police stopped the coaches and searched them. The police decided to send the coaches back to London with a police escort in order to prevent a breach of the peace occurring at the RAF base.	Appeal allowed. On the facts, there was no reasonable belief held that a breach of the peace was imminent. Even if there had been a reasonable belief that a breach was imminent the action still had to be proportionate. The police failed to show that the action taken was the least restriction necessary and so was disproportionate under Article 11 and 10.
Tabernacle v Secretary of State for Defence [2009] EWCA Civ 23	The applicants were members of a long-established women's protest camp outside an atomic weapons site. The Secretary of State used a byelaw to ban camping in the controlled area around the site.	Appeal allowed. Restricting the manner and form of a protest may in itself put restrictions on the nature and quality of the protest. The state had to justify the restriction and on the facts, there was no threat of disorder or a breach of the law.

Case	Facts	Principle
United Communist Party of Turkey and others v Turkey (1998) 26 EHRR 121	The applicant political party was disbanded by the state who claimed it posed a threat to the state.	Violation of Article 11. Political parties are essential to democracy. The only compelling reason for dissolving a political party was a threat to democracy. Parties that question the organisation of the state have a right to do so as long as they do so within democratic principles. The ban was disproportionate.

💬 Key debates

Topic	'Strasbourg discovers the right to counter-demonstrate—a note on Ollinger v Austria'
Author	David Mead
Viewpoint	The article examines the *Ollinger* case and argues that it was a step forward by the state in recognising the importance of **Article 11**.
Source	(2007) *European Human Rights Law Review* (2) pp 133–145

Topic	'The right to form and to join trade unions for the protection of his interests under Article 11 ECHR: an attempt "to digest" the case law (1975–2009) of the European Court of Human Rights'
Author	Filip Dorssemont
Viewpoint	The article reviews the ECtHR case law on trade unions under **Article 11** including collective rights, the right to strike, public servants, and positive obligations.
Source	(2010) *European Labour Law Journal* 1(2), pp 185–235.

? Exam questions

Problem question

Amy is a member of an anti-racist organisation. The organisation wishes to march through the local town centre to protest against the election of a member of the People's National Party (PNP) to the local council. The PNP is a far right organisation which advocates the expulsion of all immigrants from the state.

Exam questions

✱✱✱✱✱✱✱✱✱✱

Amy's organisation gives notice of the march to the police and permission is given. On the same day, an unauthorised counter-demonstration is held by the PNP in another part of the town. During the anti-racist march, some members of the PNP counter-march throw bottles and bricks at the march causing injuries to anti-racism protesters. At this point, there were only a few police officers present. Later, more police officers arrive and the anti-racist organisation is surrounded by police and made to wait in a car park in the town centre for several hours. The PNP protest had dispersed some time earlier.

When Amy complained after several hours in the car park, a police officer told her that the 'kettling' (containment of the march) was necessary and that a breach of the peace was imminent.

Amy wishes to bring a case against the police.

Examine what principles the Court would apply when examining Amy's application claiming the police action was unlawful and what the outcome may be, considering the HRA and the ECtHR jurisprudence.

An outline answer is included at the end of the book.

Essay question

'The European Court of Human Rights has given inadequate protection to the rights of trade unions under article 11.'

 Scan here

Scan this QR code image with your mobile device to see an outline answer to this question or log onto www.oxfordtextbooks.co.uk/orc/concentrate/

#9
Freedom from discrimination

Key Facts

- Equality is a contested concept.
- There are different forms of equality: formal and substantive.
- The United Nations has developed specific treaty and charter mechanisms to give protection from discrimination.
- **Article 14 ECHR** gives limited protection against discrimination but has been expanded by the ECtHR and **Protocol 12**.
- The **Equality Act 2010** has consolidated and expanded equality laws in the UK.

Chapter overview

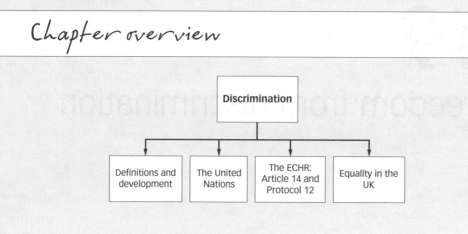

Definitions and development

Freedom from discrimination derives from the concept of equality. This concept has proved difficult to define and is contested. There are different *forms* of equality which will be noted below. However, the notion of equality is integral to the protection of human rights. To treat a person or group differently simply because of a characteristic that they possess undermines the dignity of that person or group and can lead to the violation of both civil/political and social/economic rights. The discriminatory treatment which led to the Holocaust and atrocities of the Second World War meant that the United Nations put non-discrimination at the centre of its human rights developments.

✅ *Looking for extra marks?*

For further discussion on this see academic articles and other writings on this issue.

From non-discrimination to equality of opportunity/outcome

Non-discrimination: formal equality

Discrimination can be described as the negative aspect of equality and is:

- Unjustified, less favourable treatment of a person because of a personal characteristic or because they belong to a group within society.

It is negative in the sense that non-discrimination laws ask the state to refrain from discriminating. They are also reactive; the law acts to compensate a person after past discriminatory practice. Equal treatment is the premise for the formal protection of the law such as the Fourteenth Amendment to the US Constitution which declares that all are equal before the law. This form of non-discrimination law is embodied in the idea of direct discrimination where it is clear a person has been treated unequally. However, this cannot happen in a vacuum and there must be someone that the person can be compared to, in order to demonstrate unequal treatment.

Direct discrimination

- A person is treated differently compared to a person in a similar situation on the basis of a personal characteristic (aim/motive and effect).

Direct discrimination can provide a means of redress for deliberate discriminatory practice for the individual but formal equality has limitations:

- need for comparator: focused on individual position and not deal with a general practice;
- does not remove underlying barriers that are the result of past discriminatory practice or attitudes;
- groups can receive equal treatment but this may mean separate treatment that may be discriminatory in practice, eg establish different schooling systems for different groups where one group's schooling system is inferior.

Equality of opportunity: substantive equality

Equality of opportunity is the positive aspect of equality. It addresses the underlying causes of inequality in society and attempts to undo the effects of past discriminatory practice by focusing on the *effect* rather than the motive or aim of a policy. This concept takes different forms and can be controversial. Substantive equality has a greater impact on state resources and policy decisions. It can blur the lines between civil/political and social/economic rights and it can have an adverse effect on the dominant groups in society.

Indirect discrimination

- Where law or policy, which is applied equally to everyone, has an adverse and disproportionate impact on a particular group.

Indirect discrimination occurs when a measure may be neutral, ie the state does not deliberately set out to treat a group differently but the effect of the policy is that it places a group in an unfavourable position. The focus has moved from the individual to the group. A classic example is a policy that imposes a height restriction on employees:

Scenario 1: the state passes a law which states that only 10% of the police force can be female. Motive and effect can clearly be identified. There is a clear intention to treat women differently—direct discrimination.

Definitions and development

✳✳✳✳✳✳✳✳✳✳

Scenario 2: The state passes a law which states a person must be over 6 feet tall to join the police force. The law applies equally to men and women so there is no clear evidence of intention to treat women differently. However, more women are less than 6 feet tall compared to men. The effect of the policy may be that only 10% or so of women can join the police force—Indirect discrimination

....

Brown v Board of Education (1954) US Supreme Court

In some American states, public schools were racially segregated. The Education Board of the state in question argued that this did not infringe the Fourteenth Amendment of the US Constitution with regard to equal treatment as all children were provided equal access to education. This was known as the 'separate but equal' doctrine. The plaintiffs argued that this formal interpretation of the amendment meant in reality persons were not equal due to the superiority of white only public education.

The Supreme Court decided that separate schooling violated the Fourteenth Amendment. It found that 'separate educational facilities are inherently unequal'. The separation of schools based on race 'retards the development of black children and deprives them of benefits of a racially integrated system'.

....

The *Brown* judgment recognised the concept of indirect discrimination as all were provided with equal access to education generally, but in practice the effect was to treat a group unfavourably because of their race. Most international bodies and most states now recognise indirect discrimination (see 'The European Convention on Human Rights (ECHR)', p 163, below).

Positive discrimination

This takes equality of opportunity a step further. Positive discrimination:

- allows a difference of treatment between groups if the purpose is to remove barriers to equality or redress past discriminatory practices.

An example is fair employment legislation. Northern Ireland had a history of discriminatory practice in the workplace. In order to redress this practice, the fair employment laws allowed a company to treat the discriminated group more favourably. However, this was still based on merit. If two applicants with the same qualifications applied and it was shown that the workforce was predominately from one religious/political community in Northern Ireland, then the employer should employ the minority candidate. This can be controversial but is designed to promote equality and remove past inequality. Most equality laws now allow for some form of positive discrimination.

Equality of outcome?

Equality of opportunity measures can also be used further to attempt to achieve an equality of outcome. This is highly controversial. Forms of positive discrimination can go further than above. One example is the use of quotas, where a percentage of jobs or university places for example, are held for a minority group.

Positive duties: equality of opportunity and equality of outcome

These are duties placed on public bodies. Public bodies must have due regard to the impact of policies of different groups within society when making policy decisions. The duties aim to promote and achieve equality in the longer term. The idea of 'mainstreaming' equality aims to change the culture of decision-making so as to achieve greater equality across all groups. An example can be found in **s 75 Northern Ireland Act 1998** and the **Equality Act 2010.**

Exam tip

To be able to answer an exam question on how the European Court of Human Rights has developed non-discrimination, you will need to be aware of the differences between direct and indirect discrimination.

The United Nations

The United Nations placed non-discrimination at the heart of human rights protection in the aftermath of the mass discrimination of the Second World War. The Universal Declaration of Human Rights 1948 contains a non-discrimination clause, as does the **International Covenant on Civil and Political Rights (ICCPR) 1966, Article 2(1)** and the **International Covenant on Economic, Social and Cultural Rights (ICESCR) 1966, Article 2(2).**

Specific treaties

- UN Convention on the Elimination of All Forms of Racial Discrimination, 1966
- UN Convention on the Elimination of All Forms of Discrimination Against Women, 1979
- UN Convention on the Rights of the Child, 1989
- UN Convention on Rights of Migrant Workers and their Families, 1990
- UN Convention on the Rights of Persons with Disabilities, 2008.

Declarations

- Declaration on the Elimination of All Forms of Intolerance and of Discrimination Based on Religion or Belief, 1981
- Declaration on the Rights of Persons Belonging to National or Ethnic, Religious and Linguistic Minorities, 1992.

Charter-based bodies

Under the special procedures of the Human Rights Council (see Chapter 1, 'United Nations Human Rights Council', p 8), special rapporteurs have been appointed to examine specific topics and investigate compliance with state obligations. The rapporteurs report back to the Human Rights Council. These include:

- Special rapporteur on contemporary forms of racism, racial discrimination, xenophobia, and related intolerance
- Working Group on the issue of discrimination against women in law and in practice
- Special rapporteur on adequate housing as a component of the right to an adequate standard of living, and on the right to non-discrimination in this context
- Independent Expert on minority issues.

Special rapporteurs may be appointed with a country mandate and they may also investigate claims of discrimination against groups within that state.

The European Convention on Human Rights (ECHR)

The Council of Europe has Conventions dealing with human trafficking, minority protection, children, and violence against women (see Chapter 2, 'Other human rights instruments', p 22). The ECHR has a non-discrimination clause and a protocol on discrimination.

Article 14

Article 14

'The enjoyment of the rights and freedoms set forth in this Convention shall be secured without discrimination on any ground such as sex, race, colour, language, religion, political or other opinion, national or social origin, association with a national minority, property, birth or other status.'

The ECtHR may approach the question of discrimination under **Article 14** by asking:

- Does the issue fall within the ambit of a Convention right?
- Is there a distinction between the applicant and similarly situated persons?
- Is it on a specified ground or any other status (personal characteristic)?
- Is it justifiable?

Does the issue fall within the ambit of a Convention right?

Article 14 is sometimes described as 'parasitic' because it cannot be argued as a freestanding right. It can only be argued before the ECtHR if it is attached to a substantive right such as **Article 3**. **Article 14** explicitly states that it only applies to the rights set out in the Convention (*Belgian Linguistics Case* (1968) (1979–80)).

'Within ambit'

However, this does not mean there has to be a violation of the substantive article for **Article 14** to be engaged. A state may operate a policy or measure that does not violate the substantive Convention right, but it may be carried out in a discriminatory way. In the *Belgian Linguistics Case,* the ECtHR concluded that **Article 14** could be raised if the applicants can show it is within the ambit of the substantive right.

A case example is:

....

Abdulaziz, Cabales and Balkandali v UK (1985) 7 EHRR 471

UK immigration rules allowed the wives of men with a right to remain to also have leave to remain in the UK whilst the same was not true with regard to the husbands of women in the same position. The applicants argued this violated the right to family life under **Article 8** with **Article 14**.

The ECtHR held that there was no violation of **Article 8** alone. However, when a state puts rules in place it must do so in a non-discriminatory way. There was no justification for the different rules that applied to men and women. There was a violation of **Article 14** taken with **Article 8**.

....

Note: **Protocol 12** has now created a freestanding non-discrimination right (see 'Protocol 12—removing the link to a substantive right', p 165, below).

Exam tip
If Article 14 is part of a problem question, you must be clear that you are linking it to an arguable substantive right in the Convention.

✔ Looking for extra marks?
There has been academic criticism of the need to link discrimination to a right within the ECHR. This would be useful for any discussion of the effectiveness of Article 14 protection.

Is there a distinction between the applicant and similarly situated persons?

Like direct discrimination, the applicant needs to demonstrate that there is a comparator ie a difference of treatment compared to someone in an 'analogous position' (*Lithgow v UK*

(1986)). The ECtHR does not take a formalistic approach to finding a **comparator** and the issue is usually subsumed by arguments dealing with justification for differential treatment. However, a recent example where the applicants were found not to be analogous is:

Burden v UK (2008) 47 EHRR 857

The applicants were sisters living together. They argued that they suffered from discrimination because on death, the property could not pass from one sister to the other without payment of inheritance tax. However, spouses and civil partners were exempt.

The ECtHR found that siblings and partners were not analogous as the relationships were qualitatively different. Blood ties were different from choosing to be in a relationship. The choice allowed the state to confer special status on spouses and partners.

Is it on a specified ground or any other status?

Expanding protection

Article 14 lists a number of prohibited grounds. However, the list is not exhaustive as it includes 'other status'. The ECtHR has used the open-ended nature of the term 'other status' to add to the characteristics accepted as grounds for protection from discrimination. Thus, the ECtHR has expanded protection into areas the drafters of the ECHR may not have contemplated, recognising changing social attitudes and state consensus. The expansion of the grounds for discrimination is a good example of the **'living instrument'** principle. (See Chapter 2, 'Evolutive interpretation: the 'living instrument principle', p 28). For example,the ECtHR has found discrimination based on marital status (*Rasmussen v Denmark* **(1985)**), illegitimacy (*Marckx v Belgium* **(1979–80)**), and sexual orientation (*Salgueiro da Silva Mouta v Portugal* **(2001)**).

Importance of grounds

The Court has also stated that the protected ground may influence its decision. This will affect the ability of the state to justify a difference of treatment (see 'Is it justifiable', p 161 below). 'Very weighty' reasons need to be given by the state before it can justify treating individuals differently based on certain grounds. In these cases, the margin of appreciation given to the state will be very narrow. The grounds identified so far by the ECtHR as particularly serious forms of discrimination are:

- sex (*Abdulaziz, Cabales and Balkandali v UK* **(1985)**),
- nationality (*Gaygusuz v Austria* **(1997)**),
- religion (*Hoffman v Austria* **(1994)**);
- illegitimacy (*Marckx v Belgium* **(1979–80)**);
- sexual orientation (*Salgueiro da Silva Mouta v Portugal* **(2001)**); and
- race (*Nachova v Bulgaria* **(2005)**).

Grounds not given the same amount of weight when deciding on the justification for different treatment include property and education.

Is it justifiable?

In domestic law in the UK, direct discrimination is not justifiable unless it comes under specified exceptions (**Equality Act 2010**). The ECtHR allows the state to justify a difference of treatment if the state can demonstrate that there is a reasonable and objective justification for the treatment:

Does it pursue a legitimate aim which is objective and reasonable?

In order to measure the reasonableness and objectivity of a difference of treatment, the Court will consider the aim sought, and the proportionality of the measure given the state's margin of appreciation:

- Is there a legitimate aim? Usually this is a not difficult hurdle for the state. One example where this was not accepted is ***Darby v Sweden* (1991)**, where it was found that administrative convenience was not a legitimate aim.

- Is the measure proportionate to the legitimate aim? The Court will consider the relationship of the measure to aim, whether a less restrictive measure could have been used, and the nature of discrimination—certain grounds require greater justification (see p 160 above).

- Margin of appreciation—vary according to circumstances, nature of discrimination, and background. In ***Frette v France* (2004)**, a case involving different treatment based on sexual orientation when applying for adoption, the ECtHR gave a wide margin of appreciation, taking into account the interests of the child and lack of consensus. However, in a similar later case, ***E.B. v France* (2008)**, the ECtHR found discrimination, recognising that very weighty reasons were needed in a case involving sexual orientation.

Revision tip

There are many cases you can use to illustrate the points above. It is best to concentrate on one or two cases as illustrative of each point.

Limitations of above approach to Article 14

Using direct discrimination?

As noted above, direct discrimination is seen as a type of formal equality. A finding of direct discrimination allows the individual to get redress where a state measure is designed to treat a person differently based on a personal characteristic. This type of non-discrimination clause makes it difficult for groups to access the protection of Convention rights as direct discrimination does not focus on social inequality.

The European Convention on Human Rights

✳✳✳✳✳✳✳✳✳✳

Burden of proof?

Like many of the rights in the ECHR, the burden of proving a difference of treatment is on the applicant. The applicant will have to demonstrate that he or she has been treated differently based on one of the grounds, compared to another in a similar situation. Only then does the burden shift to the state to justify the difference of treatment. By treating **Article 14** as a form of direct discrimination, the applicant will have to demonstrate motive and effect. In cases where the measure or policy may seem neutral or the case involves proving the state of mind of a state agent, it is very difficult to demonstrate motive. This makes it difficult for minorities or other groups to demonstrate the discriminatory impact of state policy in the absence of a clear motive, making substantive equality difficult to achieve.

Revision tip

This has been an issue in cases involving the Roma and it is important to see the development of the law in this area as noted below (**D.H.** case, see p 164; 'Development of indirect discrimination in ECtHR case law', see p 163).

The need to link to a substantive right?

This has been criticised as a weakness in protection from discrimination. Linking **Article 14** to Convention rights which are predominantly civil and political rights means that groups who are more likely to suffer social inequality owing to the cumulative effect of state economic and social policies find it difficult to access **Article 14**.

Also, if the ECtHR finds a violation of the substantive Convention right, it usually does not go on to consider **Article 14** (*Dudgeon v UK* (1982)). Arguably, this has undermined the importance of preventing discriminatory practice by failing to recognise its effects. However, in some cases it has examined **Article 14** where it has found a violation of the substantive right if the discrimination constitutes 'a fundamental aspect of the case' (*Marckx v Belgium* (1979–80)).

Example—race

In *Anguelova v Bulgaria* (2004), the dissent heavily criticised the majority for not examining **Article 14** after finding a violation of **Article 3** in a case involving Roma. It was argued that the Court gave the impression that Europe lives in racial harmony and discrimination does not take place. In *Nachova v Bulgaria* (2005), the applicants claimed a violation of **Article 2** with **Article 14**. Two Roma men were shot in the back whilst resisting arrest. Possibly in response to criticism, the ECtHR found a violation of **Article 2** but then went on to consider **Article 14** as a 'fundamental aspect of the case'. The ECtHR found a violation of **Article 14** with the procedural obligation to investigate under **Article 2**.

Developments—expanding protection

Recent developments have expanded the protection from discrimination under the ECHR.

Indirect discrimination

Unlike the USA (*Brown*), many domestic jurisdictions like the UK, and many international instruments, the ECtHR did not explicitly recognise indirect discrimination until recently. The Court may have been reluctant to place excessive burdens on states as substantive equality involves state social and economic policy. However, this was not sustainable given the widespread recognition elsewhere.

Development of indirect discrimination in ECtHR case law

Case law had implied that indirect discrimination was covered by the ECtHR—the *Belgian Linguistics Case* stated that **Article 14** prohibits measures whose object or result/effects is discriminatory. However, the ECtHR did not find a violation on these grounds.

··

Thlimmenos v Greece (2001) 31 EHRR 411

The applicant claimed discrimination along with **Article 9**. A criminal conviction barred all applicants from an area of employment. The applicant's criminal conviction was based on his religious belief. As a Jehovah Witness, he had refused to take part in compulsory military service. He argued that the state failed to consider the fact that his conviction stemmed from his religious beliefs.

The ECtHR held that **Article 14** was engaged when the difference of treatment results from a failure to treat two different situations differently. In this case the state should have treated the applicant differently instead of applying a neutral measure to all.

··

The ECtHR was implicitly recognising the effect of a measure even if different treatment is not the aim, in other words indirect discrimination. The Court did not mention indirect discrimination in the case. Applicants continued to argue for a form of indirect discrimination to be recognised by the ECtHR:

··

Nachova v Bulgaria (2005) 42 EHHR 933

Two young Roma men were killed when resisting arrest for a minor offence. There was an ineffectual investigation into the deaths. The applicants claimed a violation of **Article 2** with **Article 14**. The applicants argued that the burden of proof made it very difficult to prove 'motive and effect' for the shooting. Therefore the general discriminatory practices against the Roma should be enough to shift the burden of proof onto the state to demonstrate the shootings were not racially motivated (similar to indirect discrimination).

The ECtHR found that there was a violation of **Article 2** with **Article 14** on the procedural aspect (lack of effective investigation). However, it found no violation of **Article 2** with **Article 14** on the substantive aspect. Shifting the burden of proof onto the state at an earlier point meant there would be a presumption of racial motives and the state would have to prove a negative; ie that the men who shot the victims were not racist. This would be too high a burden on the state; the applicant should have to demonstrate motive and effect (applying direct discrimination principles).

✅ Looking for extra marks?

Note the Chamber disagreed with the Grand Chamber in **Nachova**. The Chamber agreed with the applicants regarding the substantive breach of **Article 2** with **Article 14**. The cogent evidence of discriminatory practice was enough to shift the burden onto the state to demonstrate the killings were not racially motivated so recognising implicitly a form of indirect discrimination.

The ECtHR finally explicitly recognised indirect discrimination in:

D.H. and Others v Czech Republic (2008) 47 EHRR 59

Roma children were placed in special schools for children with learning difficulties based on IQ tests. The tests were taken by all school children. The applicants argued that this practice discriminated against them as a high percentage of Roma children were sent to special schools. The policy had disproportionately prejudicial effects on Roma children and was a violation of **Article 14** in conjunction with **Protocol 1, Article 2** (education). It was difficult to produce evidence of individual impact or to demonstrate a deliberate policy of differential treatment, so they argued that statistical evidence of an adverse impact should be enough to shift the burden of proof to the state.

The ECtHR held by a majority of 12 votes to 4 that there was a violation of **Article 14**. The burden of proof shifted to the state to justify difference of treatment if the applicants could demonstrate a discriminatory impact. The applicants did not have to prove motive, as compelling statistical evidence of adverse impact could be enough to shift the burden. The state could not justify treatment so there was a violation under **Article 14** with **Protcol 1, Article 2**.

The Grand Chamber in **D.H.** overturned the Chamber which had applied the **Nachova** approach: the need for the applicant to prove motive and effect. The Grand Chamber for the first time *explicitly recognised indirect discrimination*. The ECtHR found that:

- Prime facie evidence is needed to shift burden of proof, there is free evaluation of all evidence.
- Statistics: if reliable and significant, they can be used to establish prime facie evidence of discriminatory effect—rebuttable presumption and burden then shifts to the state.

Significance of *D.H.*

The recognition of indirect discrimination expands the protection of the ECHR. It gives greater protection to minority groups and may have an impact on the economic and social policy of states. It has been described as the most important discrimination case yet decided by the ECtHR. It was followed in *Orsus v Croatia* **(2010)**.

✅ *Looking for extra marks?*

Note the strong dissenting judgments in both *D.H.* and *Orsus*: a reluctance from some of the judiciary of the ECtHR to place extra burdens on states by recognising indirect discrimination. They argue that the Court has gone too far in interfering in the social policy of states as the Convention is primarily for the protection of individuals from discrimination.

Protocol 12—removing the link to a substantive right

Protocol 12 of the ECHR has removed the limitations noted above in regard to bringing a case within the ambit of a Convention right. The protocol makes non-discrimination a free-standing right:

Article 1

1 The enjoyment of any right set forth by law shall be secured without discrimination on any ground such as sex, race, colour, language, religion, political or other opinion, national or social origin, association with a national minority, property, birth or other status.
2 No one shall be discriminated against by any public authority on any ground such as those mentioned in paragraph 1.

The explanatory report notes that **Article 1(2)** refers to any rights granted in national law, obligations of public authorities, by exercise of public authority discretion, or any act of a public authority.

Although in force, the Protocol has only been ratified by 18 member states (the UK has not signed or ratified the Protocol). There has only been one case before the ECtHR under the protocol:

. . . .

Sejdic v Bosnia and Herzegovina (2011) 28 BHRC 201

The applicants complained that their ineligibility to stand for election to the House of Peoples and the Presidency of Bosnia and Herzegovina breached **Article 14** in conjunction with **Protocol 1, Article 3** and under **Protocol 12, Article 1** (P12–1). The applicants were of Roma and Jewish origin. In the Preamble to the Bosnian Constitution, Bosniacs, Croats, and Serbs were described as 'constituent peoples'. As the applicants did not declare affiliation with these groups, they were ineligible to stand for election.

The ECtHR held there was no longer a reasonable and objective justification for the difference of treatment with regard to elections to the House of Peoples (which fell under the ambit of **P1–3** so it was discriminatory under **Article 14 with P1–3**). The ECtHR went on to examine **P12–1** in relation to elections for the presidency. It was not argued that this fell under **P1–3**. The ECtHR found a violation of **P12–1**. The presidential elections were a right set forth in law.

Sejdic does not go into detail about the application of the Protocol but it does make it clear that the same principles of application apply to **Article 14** and **Protocol 1, Article 2**.

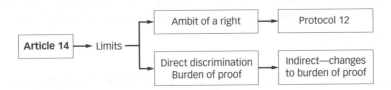

Fig 9.1 Expanding Article 14 protection

Equality in the UK

European Union

The European Union has been a source of UK anti-discrimination law:

- **Article 119 EC Treaty** on equal pay between men and women (now **Article 157 Treaty on the Functioning of the European Union** (TFEU)).

- **Article 13 TFEU**: source of equal treatment **directives**—eg religion, race, age, sexual orientation.

- **Article 21 Charter for Fundamental Rights**—equality provision.

- Case law of the European Court of Justice, eg *Coleman v Attridge Law* (2008), which found that disability discrimination also included association with disability, in this case a carer of a disabled person. This has now been reflected in the **Equality Act 2010, s 13**.

EU legislation and the case law of the European Court of Justice have significantly influenced UK law, especially the expansion of the grounds for protection from discrimination. These have expanded from the limited grounds in the initial EC treaty provisions (equal pay, nationality) to the more expansive grounds that are now part of UK law. EU directives covering grounds such as age, religion, and sexual orientation directly led to the UK enacting legislation in these areas.

Equality Act 2010

The **Equality Act 2010** replaced several pieces of legislation dealing with different grounds for discrimination (it does not apply to Northern Ireland.) The different pieces of legislation dealt with the different grounds in different ways. For example, indirect discrimination applied to race and sex but not to disability. The different Acts also covered different forms of treatment in different ways; direct and indirect treatment, harassment, and victimisation. These are all included in the new Act (with some exceptions). The Act is currently being brought into force through regulations. There is still some debate on full implementation. For example, **s 1** on a duty for public bodies to have due regard to socio-economic considerations is not yet in force.

Legislation replaced by the Equality Act 2010

- Equal Pay Act 1970
- Sex Discrimination Act 1975
- Race Relations Act 1976
- Disability Discrimination Act 1995
- Employment Equality (Religion or Belief) Regulations 2003
- Employment Equality (Sexual Orientation) Regulations 2003
- Employment Equality (Age) Regulations 2006
- Equality Act 2006
- Equality Act (Sexual Orientation) Regulations 2007

The **Equality Act 2010** includes the previously protected grounds and adds several others. The Act now covers:

- sex
- race
- disability
- religion or belief
- sexual orientation

Equality in the UK

****

- age
- gender reassignment
- marriage and sexual partnership
- pregnancy and maternity.

Enforcement

Equality and Human Rights Commission

The Equality and Human Rights Commission was established in 2006 to monitor the implementation of equality legislation. It replaced the separate Commissions that were in place before 2006. The Commission promotes equality and human rights awareness.

As part of its equality role, it also has enforcement powers which include conducting an inquiry, and conducting a formal investigation into persons suspected of an unlawful act. The investigation can lead to an unlawful act notice. Failure to comply with the notice may lead to a court order and a fine (**s 21, Equality Act 2006**). The Commission can also institute or intervene in legal proceedings (**s 30, Equality Act 2006**).

Case law

There is a wealth of case law under the previous legislation on the application of the Acts. The cases below are illustrative of some of the important issues that have come before the courts recently:

Direct discrimination

....

R (on the application of E) v Governing Body of JFS [2009] UKSC 15

JFS was a faith school of Orthodox Jewish character. Preference was given for admission to pupils whose Jewish origin was recognised as being Jewish through maternal descent. The claimant's son was not admitted because his mother had converted to Judaism. It was argued that this was discriminatory on grounds of ethnicity (race).

The appeal was dismissed. The Supreme Court decided that the case was based on race and not religious belief and therefore came under the **Race Relations Act** and was direct discrimination. The case also clarified the role of motive in the reasons for treating someone differently. Following previous case law, it found that if the criteria or decision was inherently based on a protected ground then the motive for the criteria or decision was irrelevant. If the criteria or decision was not inherently based on a protected ground (for instance if the defendant argues a child was refused admission due to merit), then the court will examine the motives carefully.

....

The House of Lords interpreted what is meant by a comparator under disability legislation in:

Lewisham LBC v Malcolm [2008] UKHL 45

The complainant had a mental illness. He was a tenant in local authority accommodation. The local authority wanted to evict him after he had sub-let against the conditions of the tenancy. He sub-let when he was not taking his medication. He claimed that he had been discriminated against on the grounds of disability. The question before the House of Lords concerned the comparator to be used.

Overruling earlier case law, (*Clark v Novacold Ltd* (1999)), the House of Lords found that the comparator was a tenant who sub-lets his flat and not just other tenants. There was no discrimination.

This decision narrowed the ability to claim disability discrimination as it would be difficult to find a 'like for like' comparator. **Section 15 of the Equality Act 2010** remedies the concerns caused by *Malcolm* by removing the need for a comparator—he or she just has to demonstrate 'unfavourable treatment' arising as a consequence of his/her disability.

Indirect discrimination

Eweida v British Airways plc [2010] EWCA Civ 80

The complainant was prevented from wearing a crucifix over her uniform. She claimed this discriminated against Christians. The policy applied to all staff but it had an adverse impact on Christians compared to non-Christians.

The Court of Appeal found that there was no discrimination. The policy did not put Christians as a group at a particular disadvantage compared to non-Christians.

✔ *Looking for extra marks?*

To get an overview of the new legislation see B Hepple, *Equality: The New Legal Framework* (Hart, 2011). Hepple also discusses the previous case law and how it is affected by the new Act.

Human Rights Act 1998

A person can bring a case under the **Human Rights Act** in the same way as under the ECHR. **Article 14** can be argued with another substantive right.

Examples (see Chapter 3, 'Which rights are covered by the HRA?', pp 44–47)

- *Ghaidan v Mendoza* (2004): housing rights of homosexual partners
- *Bellinger v Bellinger* (2003): transsexual rights
- *A v Secretary of State for the Home Department* (2005): detention of terrorist suspects

❋ Key cases

Case	Facts	Principle
D.H. and Others v Czech Republic (2008) 47 EHRR 59	Roma children were placed in special schools for children with learning difficulties based on IQ. The tests were taken by all school children. The applicants argued that this practice discriminated against them as a high percentage of Roma children were sent to special schools.	The ECtHR explicitly recognised indirect discrimination. When the applicant has shown a difference in treatment, it is for the state to show justification. Prime facie evidence is needed to shift the burden of proof. Statistics can be used if reliable and significant.
Nachova v Bulgaria (2006) 42 EHRR 933	Two young Roma men were killed while resisting arrest for a minor offence. There was an ineffectual investigation into the deaths. The applicants claimed a violation of Article 2 with Article 14 on the grounds of race.	Shifting the burden of proof onto the state at an earlier point would require the state to prove a negative. This would be too high a burden on the state; the applicant should have to demonstrate motive and effect; no violation of Article 14 with substantive breach of Article 2 (violation with procedural breach).
R (on the application of E) v Governing body of JFS [2009] UKSC 15	JFS was a faith school of Orthodox Jewish character. Preference was given for admission to pupils whose Jewish origin was recognised as being Jewish through maternal descent. The claimant's son was not admitted because his mother had converted to Judaism.	Appeal dismissed. The case was based on race and not religious belief and therefore came under the Race Relations Act and was discrimination. Clarified when motive would be relevant when determining discrimination

❞ Key debates

Topic	**'Human Rights transformed, positive rights and positive duties'**
Author	Sandra Fredman
Viewpoint	Argues that positive rights and duties should be the focus for protecting freedom and equality.
Source	*Human Rights transformed, positive rights and positive duties* (OUP, 2008)

Topic	'Constitutionalising equality: new horizons'
Author	Karon Monaghan
Viewpoint	The article examines the concept of 'constitutionalising' an equality guarantee. It examines the role of equality in the absence of a formal constitutional guarantee and suggests ways in which legal equality can be achieved.
Source	(2008) *European Human Rights Law Review* (1) pp 20–43

⑦ Exam questions

Problem question

Alma is a single mother and along with her daughter Bella, is a member of a religious group called the 'Children of Alpha Centuri'. The Alpha Centurions makes up under 0.5% of the population in the state. Alpha Centurions have separate faith schools with their own language. They also do not believe in marriage and traditionally, most women in the community are single mothers.

Alma wishes to adopt a child. However her application to adopt is refused by the local authority on the grounds that her 'background' made her unsuitable. The authority's report focuses on her marital status as the main reason for refusal, stating a lack of a 'normal arrangement of two parents'.

Bella wanted to study Law at university. Applicants have to take an entrance examination to study Law. All applicants sit the same examination in the language of the state. Bella failed the exam as did 90% of Alpha Centurions who sat the exam. Only 20% of non Alpha Centurions failed the exam. These failure rates have been similar since the examination was introduced.

Alma challenges the adoption decision and Bella challenges the use of the language exam. However, the domestic court refuses to hear the applications. Alma and Bella apply to the ECtHR.

Advise Alma and Bella as to what human rights claims could be made against the state and examine the likely outcome of the case.

An outline answer is included at the end of the book.

Essay question

Explain and analyse why *D.H. v Czech Republic* (2007) has been described as the most important case ever decided by the European Court of Human Rights.

 Scan here

Scan this QR code image with your mobile device to see an outline answer to this question or log onto www.oxfordtextbooks.co.uk/orc/concentrate/

#10
Terrorism

Key Facts

- Terrorism is a contested concept and defining terrorism has proved controversial.

- There is a debate about the relationship between anti-terror law and human rights.

- If anti-terror law is to be compatible with human rights, it should be within the rule of law and proportionate.

- The ECtHR has held **Article 3** to be absolute irrespective of conduct and will scrutinise the qualified rights for proportionality.

- States can derogate from the ECHR under certain conditions.

- Anti-terror law in the UK has been challenged in the courts.

Chapter overview

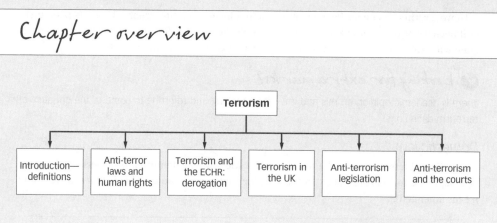

Introduction

Terrorism has always been an issue for states. However, since the terrorist attacks in the US on September 11, 2001, terrorism and the extent of anti-terror laws are now one of the biggest challenges to human rights protections. There is a wide range of source materials and criticisms of terrorism and human rights, especially the treatment of suspected terrorists in holding centres such as Guantanamo Bay, rendition of suspects, and draconian anti-terror law.

✔ Looking for extra marks?

This chapter will focus on several aspects of terrorism but it is useful to read both legal and political articles on terrorism and human rights, government reports by committees such as the Parliamentary Joint Committee on Human Rights, NGOs such as Liberty, and media coverage.

Defining terrorism

One of the difficulties with legislating for terrorism is attempting to define what terrorism is. How is terrorism differentiated from direct action, protesters, an insurrection against a totalitarian state, or an ordinary criminal act?

International law

It has proved difficult to get widespread agreement on a legal definition of terrorism. The UN Counter Terrorism Committee has attempted to define a terrorist act, as has the General Assembly in a resolution from 2004:

> criminal acts intended or calculated to provoke a state of terror in the general public, a group of persons or particular persons for political purposes are in any circumstances unjustifiable.

Introduction

****

However, this has never been established in a legally binding treaty. This has been difficult because of the political issues involved: one state may define a group as terrorists but a state with different interests may define the same group as 'freedom fighters'.

✅ Looking for extra marks?

There is academic opinion on this and it is worth reading and referring to some of the critiques of terrorism definitions.

Domestic law

Definitions of a terrorist can be found in domestic law as a definition is necessary if a state is to legislate for terrorist acts. In the UK, terrorism is defined in the **Terrorism Act 2000 s 1** (as amended):

Terrorism Act 2000 s 1

Action or threat of action (including outside the UK) designed to influence any government or an international governmental organisation or intimidate the public, in any country, for the purpose of advancing a political, religious, racial or ideological cause, which

- involves serious violence against a person,
- involves serious damage to property,
- endangers a person's life
- creates serious risk to public health/safety
- is designed to disrupt an electronic system.

The definition is controversial as it is wide-ranging, covering acts designed to 'influence' and actions including creating a risk to public safety. Critics have argued that this definition can encompass protestors and activists. Once defined as a terrorist, it can have serious implication for a person or group as the definition is used for the terrorist offences covered by UK law.

Exam tip

If a question arises about terrorism and human rights it may be important to note the width of the definition as this broadens the scope of who is affected. In a problem question based on UK law, it will be necessary to examine whether the applicant's activities fall under the definition.

✅ Looking for extra marks?

There is a wide range of criticisms of the definition. See Lord Carlile's Report on definition of Terrorism (2007) (Command Paper 7052).

Anti-terror law and human rights

Revision tip

The discussion below examines the debate surrounding terrorism and rights in context and sets out a way to measure the compatibility of legislation with human rights principles.

Anti-terror laws are usually made in response to a threat to the state and enforce more draconian measures than under ordinary criminal law. They are likely to encroach on individual human rights. States argue that this is necessary in order to protect the population, which is one of the primary responsibilities of the state. The state has a positive obligation under the ECHR to protect a person from harm, where the state knows or ought to know of an immediate risk of harm and can take reasonable steps to protect (see Chapter 4, 'UK and the right to life', p 65). However, the counter-argument is that human rights and the **rule of law** are the bedrock of democracy and without respect for these concepts, terrorism will achieve its goal of undermining the state.

Do we need anti-terror law?

Arguments for and against (this list is not exhaustive):

No:

- Criminal law enough—terrorism acts are by their nature criminal.
- Arguments that terrorism is different from ordinary crime are weak—is the complexity of terrorist threat any different from that from criminal gangs?
- Wide powers given to the state may be abused.
- May have the opposite effect from that intended and alienate communities.

Yes: criminal law not enough.

- Nature of threat—targeted at civilians, suicide bombings, etc; increases need for preventative action to avoid an atrocity.
- Sophistication of threat and groups—difficult to gather evidence and investigate groups under normal rules.
- Positive duty on the state to protect.

✓ *Looking for extra marks?*

There are academic articles on this issue which express differing views.

If we do need anti-terror law, how can compatibility with human rights and the rule of law be measured?

Proportionality

One way to measure the compatibility of terrorism legislation is by establishing if a response to terrorism is proportionate and within the rule of law. This test may be strict or it may give a wider margin of appreciation to states, depending on the rights in question.

Example

Lord Lloyd's guidelines for compatibility (Lord Lloyd's report on anti-terror legislation (1996) Command Paper 3420):

* legislation should approximate ordinary law;
* additional statutory powers must be justified but only if necessary to meet anticipated threat;
* need for additional safeguards should be considered alongside additional powers; and
* the law should comply with international obligations.

Revision tip

These criteria can be referred to when examining the jurisprudence and concept of derogation below.

Terrorism and the European Convention on Human Rights

The European Court of Human Rights (ECtHR) has adjudicated on cases involving terrorism under several ECHR articles, such as **Article 2 and 3** (Chapter 4, 'Right to life and freedom from ill treatment', p 56), **Articles 5 and 6** (Chapter 5, 'Right to liberty and right to fair trial', p 76), **Articles 8 and 10** (Chapter 6, 'Right to family and private life', p 98, and Chapter 7, 'Freedom of religion and expression', p 117).

Absolute rights

As **Articles 2 and 3** are absolute, the ECtHR treats terrorists in the same way as other victims under the Convention. The state cannot derogate from **Articles 2 and 3** in order to meet a terrorist threat (see **Article 15(2)**, 'Derogation: Article 15 ECHR', p 178, below).

Chahal v UK (1996) 23 EHRR 413

The applicant was a Sikh who had the right to remain in the UK. He was imprisoned for assault charges (later quashed). Deportation proceedings were put in place on the grounds that the applicant was a threat to national security. The applicant claimed he should not be deported as he would be subjected to torture if returned. The state argued that the positive obligation on the state not to deport should be balanced against the terrorist threat from the applicant.

The ECtHR held that it is established case law that there is a positive obligation on the state not to deport a person where there were substantial grounds for believing there is a real risk of ill treatment in the receiving state. **Article 3** is absolute and the argument that you can balance the right not to be ill treated against the threat posed by the applicant was rejected. **Article 3** is applicable *irrespective of the conduct of the applicant*. On the facts, there was enough evidence to establish a real risk of ill treatment if deported. There would be a violation of **Article 3**.

States challenged the '*Chahal* principle' in *Saadi v Italy* (**2008**). However the ECtHR upheld *Chahal*, reiterating the absolute nature of **Article 3**.

Qualified rights

When adjudicating on qualified rights such as private life and expression, the Court acknowledges that national security is a legitimate aim which may be given a wide margin of appreciation (see Chapter 2, 'Margin of appreciation', p 34), allowing the state to restrict the rights where necessary in a democratic society for the protection of others (proportionality). However, the ECtHR will still scrutinise a state measure to ensure it does not go beyond what is proportionate. (States may derogate from qualified rights but usually choose not to as a state can justify restrictions under the qualified rights and the proportionality test may be less strict than under **Article 15(1)**, see 'Derogation: Article 15 ECHR', p 178, below.)

Gillan and Quinton v UK (2010) (Application No 4158/05)

The applicants were stopped and searched by police on their way to a demonstration outside an arms fair: **s 44 Terrorism Act 2000** gave the police power to stop and search without reasonable suspicion in an authorised geographical area. London had been under a **s 44** authorisation every 28 days continuously since 2000. The applicants argued a breach of **Article 8**.

The ECtHR found there was a violation of **Article 8**. The search was a clear interference with private life which the state had to justify under **Article 8(2)**. Despite a wide margin of appreciation given for national security reasons, the ECtHR held the measures were not in accordance with law because:

- the authorisation for stop and search powers is given when 'expedient' and in practice the executive has a wide discretion;
- the independent reviewer could only report and had expressed concerns about misuse of power;
- wide discretion was given to individual police officers: there was statistical evidence of arbitrary use; and
- judicial review did not provide effective redress to counter the discretion.

In contrast in *Klass v Germany* (**1978**), secret surveillance was held not to violate **Article 8** because there were proper safeguards in place.

Limited rights

Articles 5 and 6 (see Chapter 5, 'Right to liberty and right to fair trial', p 76) are not qualified but states may choose to derogate from the rights if there is a terrorist threat (see 'Derogation: Article 15 ECHR').

....

A and others v UK (2009) (Application No 3455/05)

The applicants were held as suspected terrorists. Closed hearings were held to adjudicate on the detention of the suspected terrorists. The applicants could not attend the hearings or have access to evidence. Special advocates were used who represented the applicants. However, they could not discuss any closed evidence with the applicants. The applicants argued that this violated **Article 5(4) and Article 6**.

The Court held that closed hearings and special advocates are allowed under **Article 5** but there has to be procedural safeguards to ensure **Article 5** protection is not undermined. There has to be sufficient information available to the applicants to be able to challenge the allegations made against them. On the facts, in several of the complaints, there was enough open information for a sufficient defence, but in others there was not enough information for the applicants to provide a sufficient defence and therefore there was a violation of **Article 5(4)**. (It was not necessary to examine **Article 6**).

....

Revision tip

See UK cases below to link the ECtHR's decision with the decision of the House of Lords when it heard the *AF* case in 2009.

Derogation: Article 15 ECHR

Article 15

1 In time of war or other public emergency threatening the life of the nation any High Contracting Party may take measures derogating from its obligations under this Convention to the extent strictly required by the exigencies of the situation, provided that such measures are not inconsistent with its other obligations under international law.

2 No derogation from Article 2, except in respect of deaths resulting from lawful acts of war, or from Articles 3, 4 (paragraph 1) and 7 shall be made under this provision.

3 Any High Contracting Party availing itself of this right of derogation shall keep the Secretary General of the Council of Europe fully informed of the measures which it has taken and the reasons therefore. It shall also inform the Secretary General of the Council of Europe when such measures have ceased to operate and the provisions of the Convention are again being fully executed.

A state may derogate when certain conditions are met. There must be:

- War or other public emergency threatening the life of the nation.
- Measures taken to the extent strictly required by the exigencies of the situation.
- Provided that such measures are not inconsistent with its other obligations under international law.
- The Council of Europe must be informed.

War or other public emergency threatening the life of the nation

The ECtHR has defined 'public emergency' as an:

- Actual or imminent threat.
- Involving whole of the nation.
- Continuance of organised life of the community must be threatened.
- Must be exceptional in that normal measures are plainly inadequate.

(*Lawless v Ireland* (1961), *The Greek Case* (1969).)

The ECtHR has traditionally given the state a wide margin of appreciation to decide if there was a public emergency. A democratic state is best placed to decide this. This was reinforced in the most recent derogation case in *A and others v UK* (2009). (Note, the only case where it has been found that there was no public emergency was *The Greek Case* (1969), where there was a military regime in power.)

Measures taken to the extent strictly required by the exigencies of the situation

The ECtHR gives greater scrutiny to whether the measures taken are strictly required during an emergency. It applies a strict proportionality test. In *A and others v UK* (2009), the ECtHR found that a measure should be a:

- Genuine response to emergency.
- Fully justified in the special circumstances.
- Adequate safeguards against abuse.
- The duration of an emergency is linked to proportionality of a measure.

The UK derogated from **Article 5** with regard to seven-day detention without charge due to the conflict in Northern Ireland. This derogation followed the decision in *Brogan v UK* (1988) where the ECtHR found the seven-day pre-charge detention regime in violation of **Article 5** (see Chapter 5, 'Promptly', p 83). In *Brannigan and McBride v UK* (1993), the applicants argued that the derogation was not necessary in the circumstances. However, the ECtHR found the derogation was a proportionate response to the emergency. There were enough procedural safeguards in place. In contrast, the ECtHR held in *Aksoy v Turkey* (1996), that unsupervised detention for 14 days was not 'strictly required'.

In contrast to *Brannigan and McBride*, there were no procedural safeguards for the longer length of pre-charge detention.

Measures are not inconsistent with its other obligations under international law

The derogation must not conflict with other international treaty obligations, eg the **ICCPR**. A state should derogate from the relevant treaties it has ratified. International obligations include '*jus cogens*', ie principles of international law so fundamental that they bind all nations. These include the non-derogable rights such as the right not to be tortured.

Revision tip

Article 4 of the ICCPR allows derogation on similar grounds though is more detailed. Be aware of **Article 4 ICCPR and the UN Siracusa Principles on States of Emergency** especially if your module examines UN treaty mechanisms.

The Council of Europe must be informed

The state should inform the Council of Europe of a derogation, the reasons for it, and any changes and withdrawals of the derogation. It should be noted that the ECtHR examines derogations only if an applicant brings a case before the Court.

✅ *Looking for extra marks?*

There is academic criticism of the Court's approach to 'public emergency' and argument that there should be stricter scrutiny both by the ECtHR and by other Council of Europe bodies.

Terrorism in the UK

Background

There is a long history of anti-terrorism law in the UK. From the 1960s until the Good Friday Agreement in 1998, which signalled a transition from conflict to a peace settlement, the conflict in Northern Ireland led to anti-terror legislation. The **Emergency Provisions Act (NI) 1973–1998** and the **Prevention of Terrorism Act (GB) 1974–1999** were the main pieces of legislation. Issues that gave rise to rights concerns included powers of arrest and administrative detention (internment), stop and search powers, wide-ranging terrorist offences, non-jury trials, and the use of 'supergrass' evidence, where suspects were convicted on the uncorroborated evidence of one person. There were also questions raised about the behaviour of security forces in riots, collusion with paramilitaries, and claims of a 'shoot to kill' policy rather than arrest.

✅ Looking for extra marks?

There are many academic writings on terrorism in Northern Ireland and official government reports such as the Bloody Sunday Inquiry. Note the ECtHR jurisprudence in this chapter and other chapters involving Northern Ireland such as *Ireland v UK* **(1978)**.

Following the Good Friday Agreement, the focus moved to international terrorism and fears raised by global organisations such as Al-Qaeda. The temporary pieces of legislation in place for domestic terrorism were replaced with permanent legislation.

Anti-terrorism legislation

- **Terrorism Act 2000**: definition of terrorist, proscribed organisations, seizure powers, disclosure of information, stop and search, offences (directing terrorism).

- **Anti-terrorism, Crime and Security Act (ATCSA) 2001**: 14 parts, increased stop and search powers and disclosure of information, Part 4—indefinite detention.

- **Prevention of Terrorism Act 2005**: control orders.

- **Terrorism Act 2006**: extension of pre-charge detention to 28 days (previously 14 days under the **Criminal Justice Act 2003**), new offences—'encouragement'. (The clause allowing for 28 days' detention has now lapsed and not been renewed, so that the length of detention is again 14 days.)

- **Counter-Terrorism Act 2008**: post charge questioning, notification requirements, travel restrictions, DNA, fingerprinting of those under control orders, asset freezing.

See also:

- **Civil Contingencies Act 2004**: making of emergency regulations by order-in-council where an emergency has or will occur, regulations are necessary, and the need is urgent—where existing legislation is ineffective or causes serious delay; may be made for any purpose to prevent, control, or mitigate an aspect or effect of emergency; may make provisions of any kind—but must be proportionate; the emergency regulations may last for 30 days but are renewable; must be placed before Parliament's affirmative procedure within seven days. (Has not been used.)

- **Serious Organised Crime and Police Act 2005 Part 4**: trespass in designated sites; banning of demonstrations in designated sites, including Parliament.

Anti-terrorism legislation and the courts

Stop and search powers under Terrorism Act 2000

Under **s 44 and s 45 Terrorism Act 2000**, an authorisation allows an area to be designated for 28 days. The power allows a police constable to stop and search any person for articles of any kind that could be used for the purposes of terrorism. The power can be exercised whether or not the constable has grounds for suspecting the presence of articles. There is no need for a subjective belief or a reasonable suspicion.

....

R (on the application of Gillan and another) v Police Commissioner of the Metropolis [2006] UKHL 12

The claimants were stopped and searched by police on their way to a demonstration outside an arms fair under anti-terrorism powers: **s 44 Terrorism Act 2000** gave the police power to stop and search without reasonable suspicion in an authorised geographical area. The claimants argued the legislation was incompatible with the right to private life under **Article 8**.

The House of Lords dismissed the appeal, holding that the stop and search powers were compatible with **Article 8 of the ECHR**. The use of stop and search was an interference with the claimant's private life but this interference was held to be justified:

- It was in accordance with law because the powers were published and limited in that the constable would have to explain their actions. Judicial review was available to a claimant if they believe the power was used arbitrarily.

- It met the legitimate aim of national security and deference should be given to the executive as to the need for the power (though several of the Law Lords expressed concerns).

- It was proportionate as it was properly authorised and safeguards were in place.

....

The ECtHR disagreed with the House of Lords and found a violation due to a lack of procedural safeguards: see *Gillan and Quinton v UK* **(2010)**, p 177 above.

Government response to ECtHR decision

Following widespread criticism in the media of the misuse of the **s 44** powers and the ECtHR decision, the Government decided to repeal the powers under **s 44** and **s 45** in the **Protection of Freedoms Bill 2011** (at time of writing this is currently going through Parliament). The Bill retains the power of a constable to stop and search with reasonable suspicion. However, there are extra safeguards in place for the authorisation of the use of the power. Authorisation is only given if the senior police officer reasonably suspects an act of terrorism will take place and the geographical area and duration of authorisation is no greater than is necessary. There will also be a published code of practice.

Indefinite detention under ATCSA 2001

Under the **Anti-terrorism, Crime and Security Act 2001 Part 4,** suspected international terrorists could be held indefinitely by the state (in Belmarsh prison). The law only applied to non-nationals. They had not been convicted of any criminal offence. The law was seen as an immigration measure. It gave the state the power to deport the suspects (**s 22**). However, the *Chahal* principle (see p 176) meant they could not be deported to a state where there were significant grounds for believing there was a real risk they would be ill treated; **Article 3** is non-derogable. Instead, if the suspect could not be deported, they would be detained (**s 23**). It is possible to derogate from **Article 5** on lawful detention. Detention for an indefinite period of time would clearly violate **Article 5** (see Chapter 5, p 78).

The state derogated under **Article 15 ECHR** from **Article 5** (see 'Derogation: Article 15 ECHR', p 178, above), using the procedure under **s 14 Human Rights Act 1998**. **Article 5** was disapplied; the only way to challenge the **2001 Act** was to challenge the derogation.

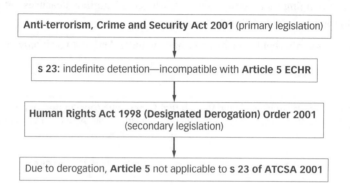

Fig 10.1 Detention and derogation under ATCSA 2001

The legislation and derogation order were challenged in:

A and others v Secretary of State for the Home Department [2005] 2 All ER 169

The claimants were detained under **ss 22 and 23 of ATCSA 2001**. They claimed the derogation order was flawed as there was not a public emergency and, if there was, the measure was disproportionate and not strictly required. Without the derogation, their detention was incompatible with **Article 5 of the ECHR**.

By a majority of 8:1 the House of Lords held the derogation order was flawed as it was disproportionate and discriminatory. With no derogation, **ss 22 and 23 of the ATCSA 2001** were incompatible with **Article 5** and **Article 14**. A declaration of incompatibility was made.

Was there a 'public emergency threatening life of nation'?

The House of Lords held by 8:1 that there was an emergency. Applying ECtHR principles, they deferred to the executive as being best placed to make the decision. Lord Hoffmann dissented, arguing the threat was not enough to be a public emergency. No other state had derogated including Spain, which had suffered from terrorist attack.

Terrorism in the UK
✳✳✳✳✳✳✳✳✳✳

Was the measure strictly required?—was it proportionate?

The House of Lords held by 8:1 that it was not proportionate:

- what of the threat posed by UK nationals?
- it allowed foreign nationals suspected of being Al-Qaeda terrorists to pursue their activities abroad if there was any country to which they were able to go
- permitted detention of non Al-Qaeda suspects
- if the threat posed by UK nationals suspected of being terrorists could be addressed without infringing their **Article 5** rights, why could similar measures not address the threat posed by foreign nationals?

The measure was also held to be discriminatory under **Article 14** as it only applied to non-nationals.

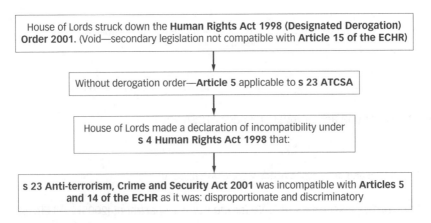

House of Lords struck down the **Human Rights Act 1998 (Designated Derogation) Order 2001**. (Void—secondary legislation not compatible with **Article 15 of the ECHR**)

↓

Without derogation order—**Article 5** applicable to **s 23 ATCSA**

↓

House of Lords made a declaration of incompatibility under **s 4 Human Rights Act 1998** that:

↓

s 23 Anti-terrorism, Crime and Security Act 2001 was incompatible with **Articles 5 and 14 of the ECHR** as it was: disproportionate and discriminatory

Fig 10.2 Outcome of *A and Others* (2005)

Exam tip

A and others is an important case and is illustrative of the judicial response to executive use of powers that may go beyond the rule of law and of the importance of proportionality.

Government response to declaration of incompatibility

In response the Government allowed the clauses in question in the **2001 Act** to lapse (they were **sunset clauses** that have to be renewed after a certain period of time) and replaced indefinite detention with the control order regime under the **Prevention of Terrorism Act 2005**.

Control orders under Prevention of Terrorism Act 2005

Control orders apply to nationals as well as non-nationals. The control order regime places certain restrictions on suspected terrorists. There are two types of orders. If the restriction amounts to a deprivation of liberty (see Chapter 5, 'Deprivation of liberty', p 79) the state should use a derogating order but if the restrictions do not amount to a deprivation then a non-derogating order should be used. Which order is used is important as they have different legal obligations. The Government has not asked for a derogating order and all orders have been non-derogating:

Derogating orders

- State must derogate from ECHR to make orders.
- **Section 4 2005 Act**: the Secretary of State must apply to court for an order in a preliminary hearing and confirm in a full hearing.
- *The court makes the decision* on the **balance of probabilities** that the person is involved in terrorism-related activity, it is necessary to protect public from risk of terrorism, and there is a *public emergency* re-designated derogation order; renewed for *six months*.

Non-derogating orders

- The state does not have to derogate from ECHR.
- **Sections 2 and 3 2005 Act**: *the Secretary of State makes the decision* on the control order.
- There must be *reasonable grounds for suspecting* the person is involved in terrorism-related activity, necessary to protect public from risk of terrorism.
- After making the decision to make the order, the Secretary of State must ask for permission from the court—the court can only refuse the application for the order if *'obviously flawed'*.
- The Secretary of State can make the order without permission if urgent, must refer to the court, which can only quash the order if 'obviously flawed'; renewed for *12 months*.

....

Secretary of State for the Home Department v JJ and Others [2007] All ER (D) 489; *Secretary of State for the Home Department v E* [2007] All ER (D) 27

(See Chapter 5, 'Deprivation of liberty', p 84.)

The applicants were controlees held under non-derogating control orders, made under the **Prevention of Terrorism Act 2005**. The control orders involved restrictions on liberty. The controlees argued that the restrictions amounted to a 'deprivation' and so Article 5 was applicable. A derogating control order should have been used.

Terrorism in the UK

✴✴✴✴✴✴✴✴✴✴

> The House of Lords held that **Guzzardi v Italy (1980)** applied. Each case had to be decided on its facts: in **JJ**, the 18-hour curfew, vetting, and the restrictions amounted to a deprivation and the order was flawed. In **E**, the 12-hour curfew, vetting, and restrictions were held to be less intrusive than in **JJ** and so there was no deprivation and the order was upheld.

The regime was also challenged under Article 6 (Chapter 5, p 94). Control order decisions are made in closed hearings by the Special Appeals Immigration Commission (SIAC). The controlees are not allowed to see the case against them and they are appointed special advocates. The system was challenged in **Secretary of State for the Home Department v MB, AF (2007)**. The House of Lords found that the controlee should have enough information to advance an effective defence. However the judgment was ambiguous and it went back to the House of Lords in **Secretary of State for the Home Department v AF (No 3) (2009)**. The House of Lords concurred with the judgment in **A and others v UK (2009)**, that the controlee is entitled to an 'irreducible minimum' of information about allegations that allows an effective defence. The House of Lords used **s 3 of the Human Rights Act** to read down the legislation to give the judge power to decide if a lack of disclosure undermines **Article 6**.

Government response to control order cases

Home Office: Review of Counter Terrorism and Security Powers (2011) (Command Paper 8004).

The Review has recommended:

- Current regime should be repealed—system to be 'less intrusive, more clearly and tightly defined'.
- Orders should only be imposed with prior permission from court (except where urgent—seven days). Home Secretary must have reasonable grounds with regard to the necessity of regime.
- Duty on police to continually review the possibility of prosecution.
- Mandatory full review by High Court with power to quash/revoke.
- Maximum limit of two years.
- More flexible and less restrictive.
- No measures allowed that would require derogation.
- Enhancements to special advocate system.
- Where there is a very serious terrorist risk, additional measures agreed upon but only used if necessary and need parliamentary approval.

These proposals aim to make the control order regime more compatible with the human rights protection and the rule of law.

Terrorism and torture

The UK courts have also been asked to examine the use of evidence possibly gathered by torture in other states and civil claims against the state for complicity in the torture of terrorist suspects overseas.

In *A and Others v Secretary of State for the Home Department (No 2)* **(2006)**, the House of Lords decided that SIAC could not hear evidence if it has been established that the evidence was obtained by the use of torture even if obtained outside UK.

Al Rawi and others (Respondents) v The Security Service and others (Appellants)
[2011] UKSC 34

The respondents were suspected terrorists held outside of the UK in holding centres including Guantanamo Bay. They claimed they were tortured and the security forces were complicit in the torture. They are pursuing a civil claim against the state. The case was on a preliminary issue as to whether the state had the power to order a closed hearing with special advocates in a civil claim where there was no statutory regime.

The Supreme Court found that there was no power at common law to introduce a closed hearing procedure. Open hearings are an important part of fair trial and open justice. If the principle of an open hearing is to be limited, it is up to Parliament to legislate to do so as it has done under anti-terror legislation.

✔ *Looking for extra marks?*

There are other issues not covered in this chapter including the freezing of suspects' assets by the state and the use of memorandums of understanding to deport suspected terrorists.

✱ *Key cases*

Case	Facts	Principle
***A v Secretary of State for the Home Department* [2005] 2 All ER 169**	The claimants were indefinitely detained. They claimed the derogation order allowing detention under the 2001 Act was flawed as there was not a public emergency and if there was, the measure was disproportionate and not strictly required.	The derogation order was flawed as it was disproportionate. It only applied to non-nationals and the threat was undermined by the fact they could leave the state voluntarily. Article 5 applied and the Act was incompatible under s 4 HRA. The court is the guardian of the rule of law.

Key debates

****

Case	Facts	Principle
Chahal v UK (1996) 23 EHRR	Deportation proceedings were put in place against the applicant on the grounds that he was a threat to national security.	Article 3 is absolute and applicable irrespective of the conduct of the applicant and a person cannot be sent to a state where there are substantial grounds for believing there is a real risk of torture. Violation.
Gillan and Quinton v UK (2010) (Application No 4158/05)	The applicants were stopped and searched by police on their way to a demonstration outside an arms fair. Section 44 Terrorism Act 2000 gave the police power to stop and search without reasonable suspicion in an authorised geographical area.	Violation of Article 8. Despite a wide margin of appreciation given for national security reasons, the ECtHR held the measures were not in accordance with the law because of a lack of proper safeguards.
Secretary of State for the Home Department v AF (No 3) [2009] UKHL 28	The claimants argued that the special advocate system under the control order scheme violated Article 6.	A controlee was entitled to a minimum of information so as to mount an effective defence. The clause in question was read down under s 3 HRA, to give the judge discretion to decide if enough information given

🌀 Key debates

Topic	'Human Rights, Terrorism and Risk: The Roles of Politicians and judges'
Author	David Feldman
Viewpoint	The author examines the UK response to terrorism and questions the necessity for such laws.
Source	(2006) *Public Law* Summer pp 364–384

Topic	'Setting the record straight: human rights in an era of international terrorism'
Author	Keir Starmer
Viewpoint	The article examines how human rights should be protected when anti-terror laws are enacted
Source	(2007) *European Human Rights Law Review* (2) pp 123–132

⑦ Exam questions

Problem question

Aisha is an asylum seeker and has leave to remain in the UK. She is a member of an animal rights organisation called the 'Animal Rights Congress' (ARC). The ARC has been involved in 'direct action', such as demonstrations. Some members of the ARC wanted to escalate the protests. A nail bomb addressed to the administrator of a laboratory carrying out animal testing was intercepted by the police.

Aisha is arrested under anti-terror legislation. She is suspected of being involved in sending the nail bomb. She is released without charge. However, the state wishes to deport her to her state of origin. Whilst awaiting deportation, Aisha is placed under a non-derogating control order, which places her under a curfew of 16 hours a day, her communication (telephone, email, etc) is under surveillance, she is placed in a flat where only security vetted persons can visit, and she is restricted in her movements. She can visit her doctor and church but cannot leave the town she lives in.

Aisha appeals against her deportation, claiming she had been ill treated in her state of origin for political activities. A report by an NGO noted widespread use of torture in her state of origin. She also appeals against the control order. However, the special advocate cannot tell her what the evidence is against her as it is 'closed evidence'. The only information she is told is that the police allege she was seen with other suspects on several occasions.

Advise Aisha as to what human rights claims can be made against the state and examine the likely outcome of the case.

An outline answer is included at the end of the book.

Essay question

'The real threat to the life of the nation, in the sense of a people living in accordance with its traditional laws and political values, comes not from terrorism but from laws such as these'. (Lord Hoffmann—*A and others* (2005).)

a)   Explain the UK's legislative response to the threat from terrorism

and

b)   Explain and analyse the challenges to these laws in the UK courts.

 Scan here
Scan this QR code image with your mobile device to see an outline answer to this question or log onto www.oxfordtextbooks.co.uk/orc/concentrate/

Exam essentials

Tips on linking the topics together

Most of the topics in this revision guide can be linked together and can overlap in an examination question. Examples:

- Knowledge of human right theories is useful if a question arises about whether the use of torture can be justified.
- Knowledge of admissibility criteria may be needed for any problem question on the substantive rights in order to identify whether a claimant can bring a case before the ECtHR.
- The concepts of proportionality and margin of appreciation link together the qualified rights in the ECtHR, and are relevant to **Article 2** and derogation under **Article 15**.
- **Article 14** cannot be raised without a substantive right, so knowledge of the rights is necessary.
- To answer a question on terrorism it may be necessary to have knowledge of the ECHR rights, especially **Articles 5** and **6** and derogation under **Article 15**.

When revising:

- Make a list of areas where topics overlap. For example, proportionality is important when discussing **Article 2(2)**, **Article 8–11**, **Article 14**, terrorism.
- Past papers: after making a list, consult past papers which should be available from your college/university—in what ways are topics linked in past questions?

Pointers for key topics/questions often tested

The key topics will have been covered by your course. You should review:

- Course materials and handouts—seminar and lecture topics.
- Lecture and seminar notes—how much time spent on each topic?
- Further reading?
- Past papers—these give a good pointer as to what type of questions will be asked. Be aware if any topics have changed on the course so that it is clear if past papers are relevant.

Material to read and reference

You should read and reference the key principles by:

- Reviewing your seminar and lecture notes, the relevant sections in your textbook, and this revision guide.

Exam essentials

✻✻✻✻✻✻✻✻✻✻

- For a good answer, you should also summarise key arguments from academics and other sources. Make a list of key principles alongside criticisms—for example, arguments for and against the use of the living instrument principle by the ECtHR.

Common mistakes to avoid

Before the examination

Do not :

- Leave revision to the last minute.
- Have an unstructured approach to revision—you need a clear timetable.
- Limit revision topics to the number of questions on the exam— topics may overlap or you may get a question you feel you can't answer.
- If you plan revision etc then there is no need to panic.

During the examination

Common mistakes such as bad timing, not answering enough questions, unstructured answers, etc, are often caused by poor technique or panic—avoid these by:

- Reading through the whole of the examination paper and decide on your questions at the beginning.
- Doing a plan: write out an outline answer, noting relevant cases and sources—doing a plan means your answer will be structured and you won't forget important cases.
- Read the instructions carefully—even if you are struggling to answer the number of questions required, an attempt at an answer is better than nothing at all.
- Timing—try to spend the appropriate/similar amount of time on each question.
- Avoid wring a 'tell all you know' answer—make sure you answer the question set; a plan should help construct a relevant answer.

Ideas for revision activities

Find out about your exam

Be clear as to length of exam, number of questions, type of questions, etc. This information should be available in a course pack or ask your tutor. Also examine past papers.

Work out what you need to know

- Review course materials, seminar, and lecture notes and you should also have notes on your reading—text book, other required reading, and further reading.
- Summarise key principles and debates for each topic; identify links and any gaps in your knowledge.
- Past papers—provide pointers as to what is expected by the tutor.

Make a revision timetable

Have a clear, workable timetable. Break up revision into manageable blocks, giving you sufficient breaks.

Have a programme of activities

- Attend any revision lectures or seminars given by your tutors. If you have a revision seminar, prepare for this—this may be the last chance to ask your tutor questions!

- Make summaries of key principles, cases, and arguments.

- Attempt past papers—one of the best ways to revise is to attempt a past paper question on a topic—do this with your notes, then attempt it without notes and within the time limit given in the exam. Practice helps to refine your technique and also can minimise exam panic.

- It may be useful to have a study group—attempt past paper questions and get others to mark them. Writing and marking can aid revision.

Outline answers

Chapter 4: Right to life and freedom from ill treatment

It is important to *apply* the legal principles and case law to the *facts* of the problem question.

1. Consider which ECHR articles are engaged

- **Article 2**—right to life—death penalty
- **Article 3**—ill treatment—death penalty, injuries in prison.

2. Is Adam's case admissible?

- Admissibility criteria—is he a victim (**Article 34**) and does he meet criteria under **Article 35**: exhaust domestic remedies etc—apply to facts.

3. If admissible (yes), the merits?

Discuss Adam's claim and arguments that would be advanced based on facts given and case law:

Article 2

Adam would argue that being sent to US where he may face the death penalty would be a violation of **Article 2**. Note the death penalty is still allowed under **Article 2(1)**. Adam can argue the general acceptance of the abolition of the death penalty has been abrogated?

- *Soering v UK* (1989)
- *Ocalan v UK* (2005)

Both cases stated **Article 2** was not violated on these grounds: However:

- *Al Saadoon v UK* (2010)—use of **Article 3** to find death penalty violation.

No violation of **Article 2** but see under **Article 3** re death penalty.

Article 3

Death penalty—argue death penalty is ill treatment under **Article 3**:

- *Soering v UK*—**Article 3** applies where substantial grounds for real risk of ill treatment in receiving state: death row; death penalty itself following *Al Saadoon v UK* (overturning *Soering*)

Treatment in prison

Adam is injured by a prisoner. How is the state liable? Positive obligation: *Osman principle*. Did the state know or ought to know of real and immediate risk of ill treatment and failed to take reasonable steps to act?

- *Osman v UK* (1998)
- *Keenan v UK* (2001)
- *Edwards v UK* (2002)

Apply to facts: does the prison know? Did it act? Was it reasonable to expect it to act?

If the state has positive obligation, does the treatment of Adam meet the threshold for **Article 3**?—Enough to be at least degrading?—factors?

- *Ireland v UK* (1978)

Conclusions

Adam can claim under **Article 2 and 3**, more likely to be successful under **Article 3**.

Chapter 5: Right to liberty and right to fair trial

It is important to *apply* the legal principles and case law to the *facts* of the problem question.

1. Consider which ECHR articles are engaged

- **Article 5**—detention—march, remand
- **Article 6**—questioning, disrepute charge

2. Can Andrew raise human rights claims?

- **HRA**—victim? (**s 7**), public authority (**s 6**) (Chapter 3)

3. Merits

Article 5

The bridge:

Andrew would argue that the restriction on the bridge ('kettling') was a deprivation of liberty under **Article 5**, applying **Article 5(1)(c)**. The police would argue that the restriction was necessary to prevent an imminent breach of the peace:

- *Guzzardi v Italy* (1980)

Outline answers

✳✳✳✳✳✳✳✳✳✳✳✳

- *Austin v Commissioner of Police of the Metropolis* (2009)
- *R (on the application of Moos) v Commissioner of Police of the Metropolis* (2011)

On the facts, consider the circumstances and length of the restriction, etc. If the 'kettling' was not necessary to prevent imminent breach of peace, then unlawful under **Article 5**.

Bail:

Apply the principles and case law under **Article 5(3)**—trial within a reasonable time. Can state justify refusal of bail? Is there a substantial risk of reoffending?

- *Matznetter v Austria* (1969)

Article 6

Questioned without a solicitor:

Andrew could argue that this was incompatible with **Article 6(1) and Article 6(3)(c)**

- *Cadder v HM Advocate* (2010)—held questioning without a solicitor was incompatible with **Article 6**

Hearing and suspension:

Does the case raise a civil right/obligation? Does it involve a private right (university is a public body). It involves employment rights so is it a civil right?

- *Le Compte v Belgium* (1981)

Andrew can raise issues over the public nature and fairness of the hearing. There was no oral hearing and Andrew can claim bias with regard to the panel. He can also claim that clear reasons should have been given:

- *Campbell and Fell v UK* (1984)
- *V and T v UK* (1999)
- *Piersack v Belgium* (1982)
- *R v Secretary of State DETR, ex p Alconbury Developments Ltd et al* (2001)

Applying the case law to the facts, discuss whether the university had any justification for its procedures and if the test for bias is met.

Chapter 6: Right to family and private life

It is important to *apply* the legal principles and case law to the *facts* of the problem question.

Injunction

Discuss whether Anne can bring a human rights claim. The injunction will be a private law measure between private parties. How can human rights claims be relevant? Discuss horizontality and the duty on the court to act compatibly with the **HRA** under **s 6**:

- eg *Campbell v MGN Ltd* (2004)

After establishing relevance, discuss the merits of the case. The judge would have to balance the **Article 8** claims of Anne against the right of the newspaper to publish. Discuss the development of the breach of confidence in English law:

- *Campbell v MGN Ltd* (2004)
- *McKennitt v Ash* (2007)
- *Douglas v Hello! Ltd (No 6)* (2005)
- *Von Hannover v Germany* (2004)

Applying the facts, Anne could argue that there is no public interest in publication and it releases private information into the public domain. **Article 8** is applicable, given the wide definition of private life, which includes photographs, etc. The court gives special regard to expression under the **HRA, s 12** and would consider the public interest as justification for publication (necessary in a democratic society).

Interception of messages

The **HRA** is applicable as interception is carried out by a public body. Discuss the principles that the court would apply. It would clearly be an interference with the right to correspondence, so the court would ask if the interception was in accordance with law (vague reasons in regulation), meets a legitimate aim, and if so, is it necessary, ie proportionate with the margin of appreciation?

- *Golder v UK* (1975)
- *Niemietz v Germany* (1993)
- *Halford v UK* (1997)
- *Copland v UK* (2007)

Applying the facts, the legitimate aim of national security is usually given a wide margin of appreciation but the surveillance would have to be in accordance with law. Is the regulation too vague to meet this requirement?

Chapter 7: Freedom of religion and expression

. . . .

It is important to *apply* the legal principles and case law to the *facts* of the problem question.

Article 10

1. Injunction: balance with Article 8

See problem answer for private life (Chapter 6) re case law.

Applying the facts and case law, the minister could argue that there is no public interest in publication. The court gives special regard to expression under the **HRA, s 12** and would consider justification (**Article 10(2).**) On the facts, the court will consider the ministerial position, newspapers as public watchdogs, etc.

2. Anne's charge

HRA is applicable (criminal charge). Discuss **Article 10** principles. Is it justified to consider Anne's opinion as incitement to hatred? Case law discusses proportionality principles to be applied:

• *Handyside v UK* (1976)
• *Sunday Times v UK* (1979)
• *Garaudy v France* (2003)
• *Surek v Turkey (No 1)* (1999)
• *Surek and Ozdemir v Turkey* (1999)
• *R (on the application of Pro Life Alliance) v BBC* (2003)

The outcome will depend on the weight given to the need to protect the rights of others (and margin of appreciation), and whether the conviction and sentence has a chilling effect on expression.

Article 9

3. Andrew's request

HRA is applicable as the school is a public body. Is his request to have time off work a manifestation of his religious belief under **Article 9(1)**? Case law would suggest that this would not be recognised as manifestation. Discuss why this is the case:

• *Kalac v Turkey* (1997)
• *X (Ahmad) v UK* (1981)

The court may consider that Andrew's request does not fall under **Article 9(1)**. If it does, consider under **Article 9(2)**.

4. Brian's pendant

HRA is applicable. Discuss the case law on the wearing of religious symbols in schools. First, is the pendant a manifestation of belief? If so, can the school justify its uniform policy? Is it proportionate?

• *Leyla Sahin v Turkey* (2005)
• *Ahmet Arslan and Others v Turkey* (2010)
• *R (on the application of Begum) v Denbigh High School* (2006)
• *Watkins-Singh v Aberdare Girls' High School Governors* (2008)

On the facts and case law, the court may give a wide margin of appreciation to the state and find the ban is justified.

Chapter 8: Freedom of assembly and association

. . . .

It is important to *apply* the legal principles and case law to the *facts* of the problem question.

Discuss the application of **Article 11** (and **Article 10**) to the facts. Two issues may arise:

1. The restriction of the demonstration

The **HRA** would apply as the police are a public body under **s 6**. **Article 11** is applicable with regard to the right to assemble. Does the action of the police interfere with that right? Discuss the general principles of assembly relevant to demonstrations. Does the need for notification under public order legislation limit assembly and if so can it be justified?

• *Cisse v France* (2002)
• *Baczkowski v Poland* (2009)

Discuss the principles applied to an imminent breach of the peace. Was the use of 'breach of the peace' justified on the facts (under **Article 11(2)**)? Discuss the necessity for imminence of breach etc.

• *R (on the application of Laporte) v Chief Constable of Gloucestershire Constabulary* (2006)

Outline answers

✳✳✳✳✳✳✳✳✳

Apply the principles to the facts of the problem, considering the length of restriction in the car park, the threat posed by the counter-demonstration, etc. Should protection of third parties be considered? (*Ollinger v Austria* (2006)).

2. Positive obligation to protect?

The attack on the demonstration by the protesters from the counter-demonstration: How is the state liable? Positive obligation: *Osman* principle. The ECtHR has recognised that if a right is to be effective, the state may have to take appropriate steps to protect the right. The state may have an obligation to ensure (when reasonable) that protestors can demonstrate without fear of harm.

• *Plattform 'Ärzte für das Leben' v Austria* (1988)

Apply the ECtHR to the facts (noting **s 2 HRA**—court must have due regard to ECtHR). Was it reasonable to expect better police protection earlier in the protest? Should the state have taken action to prevent the counter-demonstration? What would have been appropriate and reasonable?

Chapter 9: Freedom from discrimination

It is important to *apply* the legal principles and case law to the *facts* of the problem question.

Discuss the application of **Article 14** to the facts.

1. Admissibility

Is Alma's and Bella's case admissible?

• Admissibility criteria—are they victims (**Article 34**) and do they meet the criteria under **Article 35**: exhaust domestic remedies etc— apply to facts.

2. Merits

Alma

Can Alma use **Article 14**? Issue has to fall with the 'ambit' of a substantive right. In this case **Article 8**—right to family life:

• *Belgian Linguistics Case* (1968)

Discuss briefly if there has been a violation of **Article 8**. If not (and even if there is), go on to discuss **Article 14**. Applying the ECtHR principles from the case law, discuss if Alma is being treated differently from a person in an analogous position on a ground within the ECHR. The grounds could be unmarried mother under other status: (*Rasmussen v Denmark* (1985)). It could also be argued on grounds of religion given tradition of the sect.

If there is a difference of treatment, the state will have to justify the treatment as reasonable and objective—proportionate considering margin of appreciation. Consider the grounds and how they will affect the margin of appreciation given.

• *Frette v France* (2004)
• *E.B. v France* (2008)

It could also be argued that the state should have treated her application differently from other single mothers given her religious belief:

• *Thlimmenos v Greece* (2001)

Bella

Can Bella use **Article 14**? Does if fall within the ambit of another right? (right to education (**P1–2**). Discuss Bella's case with regard to indirect discrimination. The difficulty for Bella is proving that the state deliberately discriminated against her due to her religious belief. Bella would argue that the statistics in the facts are enough to shift the burden of proof onto the state. If so, the state would then have to justify the difference in the pass grade statistics (proportionality and margin of appreciation):

• *D.H. and Others v Czech Republic* (2008)
• *Orsus v Croatia* (2010)

Chapter 10: Terrorism

It is important to *apply* the legal principles and case law to the *facts* of the problem question.

Discuss the compatibility of the state action with the ECHR. Is the **HRA** applicable? Under **s 6**, the public authorities are bound by the ECHR.

1. Deportation

Discuss whether the positive obligation under **Article 3** prevents the state from deporting Aisha. Apply the case law to the facts: are there grounds to believe that Aisha faces a substantial risk of ill treatment if sent back to her state of origin? Do her alleged activities undermine her protection?

- *Chahal v UK (1996)*
- *Saadi v Italy (2009)*

2. Non-derogating order

Discuss the prevention of terrorism legislation and how this can be challenged. Aisha would argue that the order should have been 'derogating' as the restriction on her liberty amounted to a 'deprivation' under **Article 5**:

- *Guzzardi v Italy (1980)*
- *Secretary of State for the Home Department v JJ and Others (2007)*

- *Secretary of State for the Home Department v E (2007)*

3. Special advocate system

Discuss the compatibility of the special advocate system with **Article 6** and apply to the facts of the problem. Following the case law, would the information given to Aisha meet the requirements for the hearing to be fair?

- *A and others v UK (2009)*
- *Secretary of State for the Home Department v AF (No 3) (2009)*

Glossary

Abrogation (of a treaty clause): to repeal, annul, or treat as non-existent a clause of a legally binding treaty

Absolute right: A right from which no reservation or derogation can be made and there can be no justification for an interference with the right

Autonomous meaning: the ECtHR can give a legal term a meaning that is different from that given in national law

Balance of probabilities: (In ECHR case law), standard of proof, where the applicant must prove that it is more likely than not that an interference with a right has occurred

Breach of confidence: a tort in private law which protects private information conveyed confidentially

Chamber: sitting of seven judges of the European Court of Human Rights, which decides on the merits of cases found admissible

Chilling effect: term used by ECtHR to describe a state measure, act, or policy that may cause individuals to be in fear of expressing an opinion, belief, etc

Closed shop: an arrangement between an employer and a trade union which means any person wishing to be an employee or operate a profession has to be in a particular trade union

Common law: the common law consists of judge-made rules applied in cases in England and Wales through the use of precedent

Comparator: a person in an analogous position to an applicant in direct discrimination cases

Customary international law: consists of rules of law derived from the consistent conduct of states. This consistent state practice arises where states believe they have an obligation to act that way

Directive: legislative act of the European Union which requires a state to implement the act, but gives a discretion to the state as to the means by which the act is implemented. This can be done by a variety of measures depending on the subject matter of the directive

Grand Chamber: sitting of 17 judges of the European Court of Human Rights, which hears cases referred to it by the Chamber, or a panel refers cases raising serious issues of interpretation or importance

Habeas Corpus: a person can only be detained in accordance with law

High value, low value expression: as described by Sunstein, a method of differentiating between different types of expression and deciding when they can be limited by the state

Horizontality: the application of the law between private parties. Human rights law traditionally applies in a vertical relationship between the individual and the state. However the ECHR may be applied between private parties where the state has a positive obligation to regulate etc

Inherent limitations: the recognition by the ECtHR that limits may be placed on the right in domestic jurisdictional processes and are allowed for in the right itself

Injunction: discretionary court order which is used to prevent an action being carried out, to order an ongoing act to be discontinued, or to order an action to be carried out

Judicial review: judicial review allows a person with a sufficient interest in a decision or action of a public body to ask a judge to review the lawfulness of secondary legislation or decision, action, or failure to act in relation to exercise of a public function

Jus cogens: fundamental principle of international law, which is accepted by states as a principle that cannot be violated or derogated from by any state and states cannot consent in a treaty to a violation

Justiciable right: A judge is able to interpret and determine the application of a right: ability to interpret the meaning, content, and limitations attached to a right

Limited right: a right that does not allow explicit justifications for an interference with the right but may have inherent limitations and can be derogated from

Living instrument: the ECHR is open to reinterpretation over time by the ECtHR to reflect changing social attitudes and state consensus. Precedent does not apply to the ECHR

Margin of appreciation: doctrine used by the ECtHR, where the Court gives a certain amount of discretion to a state, where the state may be best placed to decide on the necessity of an act, measure, or policy

Natural rights: philosophical argument that rights should be protected due to the inherent dignity of human beings

Parliamentary supremacy: Parliament is the primary law-making body; it can make or unmake any law whatsoever and is not bound by previous legislation; nor can it bind legislation from future repeal or reform. The judiciary cannot declare primary legislation invalid

Powers of interpretation: previous to the HRA, the UK courts had developed several interpretative principles when legislation is ambiguous: these are known as the Literal Rule (plain meaning of words), Golden Rule (construing in context of statute), Mischief Rule (purpose of act/intention of Parliament)

Positive obligation: A duty placed on the state to take action to ensure the effective protection of a Convention right

Precedent: under common law, a court is bound by the decision of the higher court; the Supreme Court decisions bind all courts below it

Primary legislation: act of parliament that is made by the legislative branch of government and given Royal Assent

Proportionality: a requirement that an act or measure is proportionate to the aim it seeks to achieve; has a balance been achieved between the competing needs of the individual and the community as a whole?

Qualified right: where an interference with a right may be justified if the conditions for limitations are met; reservations and derogations can be made

Rationae loci: jurisdiction by reason of place, an applicant has to bring a case concerning an act within the territorial jurisdiction of the state

Rationae materiae: subject matter jurisdiction; the Court can only decide on a matter covered by the rights in the ECHR

Rationae personae: jurisdiction by reason of the person concerned; the applicant has to be within the jurisdiction of the Court; person has to have standing to bring the case (victim status), and act complained of can be applicable to respondent state. (Also case should be brought against state after it has ratified ECHR: may be argued as *rationae temporis*.)

Rule of law: everyone is equal before the law and bound by it; this includes the branches of government and public bodies who cannot act arbitrarily, beyond the requirements of the law

Subordinate legislation: legislation made by the executive branch under powers given to it by the primary legislation

Subsidiarity: protection of human rights is primarily the responsibility of individual states which the ECtHR will supervise

Sunset clause: A clause in primary legislation, which will lapse if not renewed by Parliament after a specified date

Utilitarianism: philosophical argument that the happiness of the many should take precedence over the needs of the few: maximisation of the happiness of the greatest number

Index

abortion
  right to life 60–1
absolute rights 32, 33
  freedom from ill
    treatment 57, 67–8
  right to life 57
  terrorism and 176–7
anti-terror law *see* **terrorism**
artistic expression
  freedom of 129–30
assembly and association,
    freedom of
  association 141, 145–6
  case law
    assembly 144–5
    association 145–6
    protests 149–50
    trade unions 146
  common law
    offences 147–8
  criminal offences 148
  ECHR text 139
  flowchart 147
  interference by state
    democratic society 143–4
    legitimate aim 143
    prescribed by law 142
  key cases 150–1
  key facts 137
  limitations 147–50
    armed forces and
      police 146
    explicit restrictions 146
    statutory 148–9
  margin of appreciation
    143–4
  peaceful assembly 139–40
  penalties 145
  positive obligations 139–40
  power to regulate 148–9
  proportionality 143
  qualified right 138, 142–4
  statutory limitations 148–9
  subject of
    demonstration 140
  third party involvement 140

  trade unions 141–2, 146
  UK domestic law 147–50
assisted suicide 61–2
association, freedom of
    see **assembly and**
    association, freedom of

bail 83
belief
  holding 119
  manifestation 119, 120–4
  non-religious 118–19
  see also **religion,**
    freedom of
bias
  fair trial right 89
Bill of Rights 1689 15
breach of confidence 112–13
burden of proof
  discrimination 162
  fairness 91
  mental illness 86
  right to life 58–9

children
  detention 81
  European Convention
    on the Exercise of
    Children's Rights
    1996 23
civil expression 129
civil rights 88–9
common law
  freedom of assembly and
    association 147–8
  human rights
    protection 14, 15–16
compensation
  unlawful detention 83
complaints
  admissibility criteria 27–8
  current structure 26–7
  reform of system 24–6
  UN procedure 8–9
constitution
  United Kingdom 14–15

  United States 4
control orders 184, 185–6
  deprivation of liberty 84–5
  derogating orders 185
  non-derogating orders 185
  proposed reform 186
Convention on Action against
    Trafficking in Human
    Beings 2005 23
Convention on Preventing
    and Combating
    Violence against
    Women and Domestic
    Violence 2011 23
correspondence
  meaning 102
  see also **family and private**
    life, right to
Council of Europe
  derogation from ECHR 180
  formation 21
  structure 21–2
  terrorism 180
  torture 69
custody *see* **detention**

damages
  Human Rights Act
    1998 48–9
death penalty 57, 58, 62–3
declaration of
    incompatibility 46–7,
    49, 184
Declaration of the Rights of
    Man and Citizen 1789 4
degrading treatment
  definition 70
  discrimination as 70
  UN Convention 1984 68–9
  see also **ill treatment,**
    freedom from
demonstrations *see* **protests**
    and demonstrations
deportation
  detention 82
  right to family life 106, 112

derogation from ECHR 33, 50
  Council of Europe 180
  fair trial right 77
  right to liberty 77
  terrorism 47, 51–2, 178–80,
    183, 184
detention
  arbitrary 80–1
  bail 83
  challenging 85–6
  compensation 83
  criminal offences 81
  freedom from ill
    treatment 71
  immigration, deportation
    or extradition 82
  impartial and independent
    judicial body 83, 85
  indefinite 182–4
  legal certainty 80–1
  mental illness 79–80, 82, 86
  minors 81
  non-compliance with court
    order 81
  non-fulfilment of legal
    obligation 81
  in prison 85–6
  procedure prescribed by
    law 80–1
  prompt action
    following 82–3
  reasons 80, 82
  review 83
  state duty to protect/
    safeguard life 64
  terrorism 81, 182–4
  UK domestic law 83–7
dignity 2–3, 57
**discrimination, freedom
    from**
  burden of proof 162
  case law 168–9
  comparators 159–60
  definition 154–5
  degrading treatment 70
  direct discrimination 155,
    161, 168–9
  ECHR text 158
  enforcement 168
  Equality Act 2010 167–8

EU law 166–7
  as freestanding
    right 165–6
  grounds 160–1
  Human Rights Act
    1998 169
  indirect discrimination
    155–6, 163–5, 169
  justification 161
  key cases 170
  key facts 153
  legitimate aim 161
  limitations 161–2
  margin of appreciation 161
  positive discrimination 156
  proportionality 161
  UK domestic law 161,
    166–9
  United Nations 157–8
  within ambit of substantive
    right 159, 162, 165
  see also **equality**
domestic violence
  Convention on Preventing
    and Combating
    Violence against
    Women and Domestic
    Violence 2011 23
  state duty to protect 64
dress
  religious 123–4, 125

environmental issues
  right to family and private
    life 110–11
equality
  duties of public
    bodies 157
  Equality Act 2010 167–8
  EU law 166–7
  formal 154–5
  of opportunity 155–6
  of outcome 156–7
  substantive 155–6
  UK domestic law 166–9
  see also **discrimination,
    freedom from**
Equality Act 2010 167–8
equality of arms
  fair trial right 90, 94

**European Charter for
    Regional and Minority
    Languages 1992** 22
**European Convention on the
    Exercise of Children's
    Rights 1996** 23
**European Convention on
    Human Rights (ECHR)**
  absolute rights 32, 33, 57,
    67–8, 176–7
  Convention rights 23–4
  declarations of
    incompatibility 46–7,
    49, 184
  derogation *see* **derogation
    from ECHR**
  formulation 22
  horizontal effect 31–2
  Human Rights Act
    1998 and 40
  interpretation by ECtHR
    28–32, 100, 160
  autonomous meanings 30
  effectiveness 30
  key cases 35–6
  key facts 20
  limited rights 32, 33, 178
  as 'living instrument'
    28–30, 100, 160
  nature of rights 32–3
  positive obligations 30–1
    effect 31–2
  freedom of
    assembly 139–40
  freedom from ill
    treatment 71–2
  right to family and
    private life 100
  right to life 63–5
  protocols 23–4
  qualified rights 32, 33
  see also **qualified rights**
  reservations 50
  terrorism and 176–80
  UK ratification 16
  vertical effect 31
  *see also individual rights
    and freedoms eg* **life,
    right to**; **ill treatment,
    freedom from**

Index

****

European Convention for the
    Prevention of Torture
    1961 22
European Court of Human
    Rights (ECtHR) 24
case law 44
complaints
    admissibility criteria 27–8
    current structure 26–7
    reform of system 24–6
interpretation of ECHR
    28–32
    autonomous meanings 30
    effectiveness 30
    as 'living instrument'
        28–30, 100, 160
    positive obligations 30–2,
        63–5, 139–40
margin of
    appreciation 34–5
    see also margin of
        appreciation
proportionality 33–4
    see also proportionality
European Social Charter
    1961 22
evidence
fair trial 91, 93
expression, freedom of
artistic expression 129–30
case law 128–31
civil/public interest
    expression 129
ECHR text 126–7
flowchart 131
hate speech 130
incitement to hatred 130–1
key cases 134–5
key facts 116
limitations 127–8
    democratic society 128
    legitimate aim 128
    prescribed by law 127
    margin of appreciation 128
    political expression 128–9,
        133
    privacy, conflict with
        99–100, 111, 113, 131,
        132
    proportionality 128

protests 133
public order 133
qualified right 117, 126,
    127–8
UK domestic law 131–3
value of expression 127
extradition
detention 82

fair trial, right to
access to court 90
adversarial trial 90
attendance at hearing 90
civil right/obligation 88–9
criminal charge 88, 92
derogation 77
determination 88
due process right 77
ECHR text 87–8
equality of arms 90, 94
evidential rules 91, 93
fairness 90–1
flowchart 93
impartiality 89, 94
independent tribunal/
    court 89, 94
key cases 95
key facts 76
legal representation 91
presumption of
    innocence 91
public hearing 90
reasonable time 89
reasoned and final
    judgment 91
right to participate 90
self-incrimination 91, 92
state obligations 90–1
terrorism and 178
UK domestic law 92–4
family and private life,
    right to
correspondence 102
deportation 106, 112
ECHR text 100
environmental
    issues 110–11
family life 101
family proceedings 104–6
flowchart 105

freedom of expression,
    conflict with 99–100,
    111, 113, 131, 132
home 101–2
immigration 106, 112
key cases 114
key facts 98
margin of appreciation
    103–4
personal information 108
positive obligations 100
privacy 112–13
private life 101
proportionality 103, 112
protected interests 100–2
protection from harm 108
qualified right 99, 102–4
removal from state 106
scope 104–11
searches and surveillance
    107, 177
sexual rights 108–9
state interference 99,
    102–4
    in accordance with
        law 102
    democratic society 103–4
    legitimate aim 102
super injunctions 113, 132
terrorism and 177
UK domestic law 111–13
United Nations 99
Framework Convention
    for the Protection of
    National Minorities
    1995 23
freedom of assembly
    and association
    see assembly and
        association, freedom of
freedom of expression
    see expression,
        freedom of
freedom from discrimination
    see discrimination,
        freedom from
freedom from ill treatment
    see ill treatment,
        freedom from
funeral pyres 126

Index

gender recognition
case law 29–30
declaration of
incompatibility 46–7

hatred
hate speech 130
incitement to 130–1
home
meaning 101–2
see also **family and private
life, right to**
homosexuality
right to private life 109
horizontal effect 41
European Convention on
Human Rights 31–2
Human Rights Act
1998 43–4
human rights
categories of rights 11–14
challenges 3
civil and political rights 12,
13, 22
current position 10–11
definition 2–3
development 3–11
key cases 17–18
key facts 1
dignity 2–3, 57
enforcement 12–14
first generation rights 12,
13, 22
natural rights 2, 67–8
second generation
rights 12, 13
social, economic and
cultural rights 12, 13
third generation rights 12
treaties protecting 22–3
*see also individual rights
and freedoms eg* **ill
treatment, freedom
from, life, right to**
Human Rights Act 1998 15, 16
application 52
bodies bound by Act 41
damages 48–9
declaration of
incompatibility 46–7, 49

derogation powers 50
direct vertical effect 41
discrimination 169
ECHR and 16, 40
ECtHR case law and 44
excluded rights 40
future of 53
horizontal effect 43–4
interpretation clause 44–6
judicial deference 51–2
judicial powers/duties 44–7
key cases 53–4
key facts 38
persons bringing case 41
political powers/
duties 49–50
proportionality 33–4, 50
public authorities 42–3
reason for 39–40
remedial action 49
remedies 47–9
reservation powers 50
rights covered 40
statement of
compatibility 49

ill treatment, freedom from
absolute right 57, 67–8
definitions 69–70
degrading treatment 68–9,
70
detention 71
ECHR text 69
inhuman treatment 68–9
key cases 74
key facts 56
positive obligations 71–2
removal of person from
state 71–2
state duties 71–2
information provision 71
legal framework 71
terrorism and 176–7
threshold 70–1
torture 68–9
UK domestic law 72–3
UN Convention against
Torture and other
Cruel, Inhuman or
Degrading Treatment

or Punishment
1984 68–9
United Nations 68–9
immigration
detention 82
right to family life 106, 112
incitement to hatred 130–1
inhuman treatment
definition 69
UN Convention against
Torture and other
Cruel, Inhuman or
Degrading Treatment
or Punishment
1984 68–9
see also **ill treatment,
freedom from**
injunctions
privacy 113, 132
**innocence, presumption
of** 91
**International Covenant on
Civil and Political
Rights (ICCPR) 1966** 6
Human Rights
Committee 7
**International Covenant
on Economic, Social
and Cultural Rights
(ICESCR) 1966** 6

judicial deference 51–2

League of Nations 5
legal representation
fair trial right 91
liberty, right to
deprivation of
liberty 79–80, 84–5
see also **detention**
derogation 77
due process right 77
ECHR text 78–9
flowchart 84
key cases 95
key facts 76
mentally ill patients 79–80
public order cases 86–7
terrorism and 84–5, 178
UK domestic law 83–7

Index

✳✳✳✳✳✳✳✳✳✳✳✳

life, right to
abortion 60–1
absolute right 57
assisted suicide 61–2
burden of proof 58–9
death penalty 57, 58, 62–3
detention 64
domestic violence 64
ECHR text 58
exceptions 59–60
    defence of person from
        unlawful violence 59
    effecting lawful
        arrest 59
    preventing escape of
        lawful detainee 59–60
    quelling riot or
        insurrection 60
key cases 73–4
key facts 56
Osman test 65–6
positive obligations 63–5
removal of person from
    state 64
right to die 61–2
state duties
    information provision 64
    legal framework 64
    to investigate deaths 65,
        66–7
    to protect/safeguard
        life 64–5
terrorism and 176
UK domestic law 65–7
United Nations 58
limited rights 32, 33
terrorism and 178

Magna Carta 1215 3, 15
margin of appreciation
    34–5
freedom of assembly and
    association 143–4
freedom of expression 128
freedom from
    discrimination 161
freedom of religion 122
right to family and private
    life 103–4
medical treatment

removal of person from
    state 72
mental illness
burden of proof 86
detention 79–80, 82, 86

natural rights 2, 67–8
Nuremburg trials 5–6

Osman **test** 65–6

parliamentary supremacy
    14, 40, 46
photographs
right to private life 107,
    111, 113
political expression
freedom of 128–9, 133
privacy *see* **family and
    private life, right to**
private life, right to *see*
    **family and private life,
    right to**
proportionality
anti-terror laws 176,
    179–80, 184
criteria 33–4
freedom of assembly and
    association 143
freedom of expression 128
freedom from
    discrimination 161
freedom of religion 121–2
Human Rights Act
    1998 33–4, 50
right to family and private
    life 103, 112
**Protection of Freedoms
    Bill** 182
protests and demonstrations
case law 149–50
criminal offences 148
freedom of expression 133
power to regulate 148–9
right to private life 177
subject matter 140
third party
    involvement 140
see also **assembly and
    association, freedom of**

public authorities
definition 42–3
discrimination 157
judicial deference 51–2
public interest expression
    129
public order
case law 149–50
deprivation of liberty 86–7
freedom of expression 133

qualified rights 32, 33, 99
freedom of association and
    assembly 138, 142–4
freedom of expression 117,
    126, 127–8
freedom of religion 117,
    121–2
right to family and private
    life 99, 102–4
terrorism and 177

rapporteurs 9, 158
religion, freedom of
beliefs
    holding 119
    limitations 121–4
    manifestation 119, 120–4
    non-religious 118–19
ECHR text 118
in education 122–3, 125
flowchart 124
funeral pyres 126
key cases 134
key facts 116
margin of appreciation 122
non-religious
    beliefs 118–19
proportionality 121–2
qualified right 117, 121–2
religion 118
religious dress 123–4, 125
sacred cows 125
state interference 121–4
    democratic society
        121–2
    legitimate aim 121
    prescribed by law 121
UK domestic law 124–6
UN declaration 117–18